# Oh My Goddess!

ああ女神さま

## FINAL EXAM

# Oh My Goddess!

ああ女神さま

## FINAL EXAM

STORY AND ART BY

## Kosuke Fujishima

TRANSLATION BY

Dana Lewis, Alan Gleason & Toren Smith

LETTERING AND TOUCH-UP BY

Jason Hvam & L. Lois Buhalis

DARK HORSE COMICS®

PUBLISHER
Mike Richardson

SERIES EDITORS
Mike Hansen & Greg Vest

COLLECTION EDITOR
Chris Warner

COLLECTION DESIGNER
Amy Arendts

ART DIRECTOR
Mark Cox

English-language version produced by Studio Proteus
for Dark Horse Comics, Inc.

*OH MY GODDESS! Vol. III: Final Exam*

This volume collects stories from issues eleven and twelve of the Dark Horse comic-book series
*Super Manga Blast!*, issue three of the Dark Horse comic-book series *Oh My Goddess!*, and issues
three through five of the Dark Horse comic-book series *Oh My Goddess! Part II.*

Published by
Dark Horse Comics, Inc.
10956 SE Main Street
Milwaukie, OR 97222

www.darkhorse.com

To find a comics shop in your area, call the Comic Shop
Locator Service toll-free at 1-888-266-4226

First edition: October 2002
ISBN: 1-56971-765-6

3 5 7 9 10 8 6 4 2
Printed in Canada

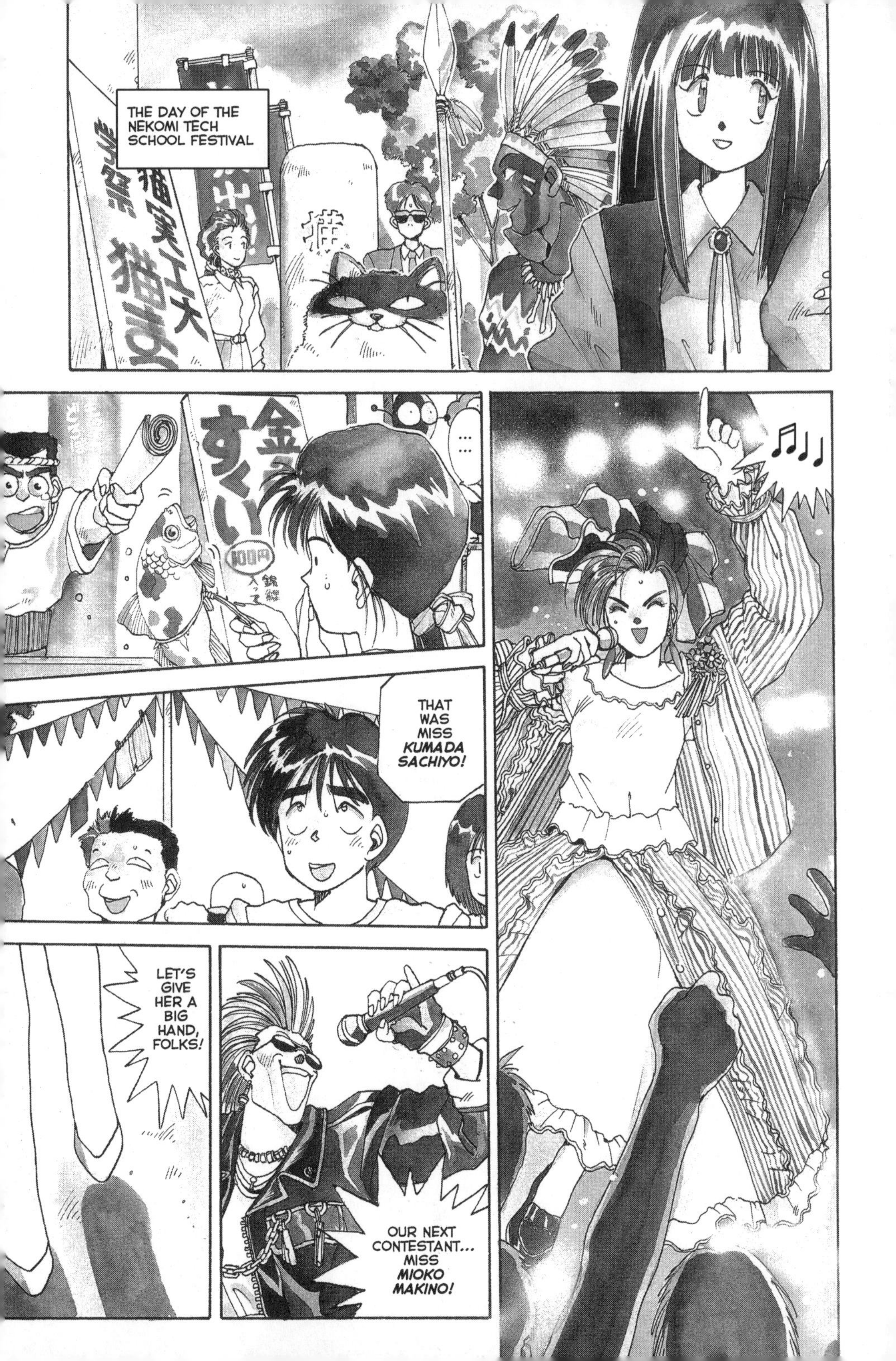
THE DAY OF THE NEKOMI TECH SCHOOL FESTIVAL
...
THAT WAS MISS *KUMADA SACHIYO!*
LET'S GIVE HER A BIG HAND, FOLKS!
OUR NEXT CONTESTANT... MISS *MIOKO MAKINO!*

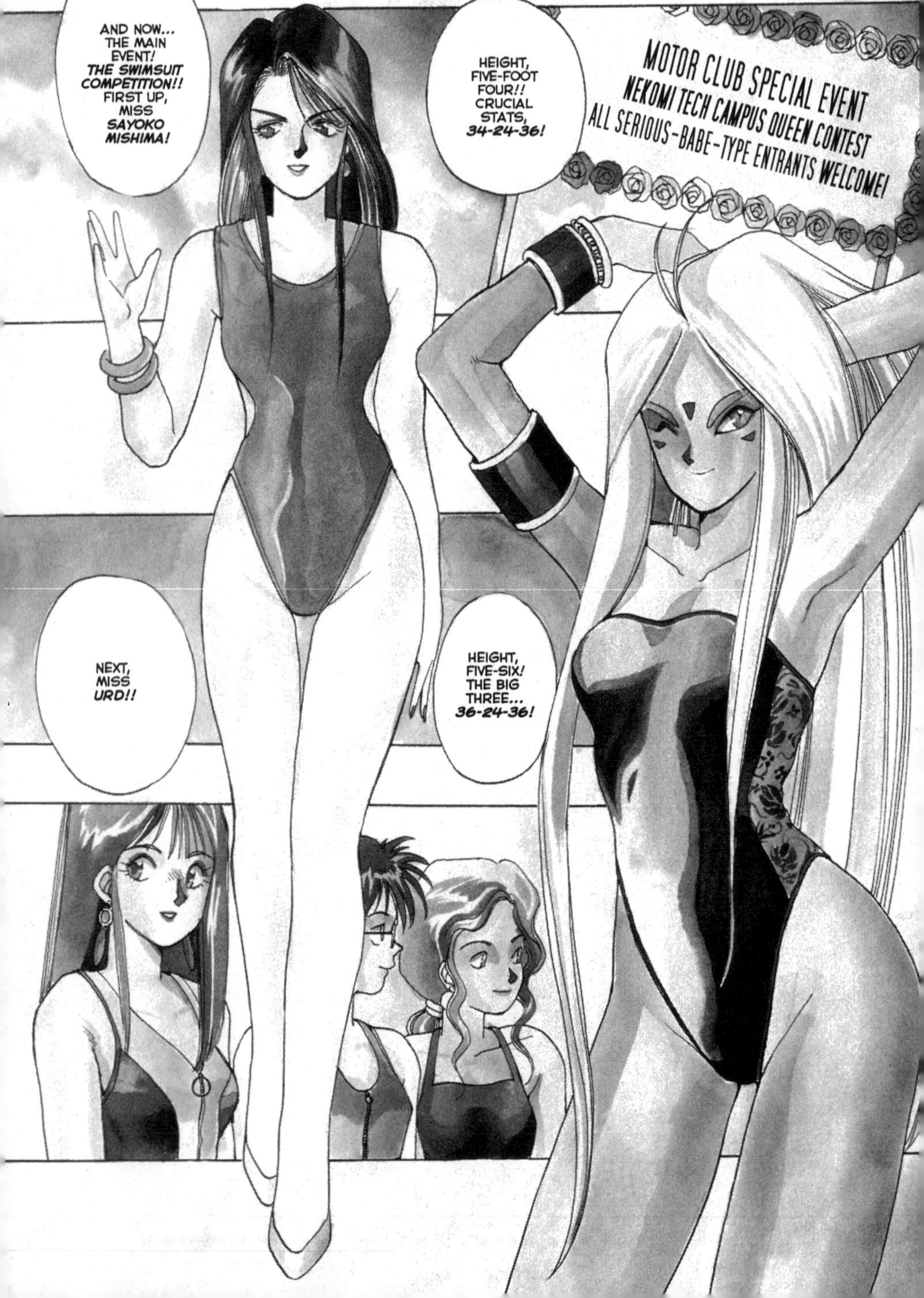

AND NOW... THE MAIN EVENT! THE SWIMSUIT COMPETITION!! FIRST UP, MISS SAYOKO MISHIMA!
HEIGHT, FIVE-FOOT FOUR!! CRUCIAL STATS, 34-24-36!
MOTOR CLUB SPECIAL EVENT
NEKOMI TECH CAMPUS QUEEN CONTEST
ALL SERIOUS-BABE-TYPE ENTRANTS WELCOME!
NEXT, MISS URD!!
HEIGHT, FIVE-SIX! THE BIG THREE... 36-24-36!

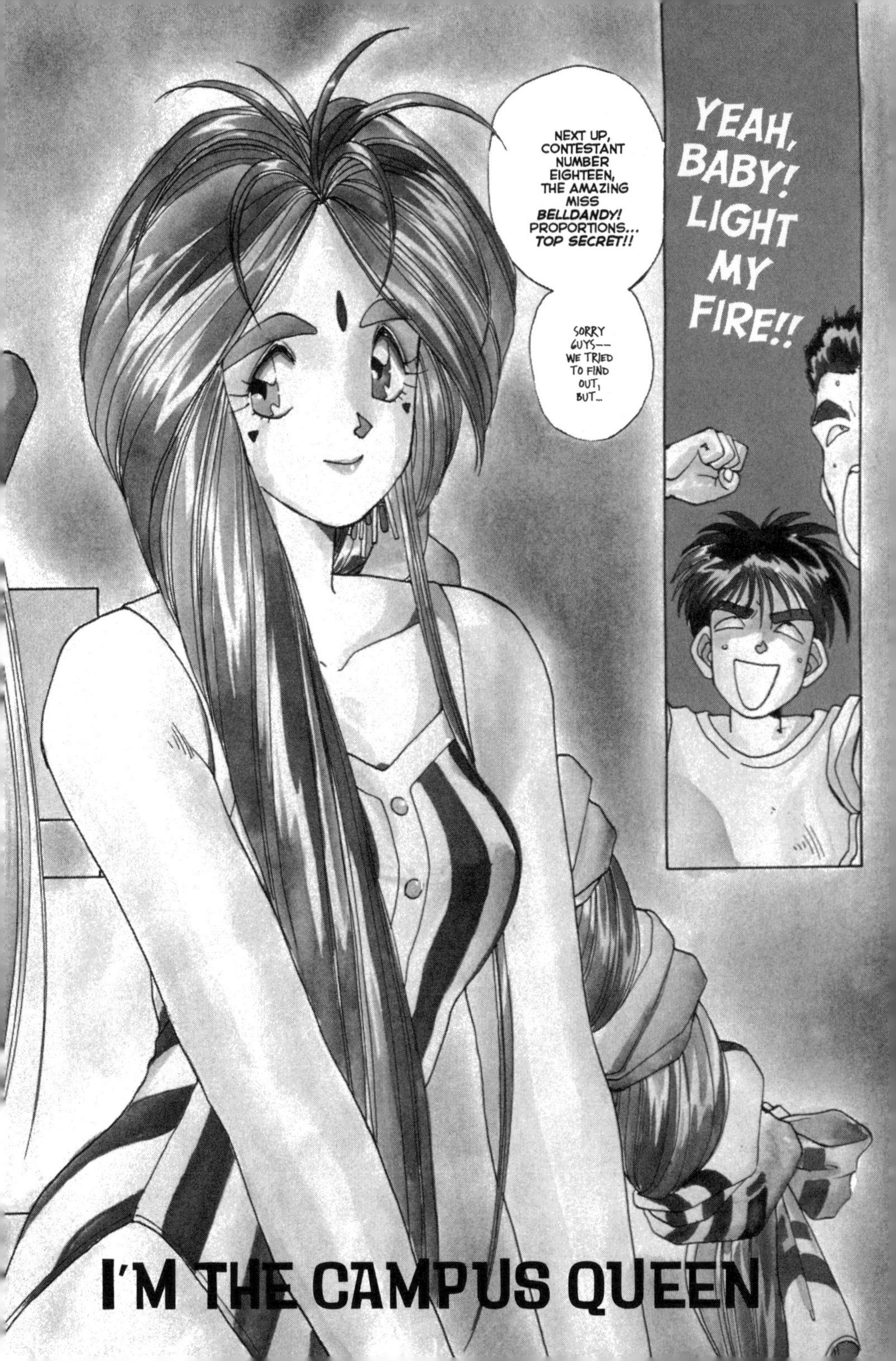
NEXT UP, CONTESTANT NUMBER EIGHTEEN, THE AMAZING MISS BELLDANDY! PROPORTIONS... TOP SECRET!!
SORRY GUYS— WE TRIED TO FIND OUT, BUT...
YEAH, BABY! LIGHT MY FIRE!!
I'M THE CAMPUS QUEEN

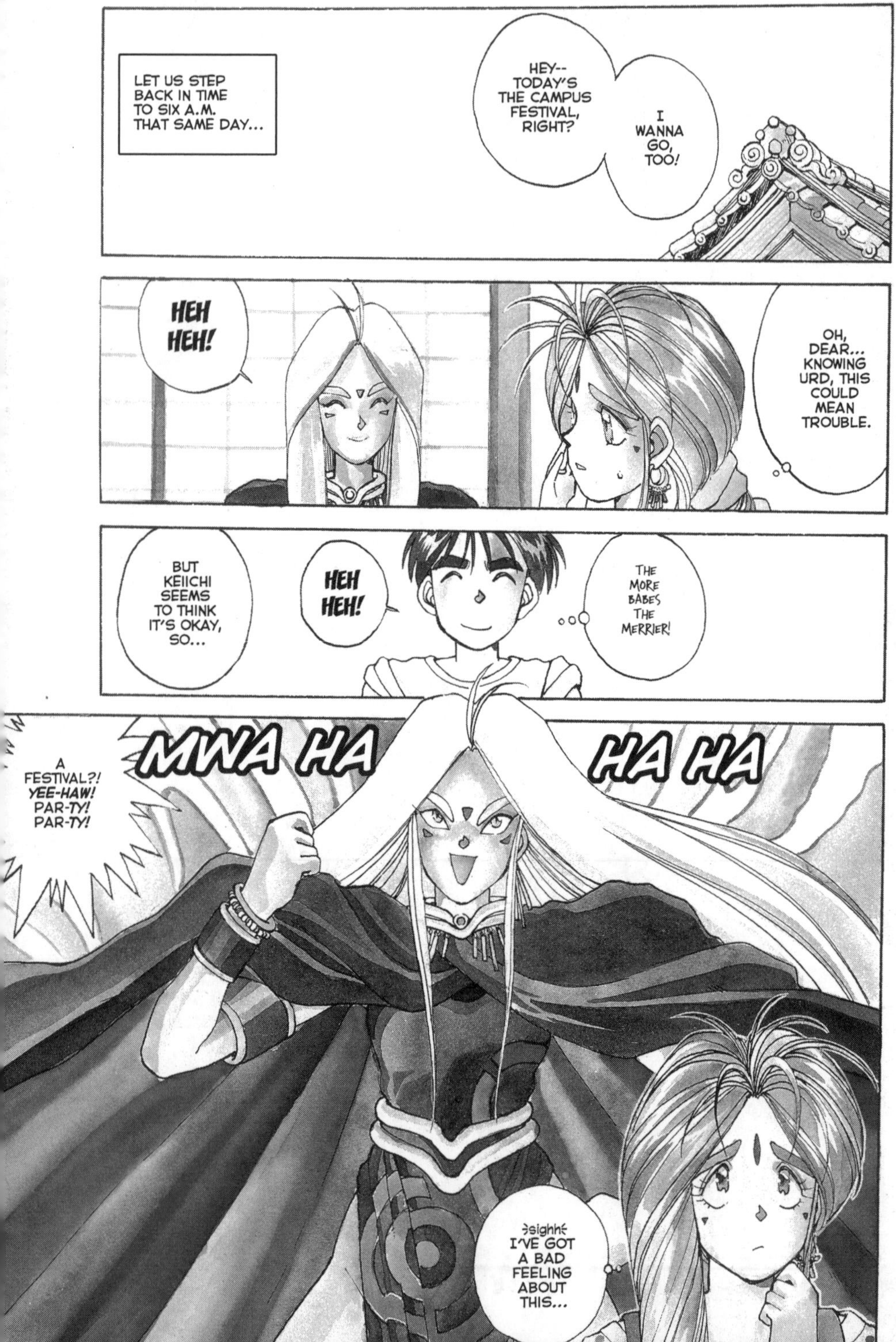

LET US STEP BACK IN TIME TO SIX A.M. THAT SAME DAY...
HEY-- TODAY'S THE CAMPUS FESTIVAL, RIGHT?
I WANNA GO, TOO!
HEH HEH!
OH, DEAR... KNOWING URD, THIS COULD MEAN TROUBLE.
BUT KEIICHI SEEMS TO THINK IT'S OKAY, SO...
HEH HEH!
THE MORE BABES THE MERRIER!
A FESTIVAL?! YEE-HAW! PAR-TY! PAR-TY!
MWA HA HA HA
*sighh* I'VE GOT A BAD FEELING ABOUT THIS...

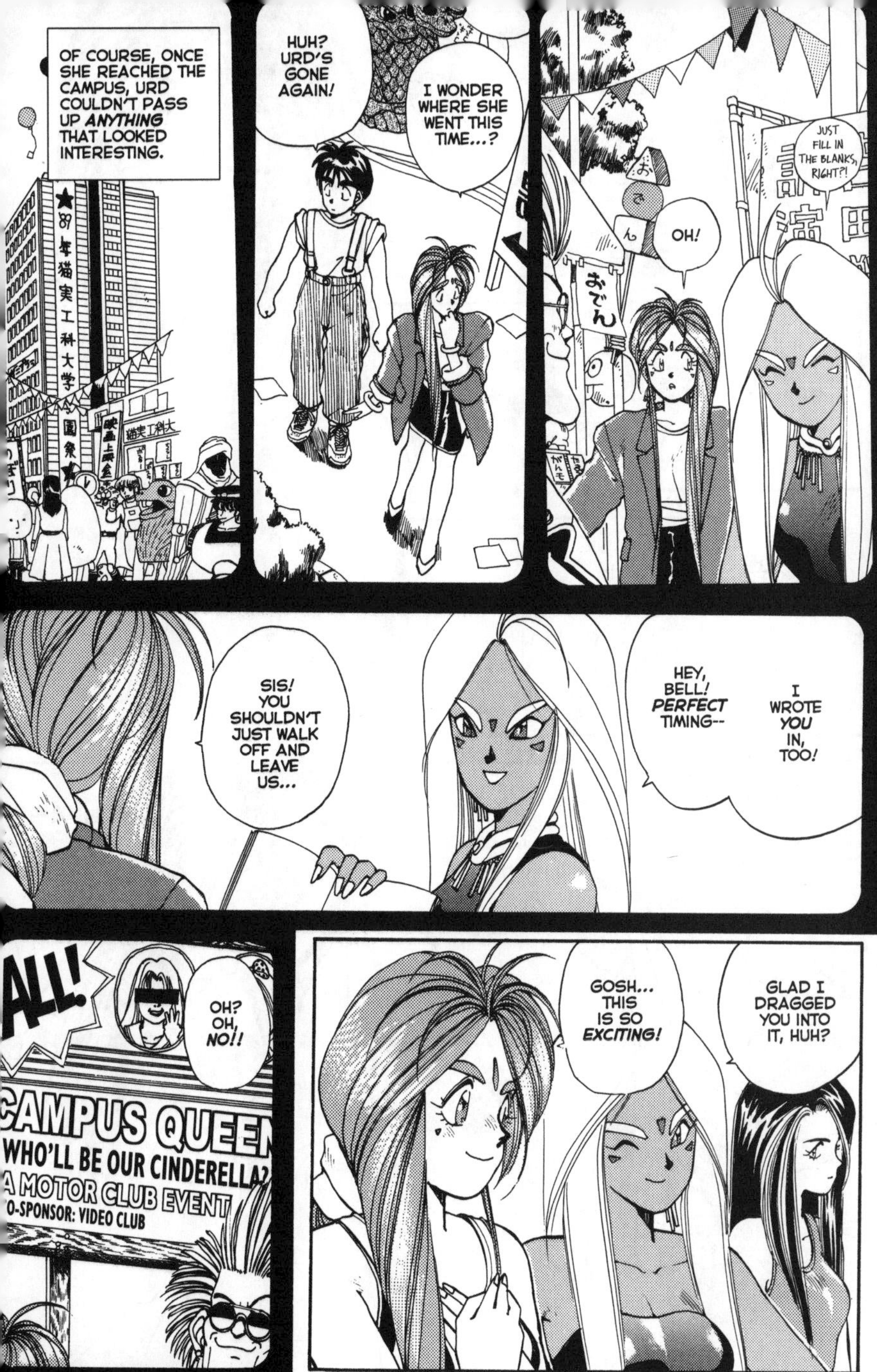
OF COURSE, ONCE SHE REACHED THE CAMPUS, URD COULDN'T PASS UP *ANYTHING* THAT LOOKED INTERESTING.
猫実工科大
HUH? URD'S GONE AGAIN!
I WONDER WHERE SHE WENT THIS TIME...?
JUST FILL IN THE BLANKS, RIGHT?!
おでん
OH!
SIS! YOU SHOULDN'T JUST WALK OFF AND LEAVE US...
HEY, BELL! *PERFECT* TIMING--
I WROTE *YOU* IN, TOO!
ALL!
OH? OH, *NO!!*
CAMPUS QUEEN
WHO'LL BE OUR CINDERELLA?
A MOTOR CLUB EVENT
O-SPONSOR: VIDEO CLUB
GOSH... THIS IS SO *EXCITING!*
GLAD I DRAGGED YOU INTO IT, HUH?

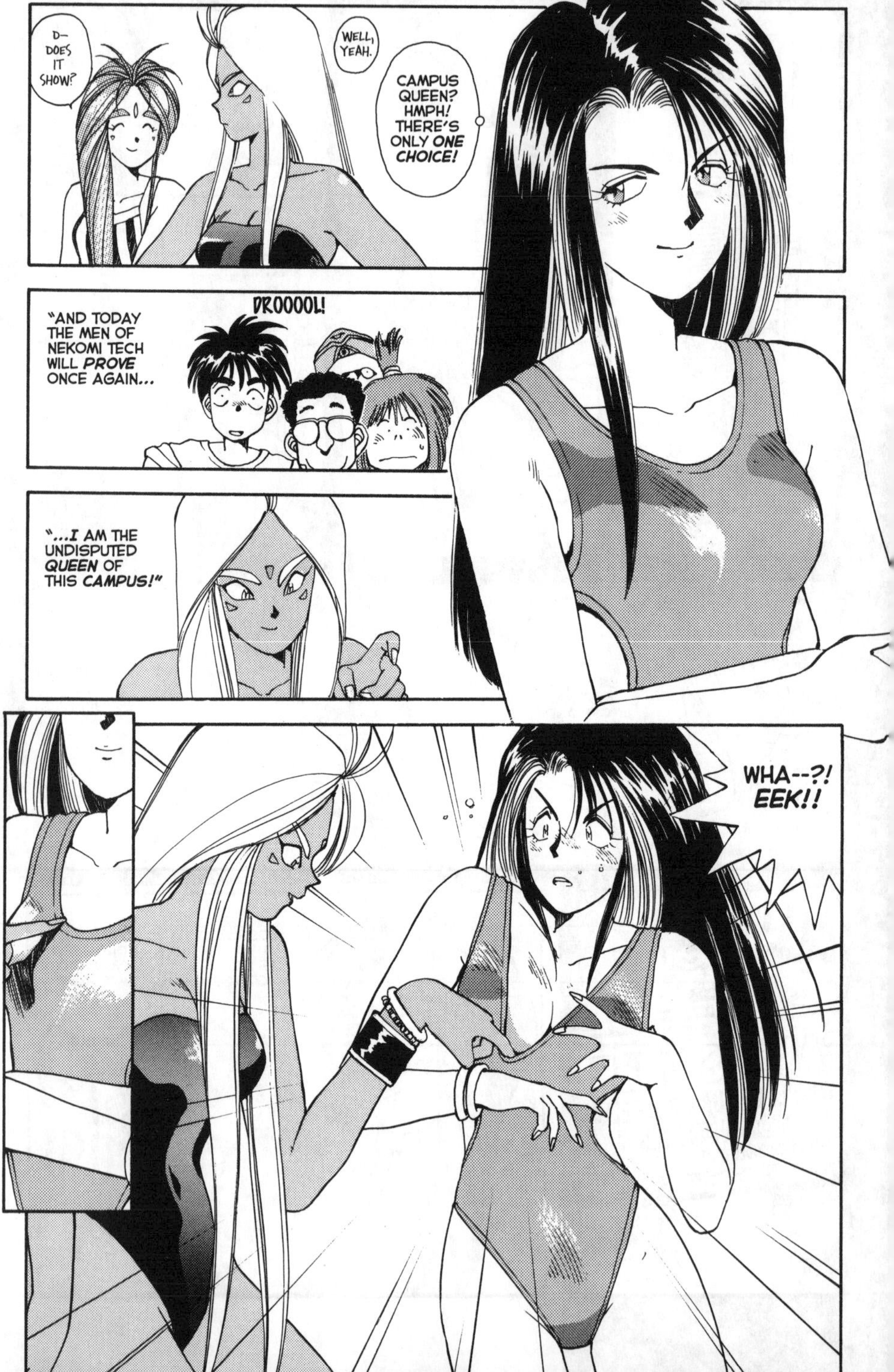
D-DOES IT SHOW?
WELL, YEAH.
CAMPUS QUEEN? HMPH! THERE'S ONLY ONE CHOICE!
"AND TODAY THE MEN OF NEKOMI TECH WILL PROVE ONCE AGAIN...
DROOOOL!
"...I AM THE UNDISPUTED QUEEN OF THIS CAMPUS!"
WHA--?! EEK!!

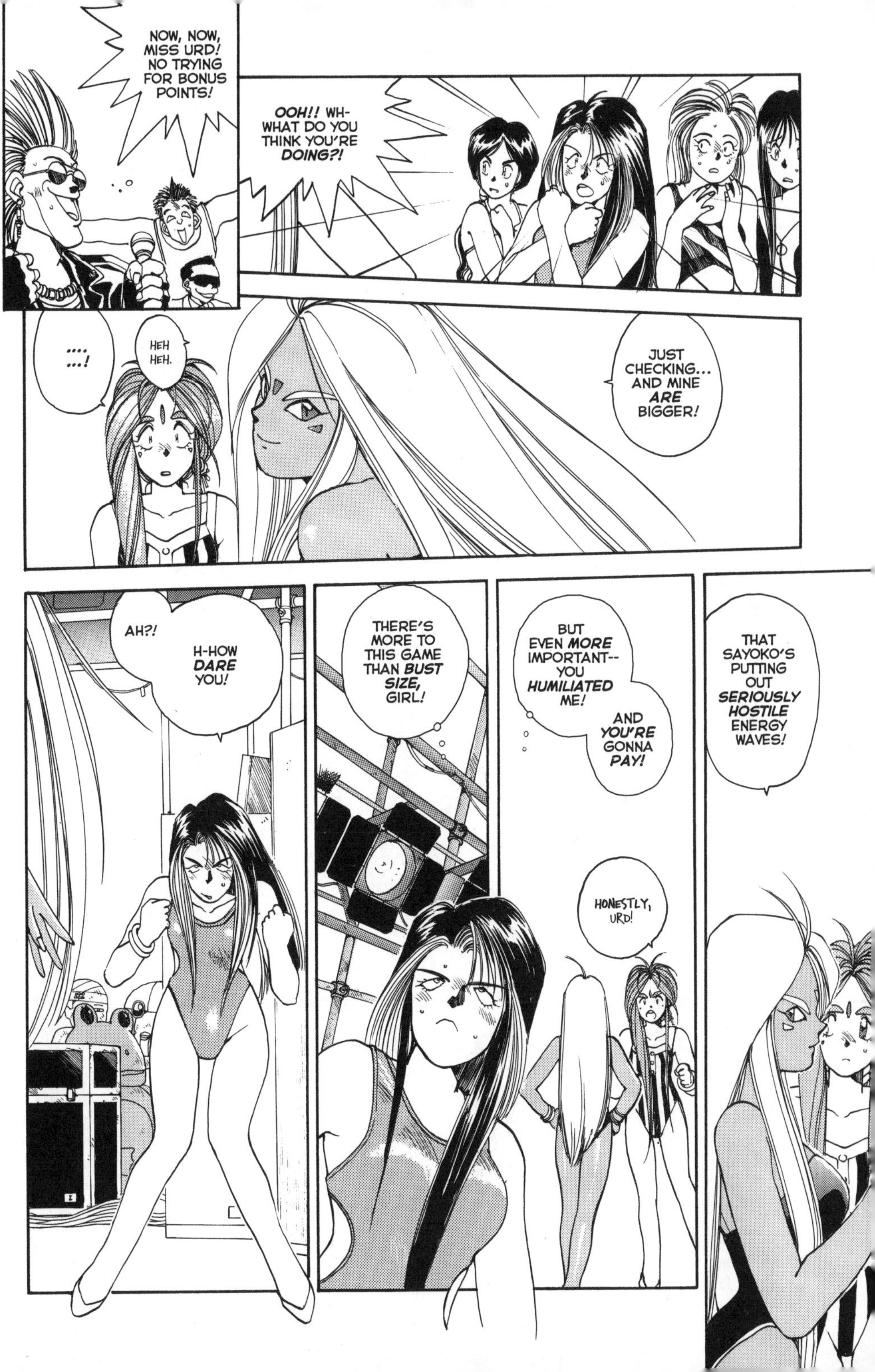
NOW, NOW, MISS URD! NO TRYING FOR BONUS POINTS!
OOH!! WH-WHAT DO YOU THINK YOU'RE DOING?!
...., ...!
HEH HEH.
JUST CHECKING... AND MINE ARE BIGGER!
AH?!
H-HOW DARE YOU!
THERE'S MORE TO THIS GAME THAN BUST SIZE, GIRL!
BUT EVEN MORE IMPORTANT--YOU HUMILIATED ME!
AND YOU'RE GONNA PAY!
HONESTLY, URD!
THAT SAYOKO'S PUTTING OUT SERIOUSLY HOSTILE ENERGY WAVES!

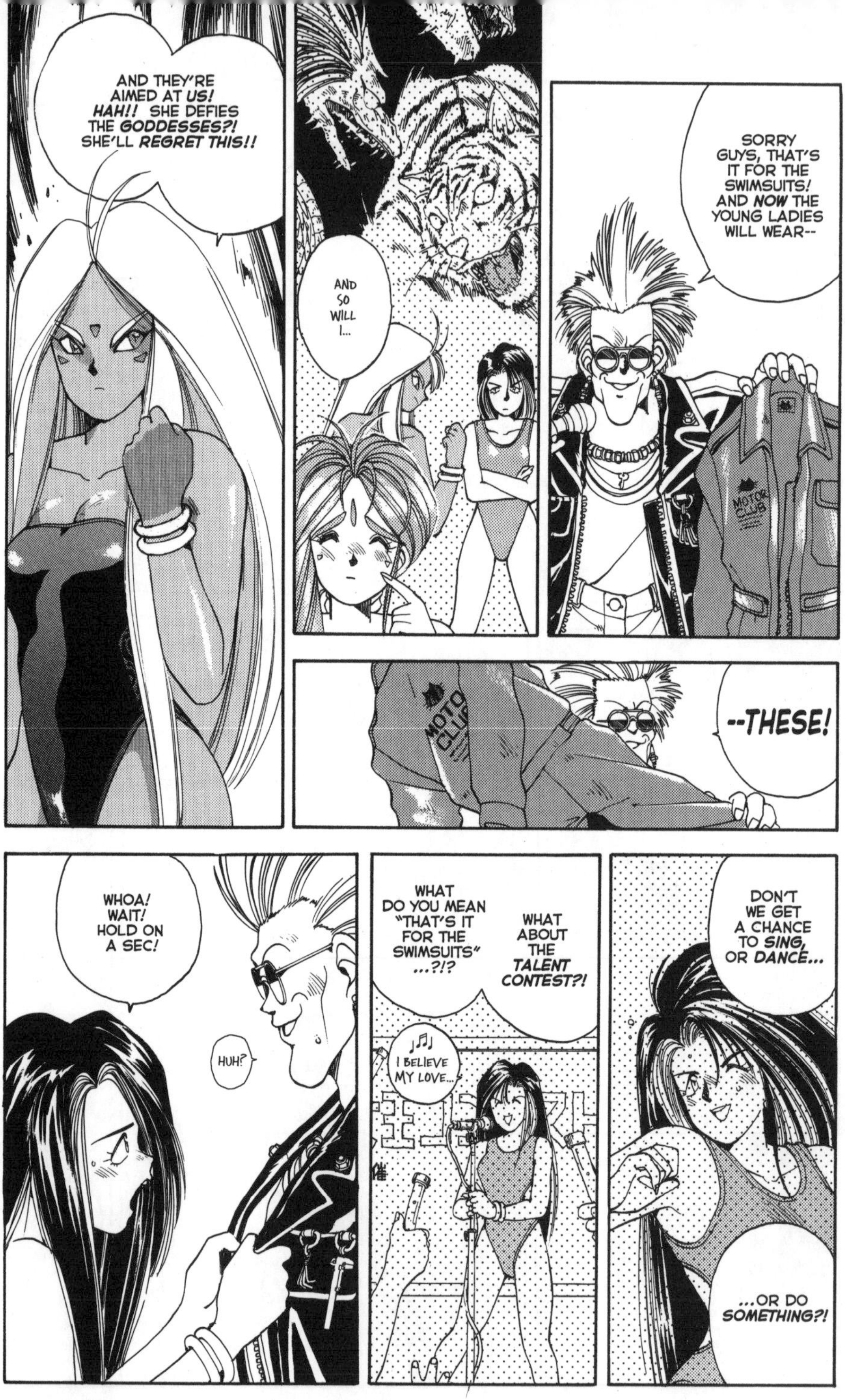
AND THEY'RE AIMED AT US! HAH!! SHE DEFIES THE GODDESSES?! SHE'LL REGRET THIS!!
AND SO WILL I...
SORRY GUYS, THAT'S IT FOR THE SWIMSUITS! AND NOW THE YOUNG LADIES WILL WEAR--
MOTOR CLUB
MOTOR CLUB
--THESE!
WHOA! WAIT! HOLD ON A SEC!
HUH?
WHAT DO YOU MEAN "THAT'S IT FOR THE SWIMSUITS" ...?!?
WHAT ABOUT THE TALENT CONTEST?!
♪♫ I BELIEVE MY LOVE...
DON'T WE GET A CHANCE TO SING, OR DANCE...
...OR DO SOMETHING?!

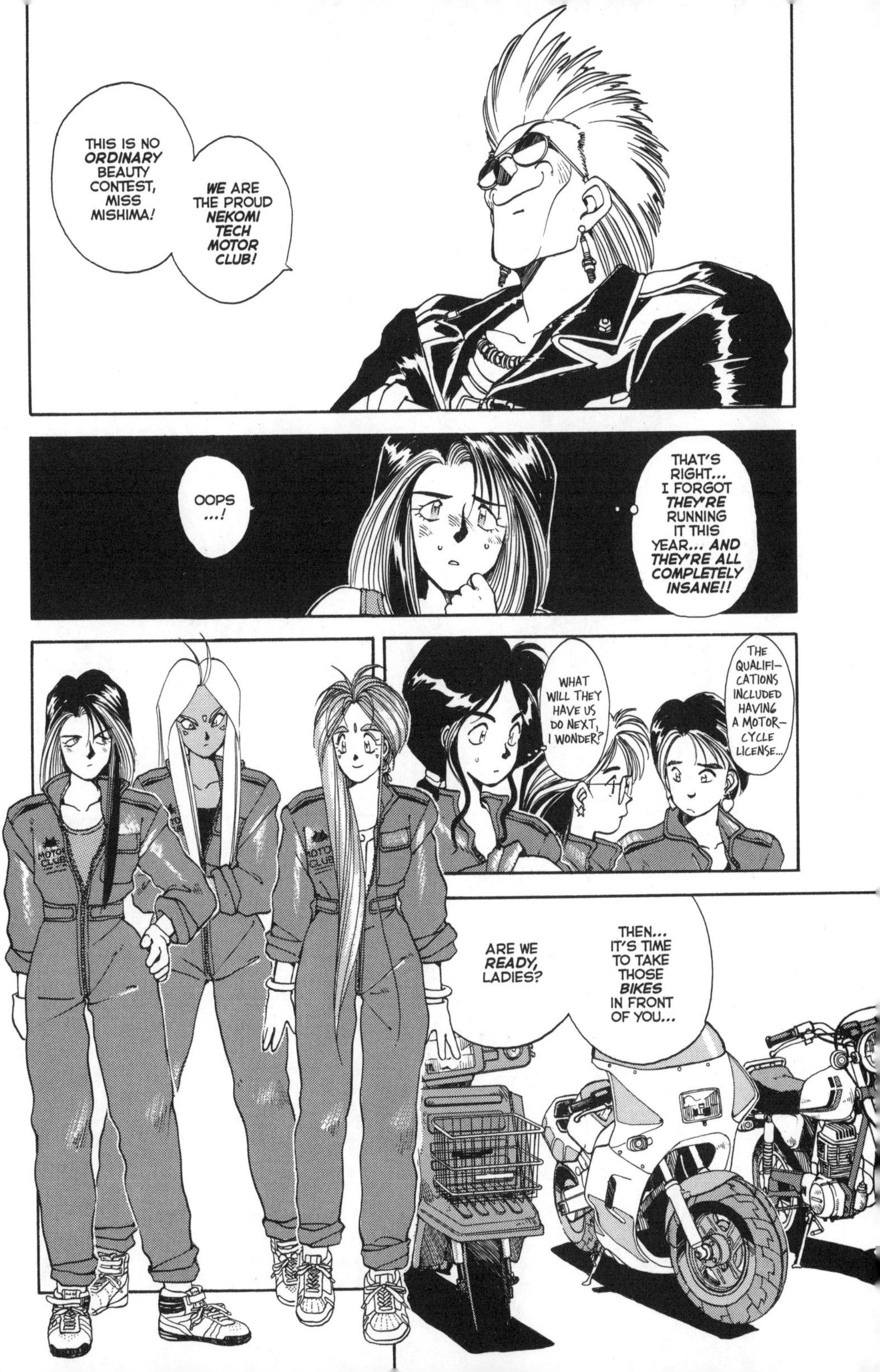
THIS IS NO ORDINARY BEAUTY CONTEST, MISS MISHIMA!
WE ARE THE PROUD NEKOMI TECH MOTOR CLUB!
OOPS ...!
THAT'S RIGHT... I FORGOT THEY'RE RUNNING IT THIS YEAR... AND THEY'RE ALL COMPLETELY INSANE!!
WHAT WILL THEY HAVE US DO NEXT, I WONDER?
THE QUALIFI-CATIONS INCLUDED HAVING A MOTOR-CYCLE LICENSE...
ARE WE READY, LADIES?
THEN... IT'S TIME TO TAKE THOSE BIKES IN FRONT OF YOU...

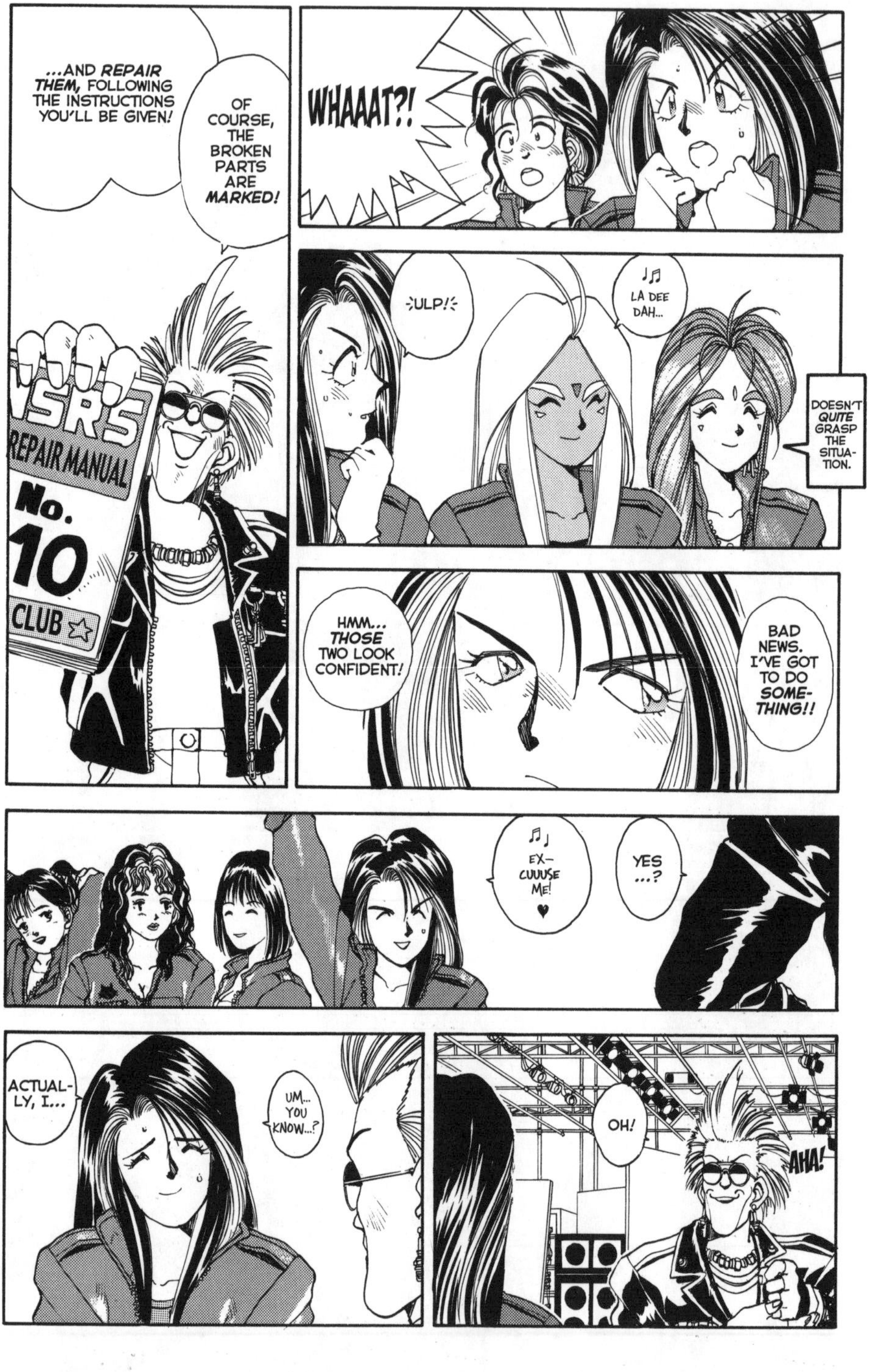
...AND REPAIR THEM, FOLLOWING THE INSTRUCTIONS YOU'LL BE GIVEN!
OF COURSE, THE BROKEN PARTS ARE MARKED!
REPAIR MANUAL
No. 10
CLUB
WHAAAT?!
ULP!
LA DEE DAH...
DOESN'T QUITE GRASP THE SITUATION.
HMM... THOSE TWO LOOK CONFIDENT!
BAD NEWS. I'VE GOT TO DO SOMETHING!!
EX-CUUUSE ME! ♥
YES ...?
ACTUALLY, I...
UM... YOU KNOW...?
OH!
AHA!

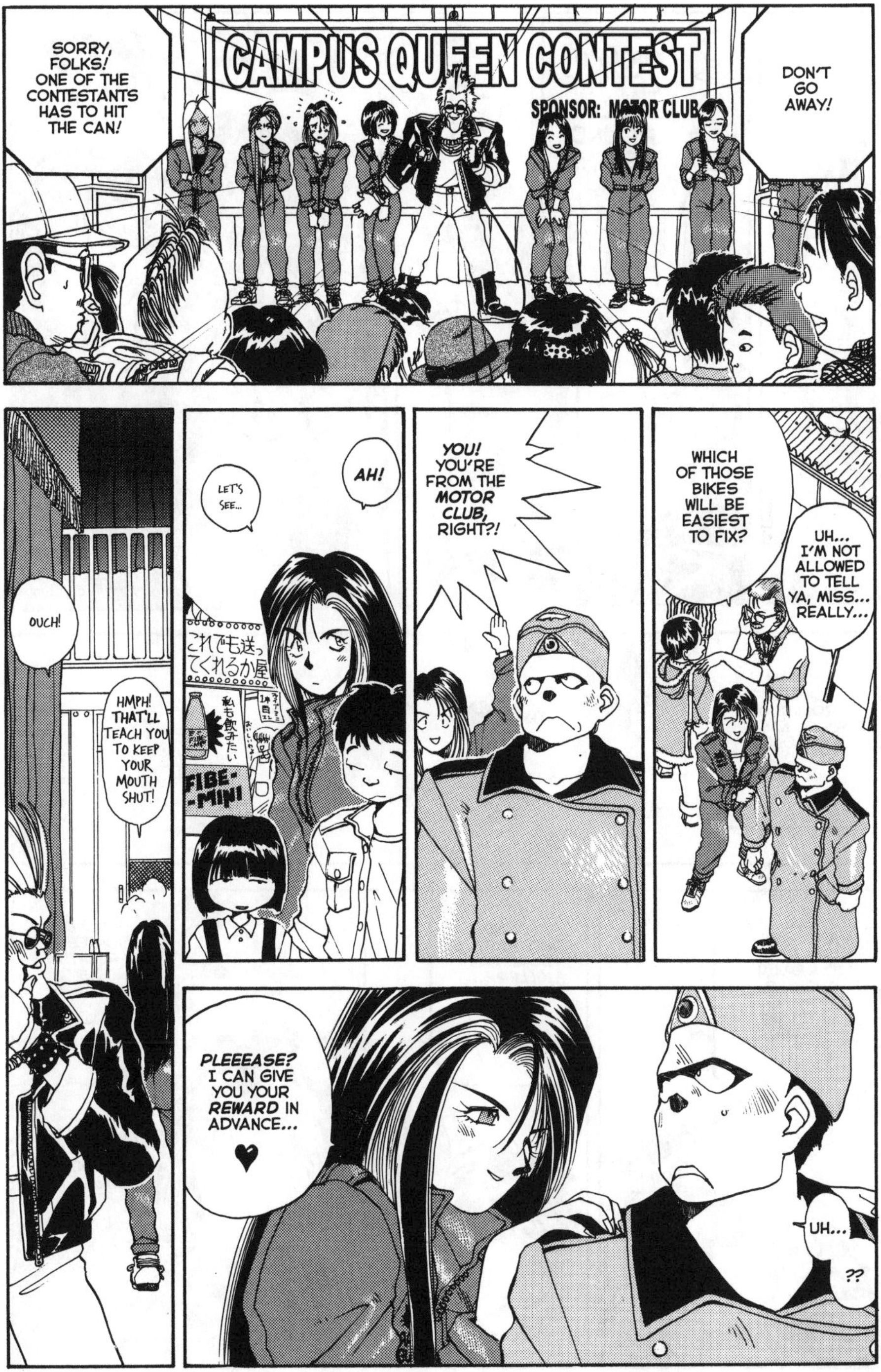
SORRY, FOLKS! ONE OF THE CONTESTANTS HAS TO HIT THE CAN!
CAMPUS QUEEN CONTEST
SPONSOR: MOTOR CLUB
DON'T GO AWAY!
OUCH!
HMPH! THAT'LL TEACH YOU TO KEEP YOUR MOUTH SHUT!
LET'S SEE...
AH!
これでも送ってくれるか屋
私も飲みたい
FIBE-MINI
YOU! YOU'RE FROM THE MOTOR CLUB, RIGHT?!
WHICH OF THOSE BIKES WILL BE EASIEST TO FIX?
UH... I'M NOT ALLOWED TO TELL YA, MISS... REALLY...
PLEEEASE? I CAN GIVE YOU YOUR REWARD IN ADVANCE... ♥
UH...
??

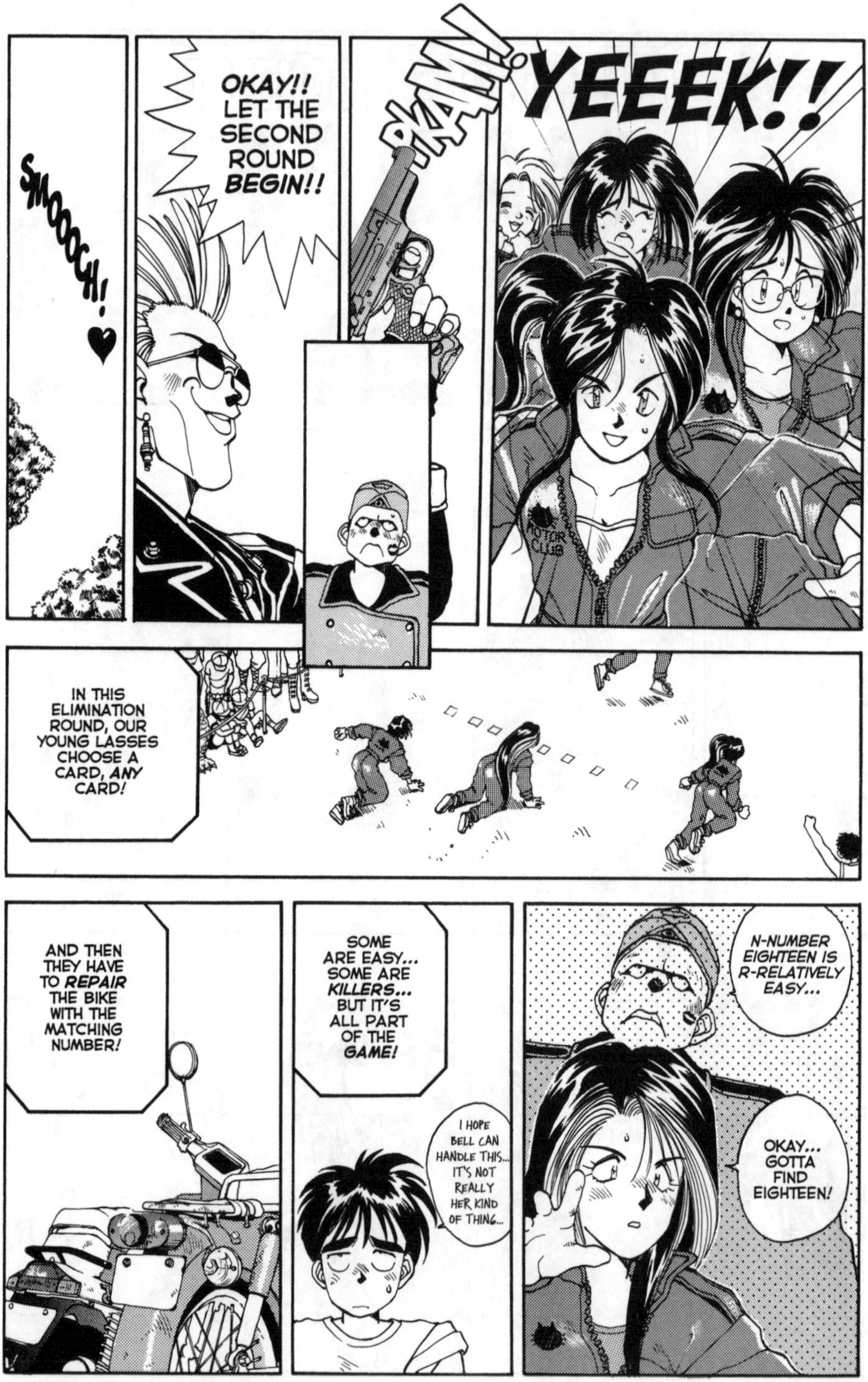
SMOOOCH! ♥
OKAY!! LET THE SECOND ROUND BEGIN!!
PKAM!!
YEEEK!!
IN THIS ELIMINATION ROUND, OUR YOUNG LASSES CHOOSE A CARD, ANY CARD!
AND THEN THEY HAVE TO REPAIR THE BIKE WITH THE MATCHING NUMBER!
SOME ARE EASY... SOME ARE KILLERS... BUT IT'S ALL PART OF THE GAME!
I HOPE BELL CAN HANDLE THIS... IT'S NOT REALLY HER KIND OF THING...
N-NUMBER EIGHTEEN IS R-RELATIVELY EASY...
OKAY... GOTTA FIND EIGHTEEN!

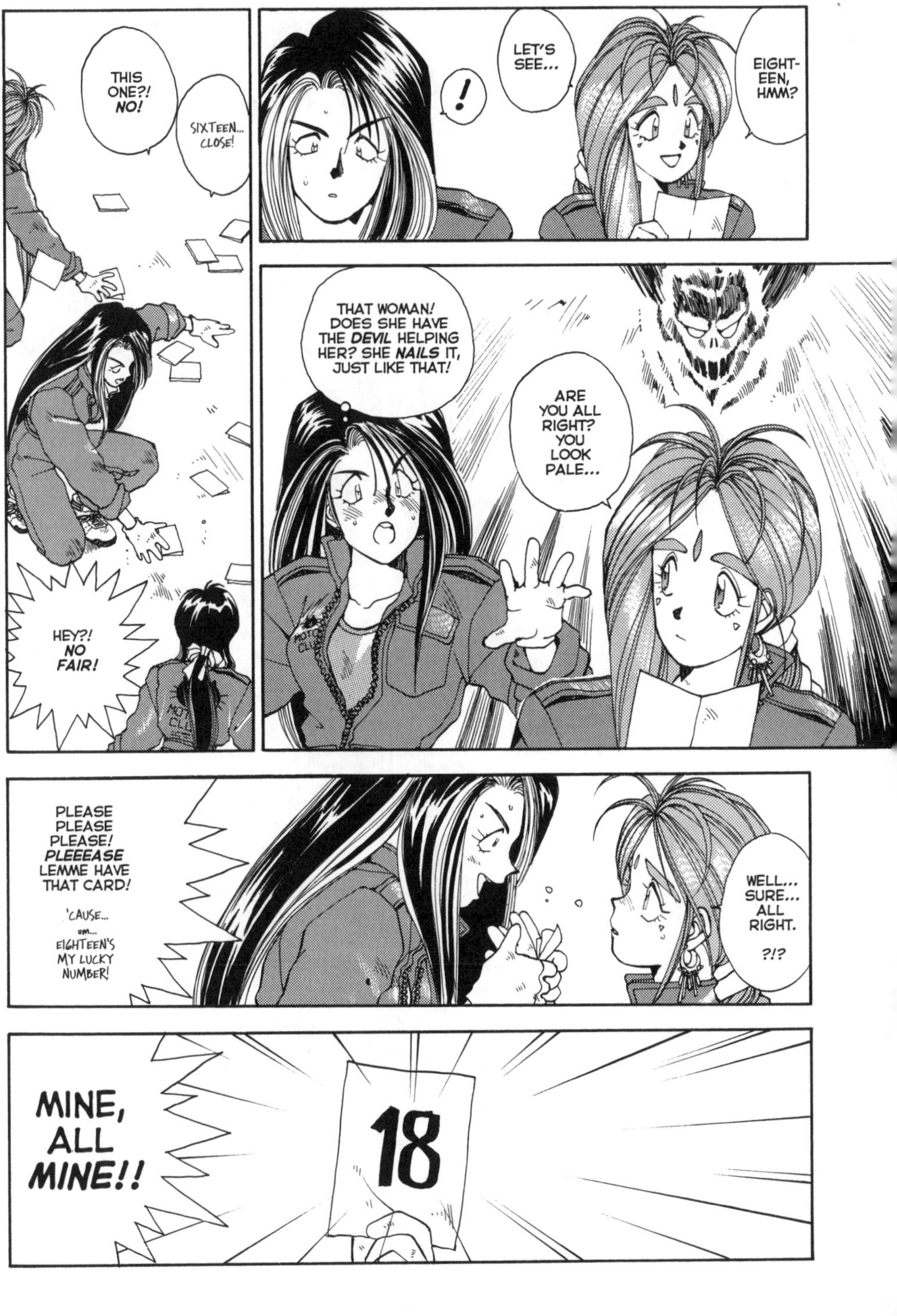

LET'S SEE...
!
EIGHTEEN, HMM?
THIS ONE?! NO!
SIXTEEN... CLOSE!
HEY?! NO FAIR!
THAT WOMAN! DOES SHE HAVE THE DEVIL HELPING HER? SHE NAILS IT, JUST LIKE THAT!
ARE YOU ALL RIGHT? YOU LOOK PALE...
PLEASE PLEASE PLEASE! PLEEEASE LEMME HAVE THAT CARD!
'CAUSE... UM... EIGHTEEN'S MY LUCKY NUMBER!
WELL... SURE... ALL RIGHT.
?!?
MINE, ALL MINE!!
18

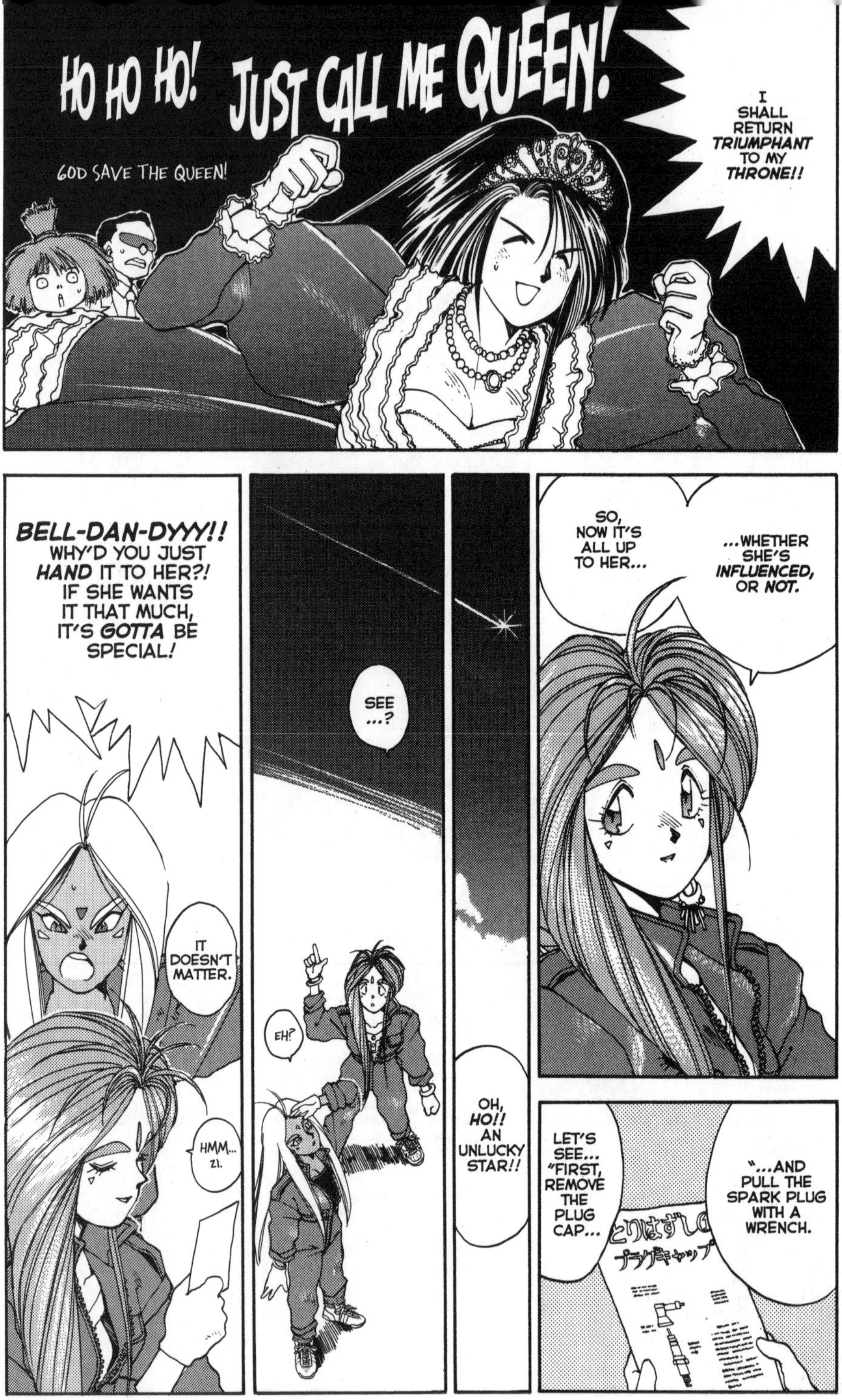
HO HO HO! JUST CALL ME QUEEN!
GOD SAVE THE QUEEN!
I SHALL RETURN TRIUMPHANT TO MY THRONE!!
BELL-DAN-DYYY!! WHY'D YOU JUST HAND IT TO HER?! IF SHE WANTS IT THAT MUCH, IT'S GOTTA BE SPECIAL!
IT DOESN'T MATTER.
HMM... 21.
SEE ...?
EH?
OH, HO!! AN UNLUCKY STAR!!
SO, NOW IT'S ALL UP TO HER...
...WHETHER SHE'S INFLUENCED, OR NOT.
LET'S SEE... "FIRST, REMOVE THE PLUG CAP...
"...AND PULL THE SPARK PLUG WITH A WRENCH.

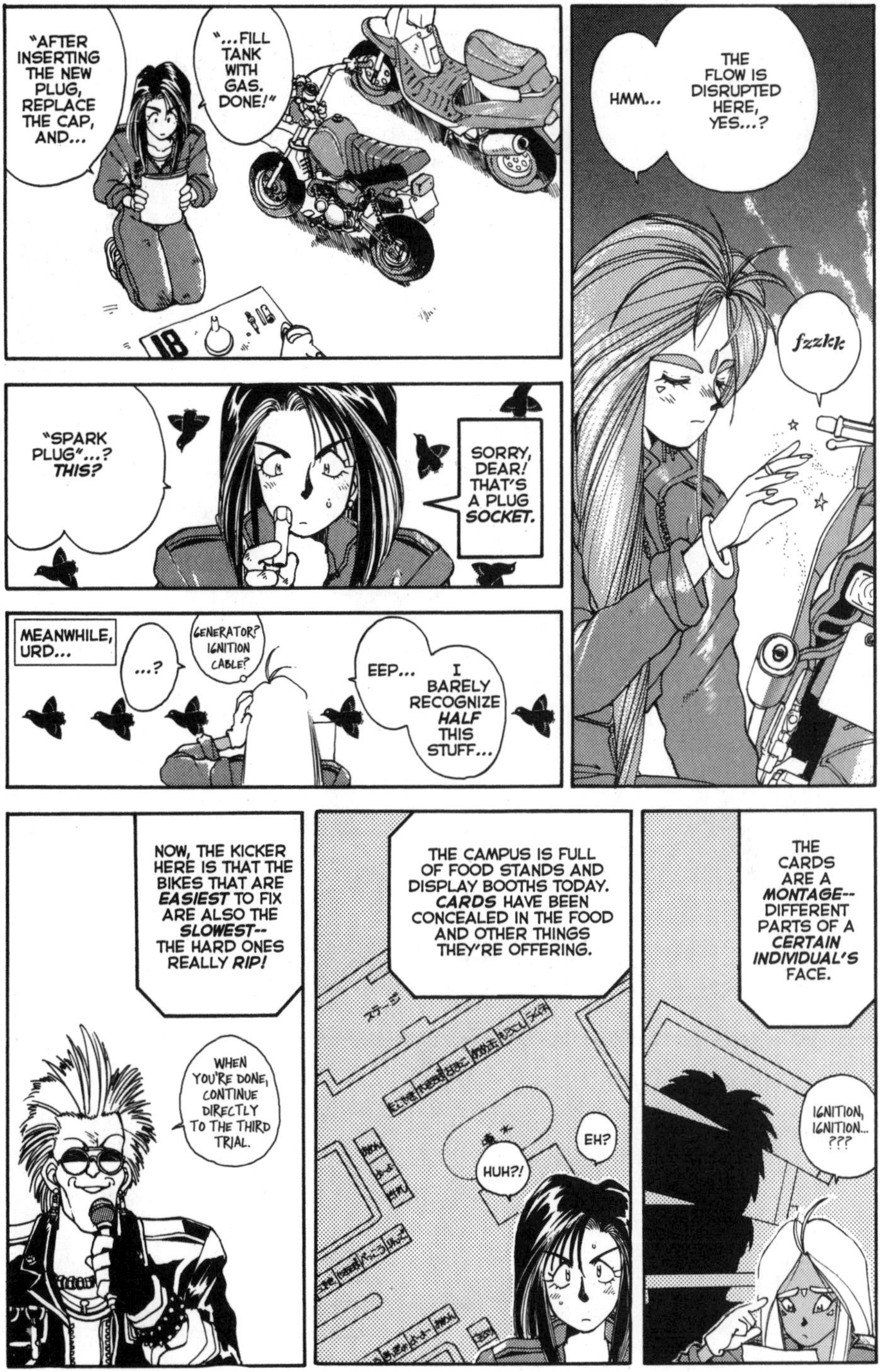
"AFTER INSERTING THE NEW PLUG, REPLACE THE CAP, AND...
"...FILL TANK WITH GAS. DONE!"
"SPARK PLUG"...? THIS?
SORRY, DEAR! THAT'S A PLUG SOCKET.
MEANWHILE, URD...
...?
GENERATOR? IGNITION CABLE?
EEP... I BARELY RECOGNIZE HALF THIS STUFF...
HMM...
THE FLOW IS DISRUPTED HERE, YES...?
fzzkk
NOW, THE KICKER HERE IS THAT THE BIKES THAT ARE EASIEST TO FIX ARE ALSO THE SLOWEST-- THE HARD ONES REALLY RIP!
WHEN YOU'RE DONE, CONTINUE DIRECTLY TO THE THIRD TRIAL.
THE CAMPUS IS FULL OF FOOD STANDS AND DISPLAY BOOTHS TODAY. CARDS HAVE BEEN CONCEALED IN THE FOOD AND OTHER THINGS THEY'RE OFFERING.
EH?
HUH?!
THE CARDS ARE A MONTAGE-- DIFFERENT PARTS OF A CERTAIN INDIVIDUAL'S FACE.
IGNITION, IGNITION... ???

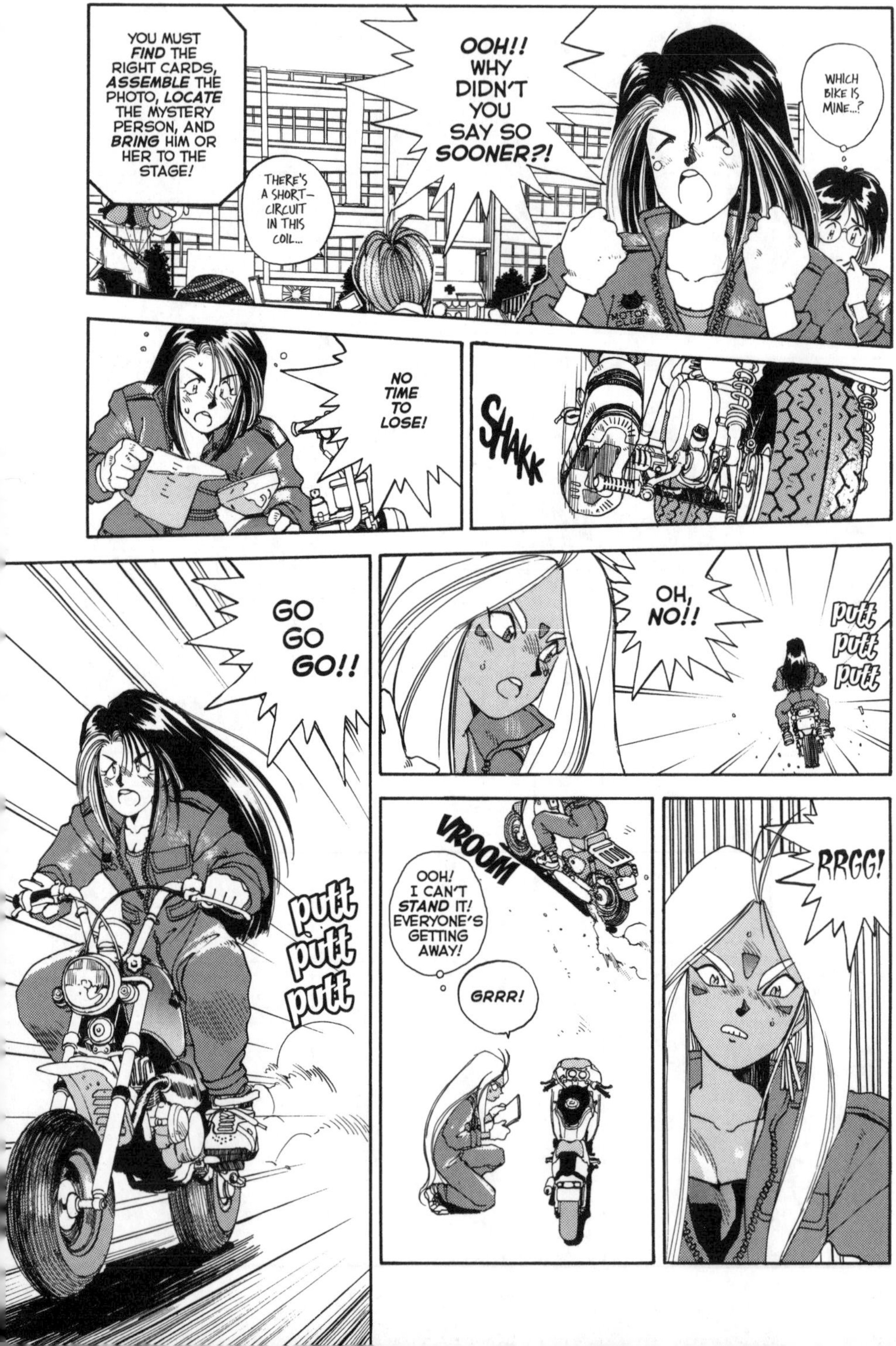

YOU MUST *FIND* THE RIGHT CARDS, *ASSEMBLE* THE PHOTO, *LOCATE* THE MYSTERY PERSON, AND *BRING* HIM OR HER TO THE STAGE!
THERE'S A SHORT-CIRCUIT IN THIS COIL...
OOH!! WHY DIDN'T YOU SAY SO SOONER?!
WHICH BIKE IS MINE...?
NO TIME TO LOSE!
SHAKK
GO GO GO!!
putt putt putt
OH, NO!!
putt putt putt
VROOM
OOH! I CAN'T *STAND* IT! EVERYONE'S GETTING AWAY!
GRRR!
RRGG!

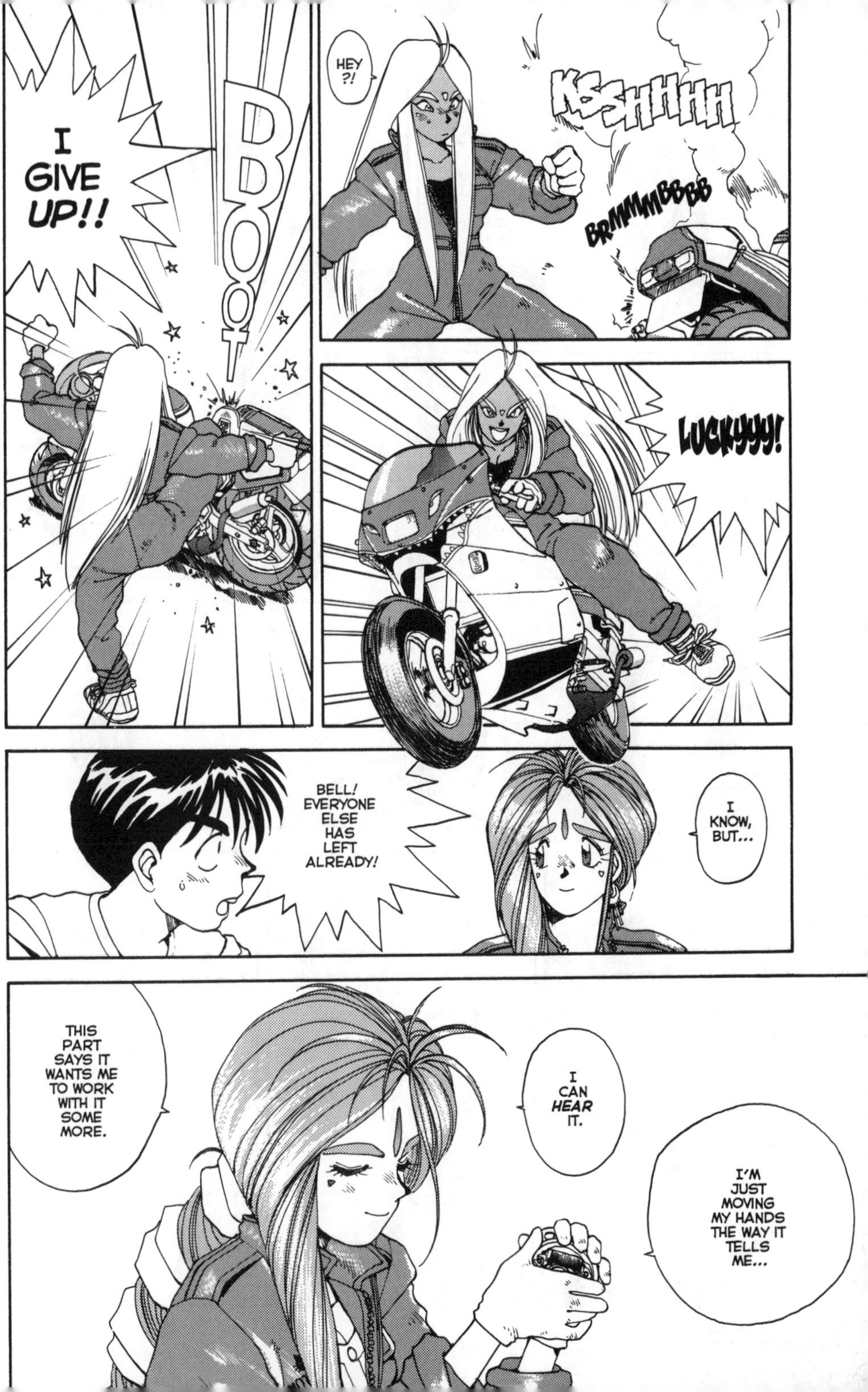
I GIVE UP!!
BOOT
HEY ?!
KSSHHHH
BRMMMBBBB
LUCKYYY!
BELL! EVERYONE ELSE HAS LEFT ALREADY!
I KNOW, BUT...
THIS PART SAYS IT WANTS ME TO WORK WITH IT SOME MORE.
I CAN *HEAR* IT.
I'M JUST MOVING MY HANDS THE WAY IT TELLS ME...

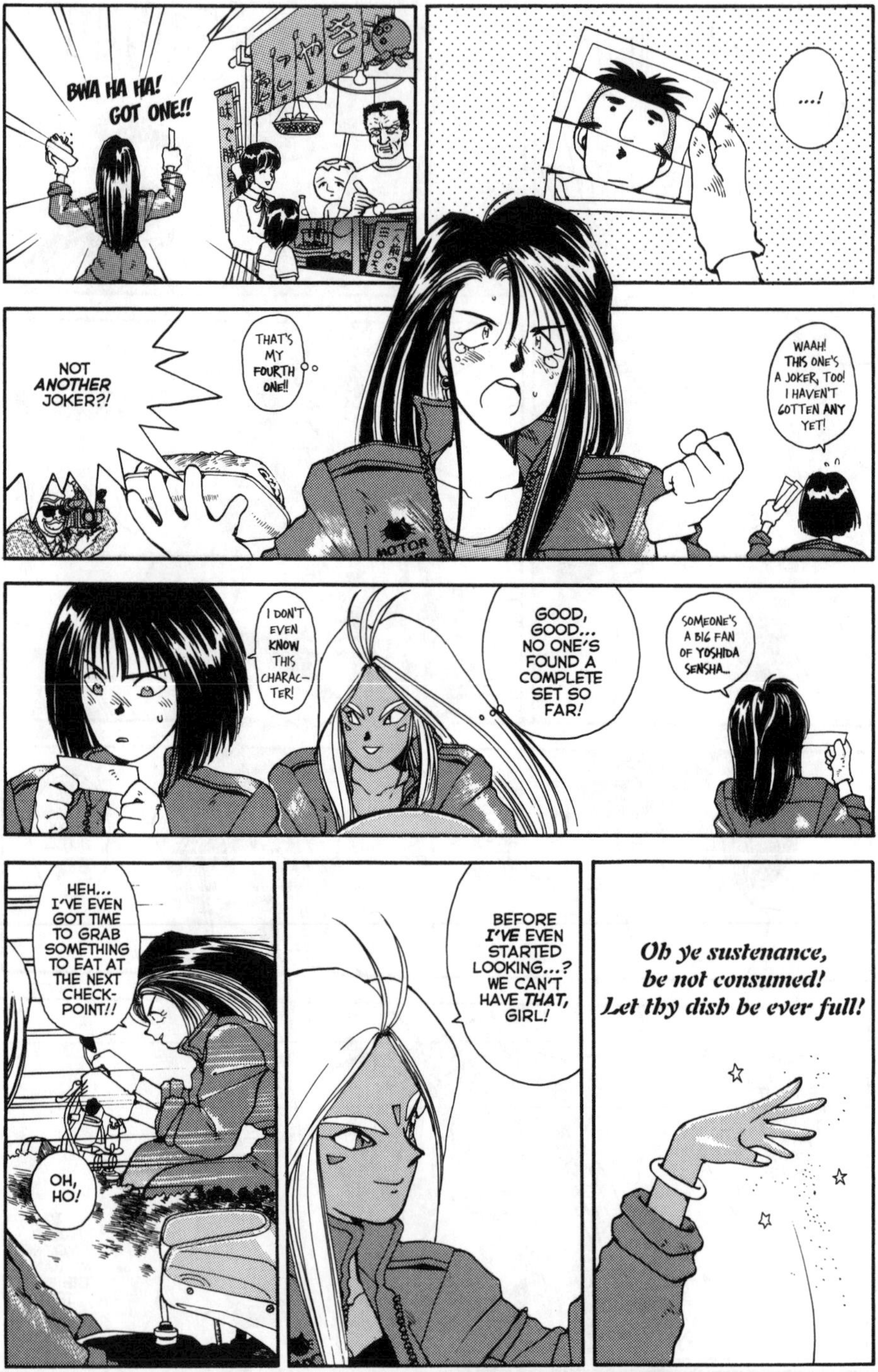
BWA HA HA! GOT ONE!!
...!
NOT ANOTHER JOKER?!
THAT'S MY FOURTH ONE!!
WAAH! THIS ONE'S A JOKER, TOO! I HAVEN'T GOTTEN ANY YET!
I DON'T EVEN KNOW THIS CHARAC-TER!
GOOD, GOOD... NO ONE'S FOUND A COMPLETE SET SO FAR!
SOMEONE'S A BIG FAN OF YOSHIDA SENSHA...
HEH... I'VE EVEN GOT TIME TO GRAB SOMETHING TO EAT AT THE NEXT CHECK-POINT!!
OH, HO!
BEFORE I'VE EVEN STARTED LOOKING...? WE CAN'T HAVE THAT, GIRL!
Oh ye sustenance, be not consumed! Let thy dish be ever full!

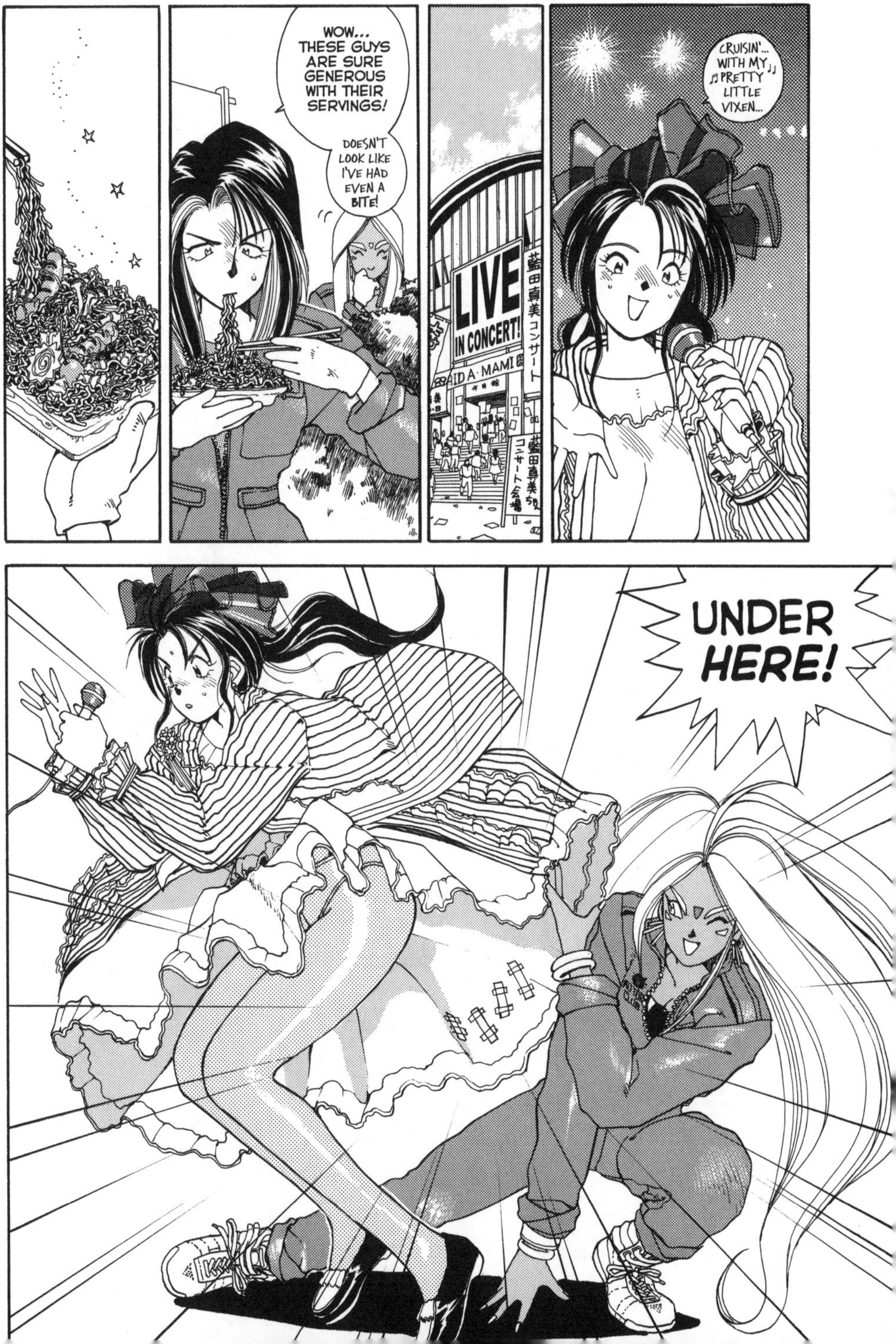
WOW... THESE GUYS ARE SURE GENEROUS WITH THEIR SERVINGS!
DOESN'T LOOK LIKE I'VE HAD EVEN A BITE!
LIVE IN CONCERT!
藍田真美コンサート
AIDA·MAMI
CRUISIN'... WITH MY ♫ PRETTY ♫ LITTLE VIXEN...
UNDER HERE!

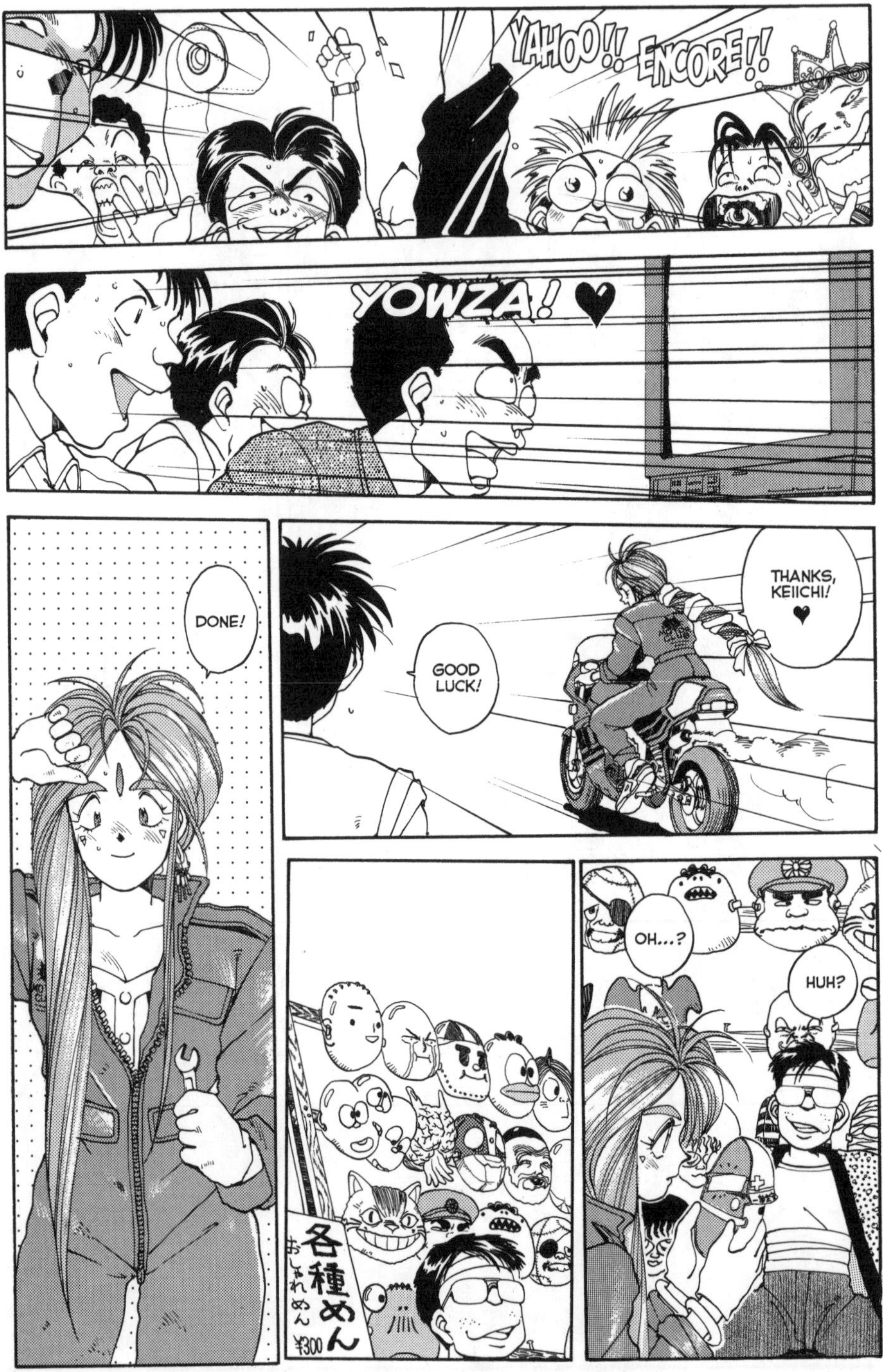
YAHOO!!
ENCORE!!
YOWZA! ♥
DONE!
GOOD LUCK!
THANKS, KEIICHI! ♥
各種めん
おしゃれめん
¥300
OH...?
HUH?

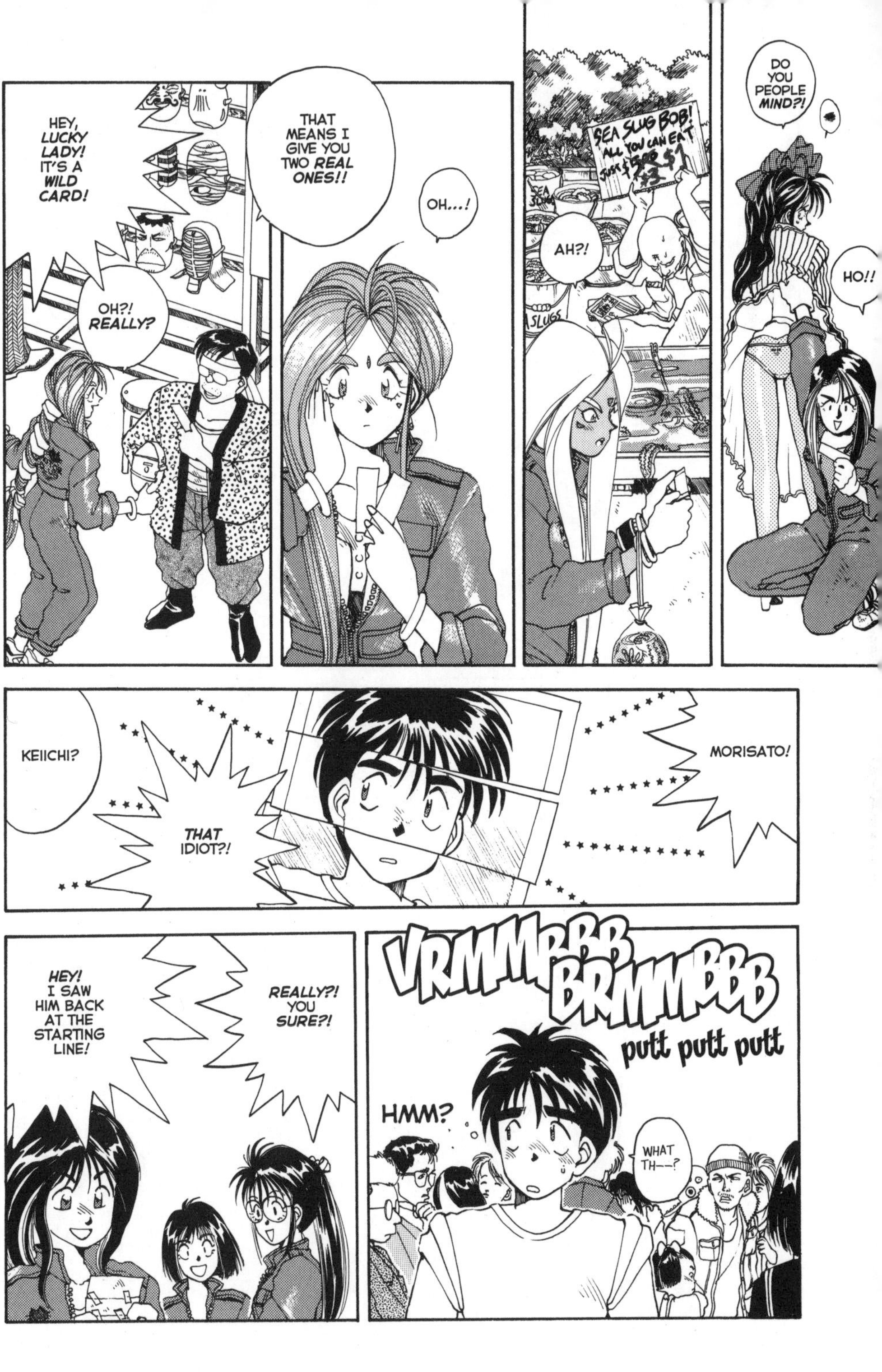
HEY, LUCKY LADY! IT'S A WILD CARD!
OH?! REALLY?
THAT MEANS I GIVE YOU TWO REAL ONES!!
OH...!
SEA SLUG BOB! ALL YOU CAN EAT
SEA SLUGS
AH?!
SLUGS
DO YOU PEOPLE MIND?!
HO!!
KEIICHI?
THAT IDIOT?!
MORISATO!
HEY! I SAW HIM BACK AT THE STARTING LINE!
REALLY?! YOU SURE?!
VRMMBBB BRMMBBB
putt putt putt
HMM?
WHAT TH--?

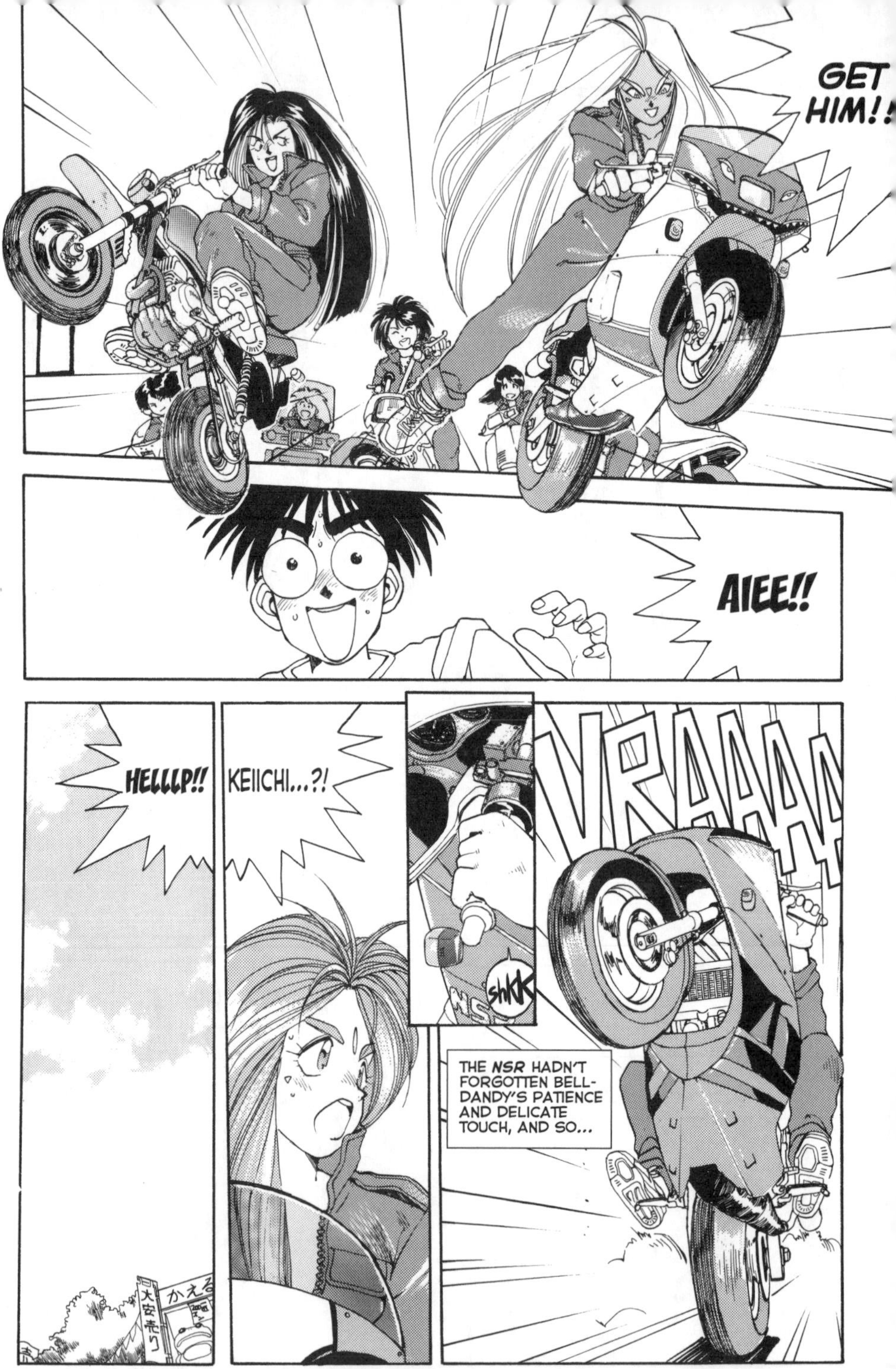
GET HIM!!
AIEE!!
HELLLP!!
大安売り
かえる
KEIICHI...?!
shKK
VRAAAA
THE NSR HADN'T FORGOTTEN BELL-DANDY'S PATIENCE AND DELICATE TOUCH, AND SO...

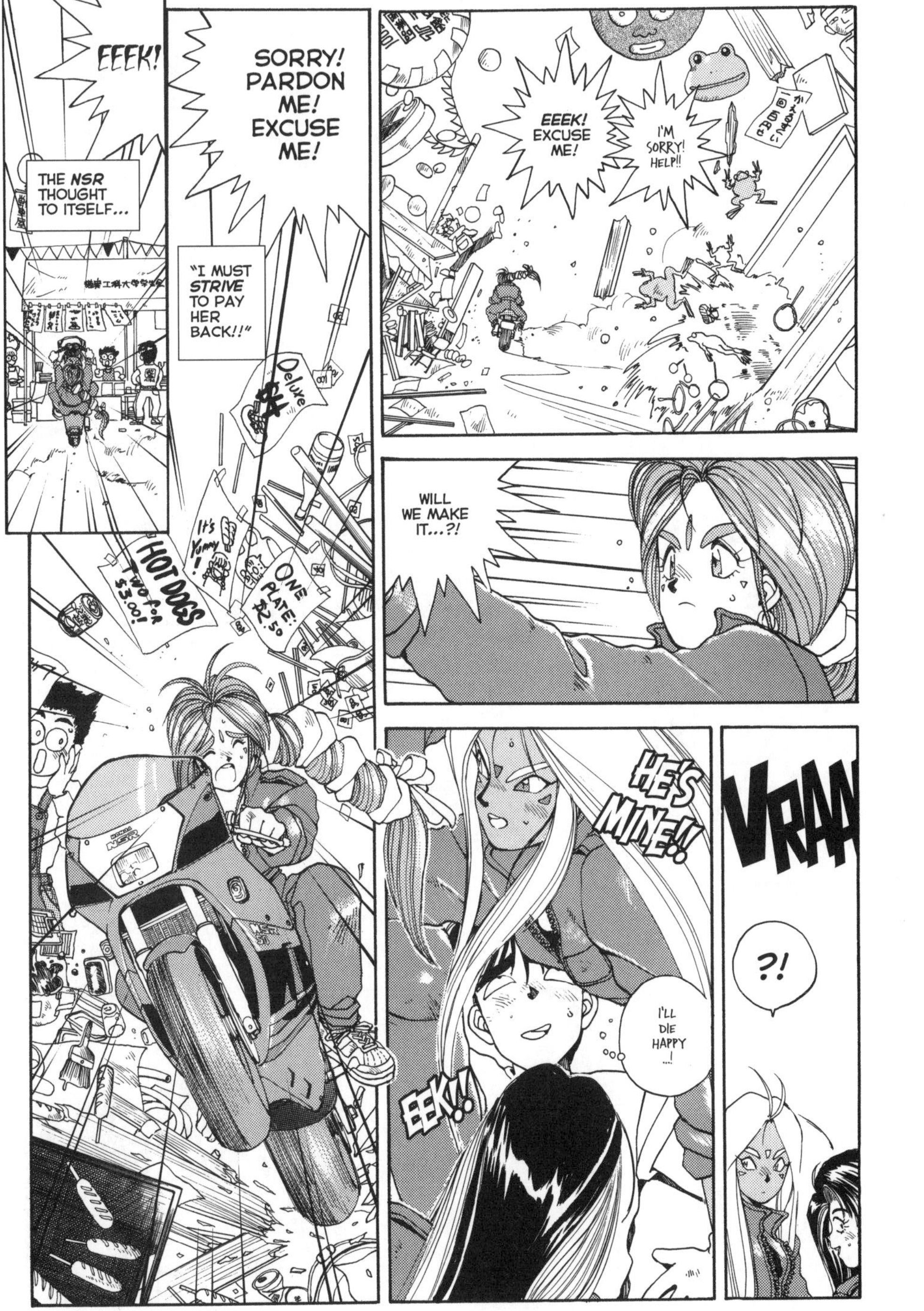
EEEK!
THE NSR THOUGHT TO ITSELF...
SORRY! PARDON ME! EXCUSE ME!
"I MUST STRIVE TO PAY HER BACK!!"
EEEK! EXCUSE ME!
I'M SORRY! HELP!!
Deluxe
It's Yummy!
HOT DOGS TWO for $3.00!
ONE PLATE $2.50
WILL WE MAKE IT...?!
HE'S MINE!!
I'LL DIE HAPPY...!
EEK!!
VRAA
?!

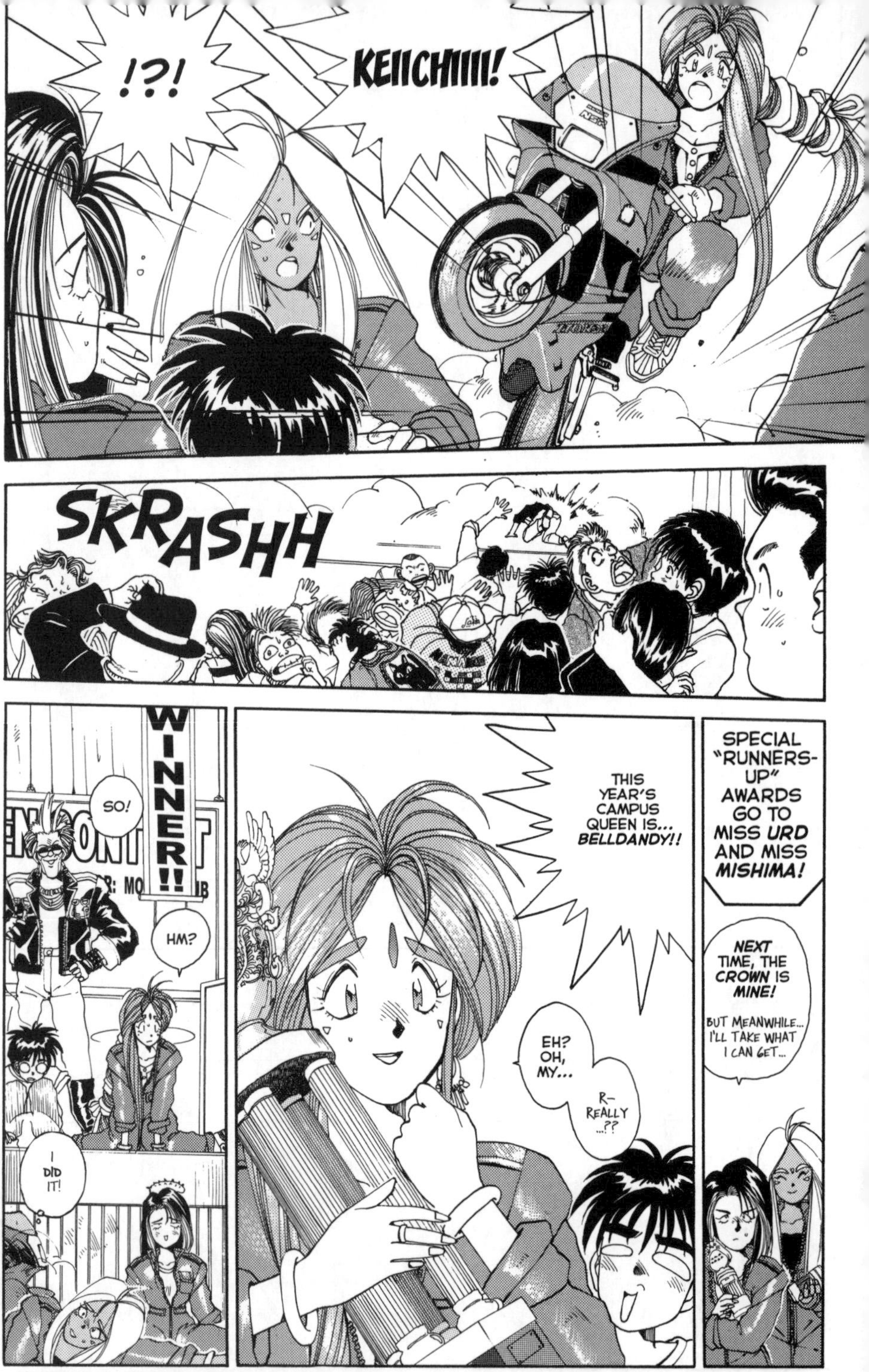
!?!
KEIICHIIIII!
SKRASHH
SO!
WINNER!!
HM?
I DID IT!
THIS YEAR'S CAMPUS QUEEN IS... BELLDANDY!!
EH? OH, MY...
R-REALLY ...??
SPECIAL "RUNNERS-UP" AWARDS GO TO MISS URD AND MISS MISHIMA!
NEXT TIME, THE CROWN IS MINE!
BUT MEANWHILE... I'LL TAKE WHAT I CAN GET...

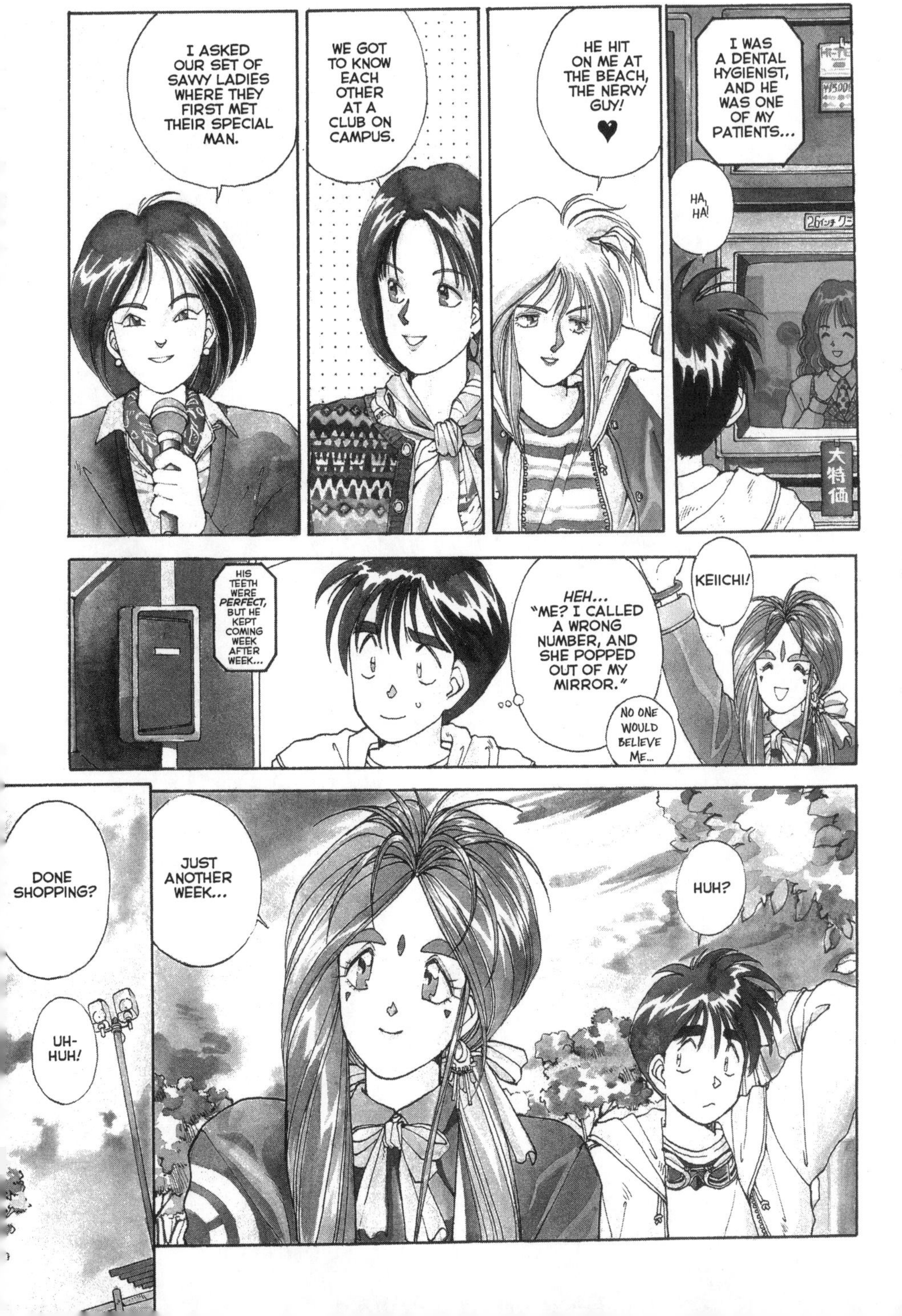
I ASKED OUR SET OF SAVVY LADIES WHERE THEY FIRST MET THEIR SPECIAL MAN.
WE GOT TO KNOW EACH OTHER AT A CLUB ON CAMPUS.
HE HIT ON ME AT THE BEACH, THE NERVY GUY! ♥
I WAS A DENTAL HYGIENIST, AND HE WAS ONE OF MY PATIENTS...
HA, HA!
大特価
HIS TEETH WERE *PERFECT*, BUT HE KEPT COMING WEEK AFTER WEEK...
*HEH...* "ME? I CALLED A WRONG NUMBER, AND SHE POPPED OUT OF MY MIRROR."
NO ONE WOULD BELIEVE ME...
KEIICHI!
DONE SHOPPING?
UH-HUH!
JUST ANOTHER WEEK...
HUH?

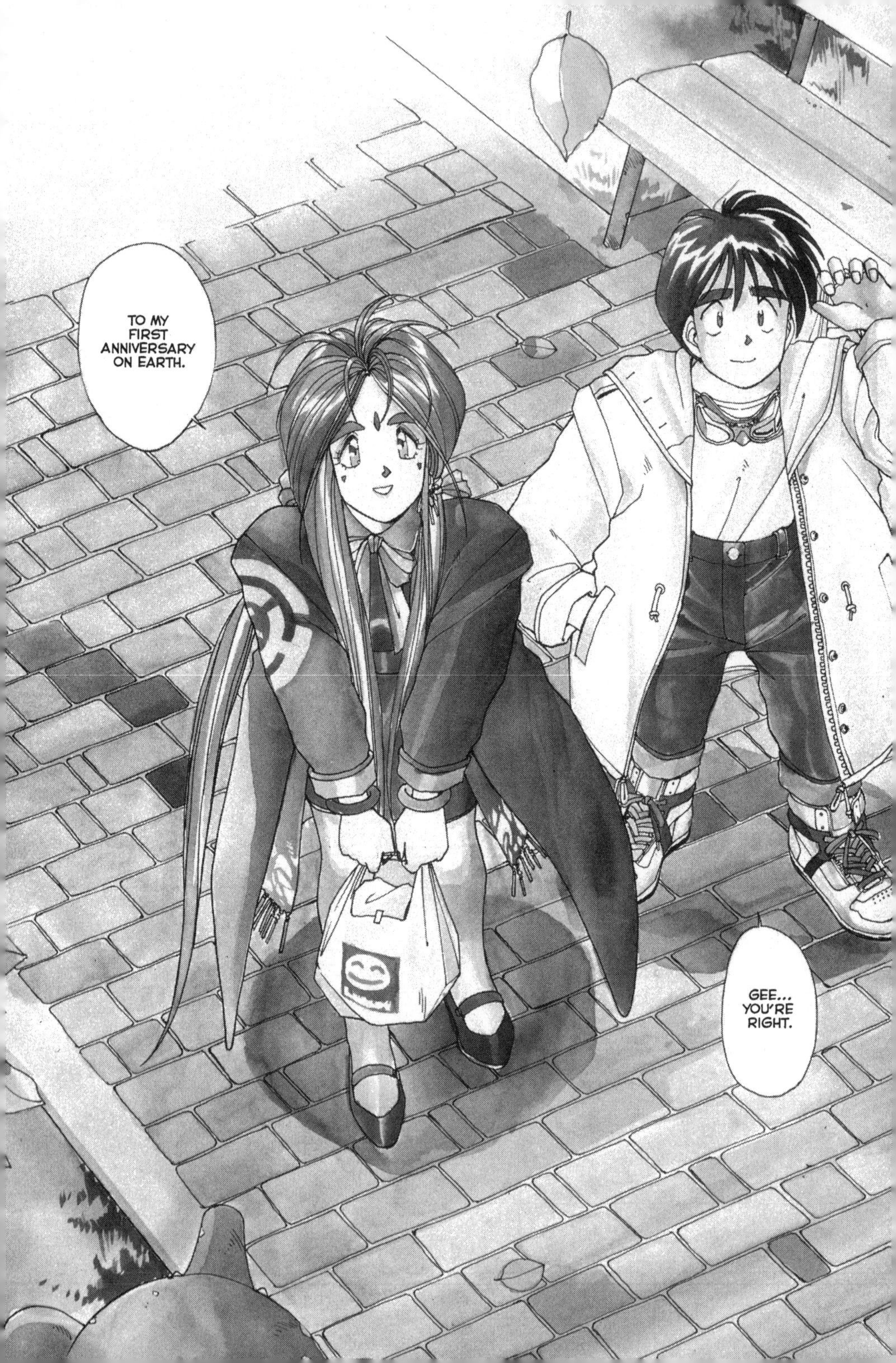
TO MY FIRST ANNIVERSARY ON EARTH.
GEE... YOU'RE RIGHT.

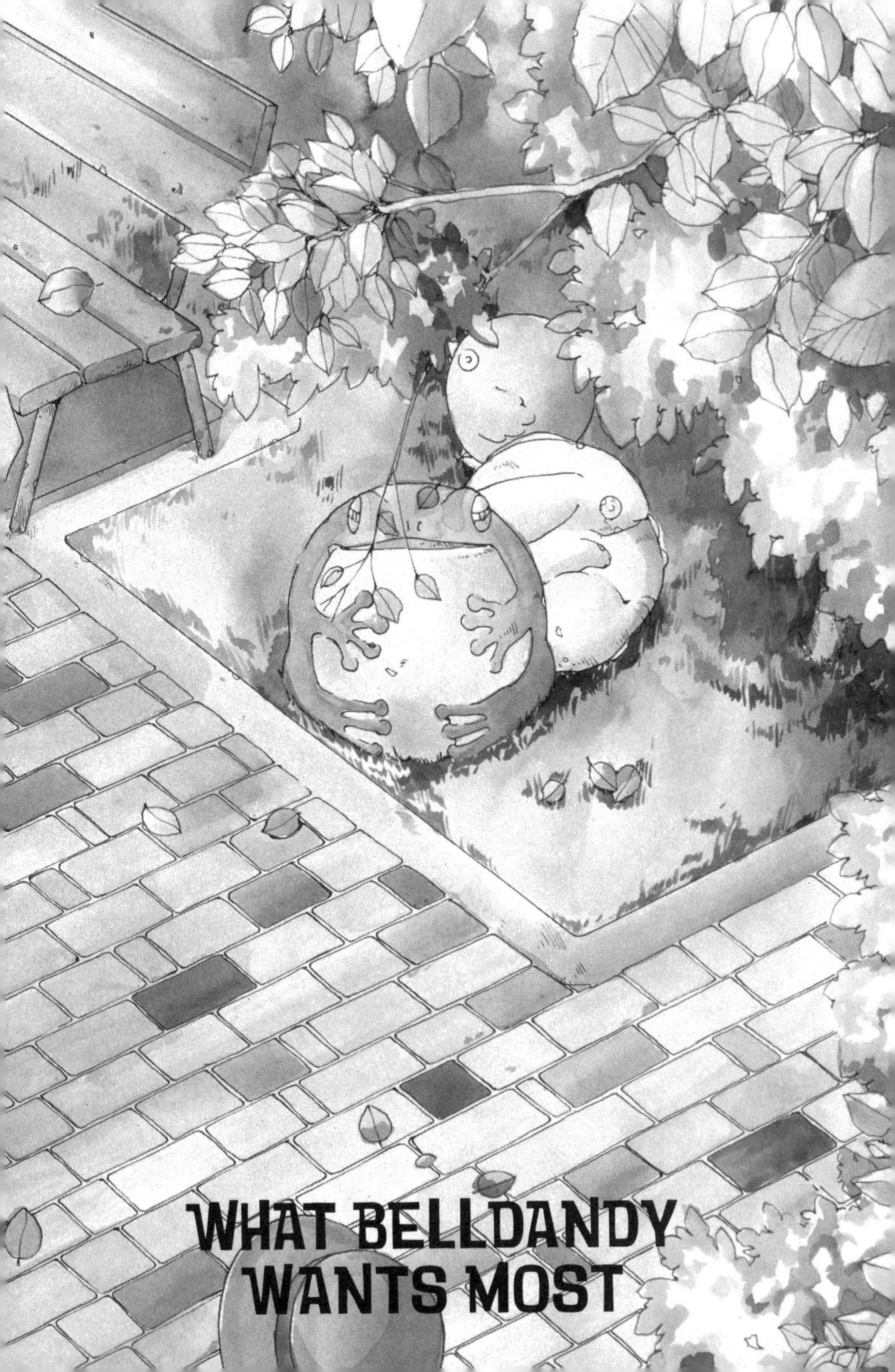
WHAT BELLDANDY
WANTS MOST

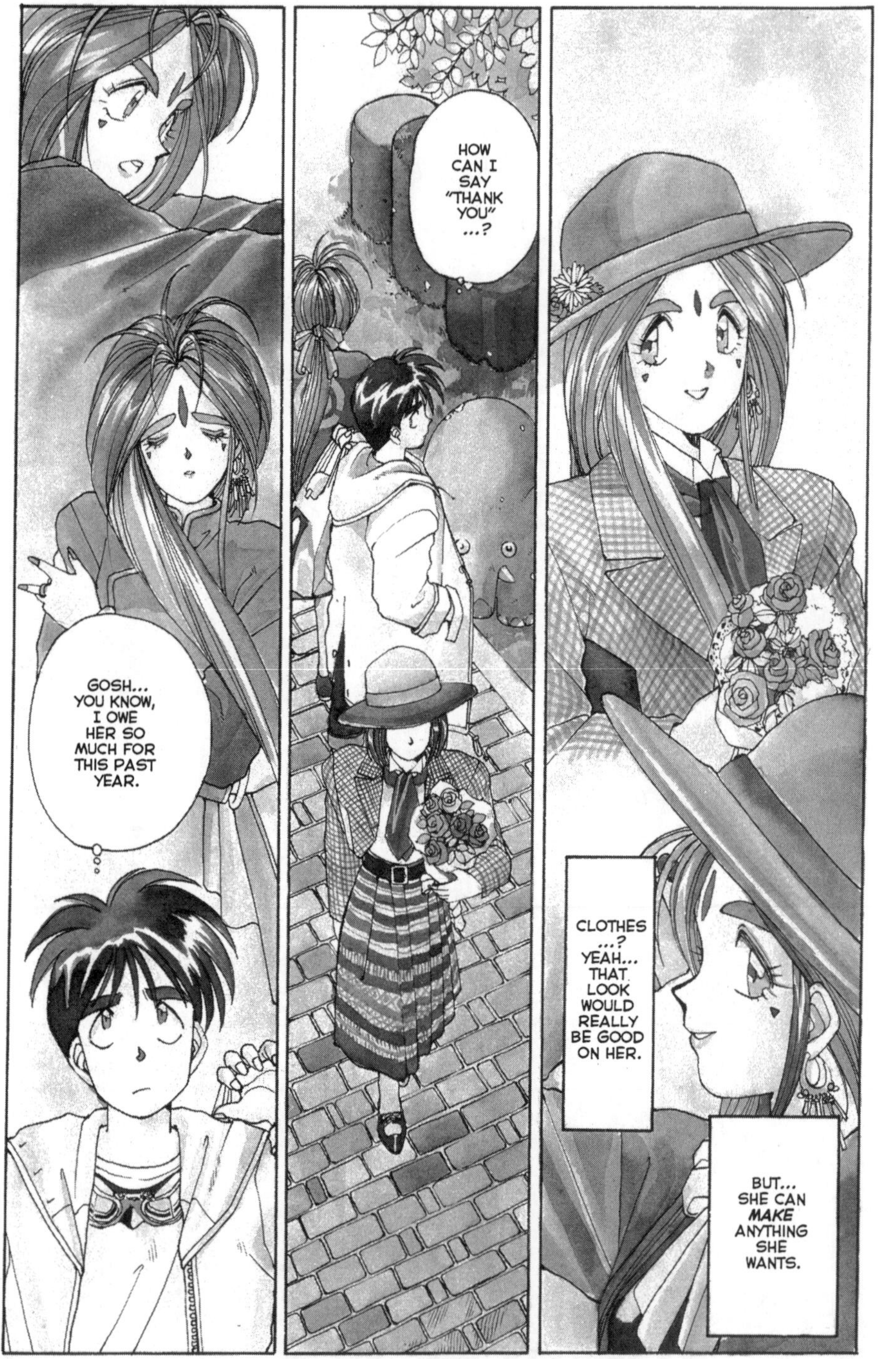
GOSH... YOU KNOW, I OWE HER SO MUCH FOR THIS PAST YEAR.
HOW CAN I SAY "THANK YOU" ...?
CLOTHES ...? YEAH... THAT LOOK WOULD REALLY BE GOOD ON HER.
BUT... SHE CAN *MAKE* ANYTHING SHE WANTS.

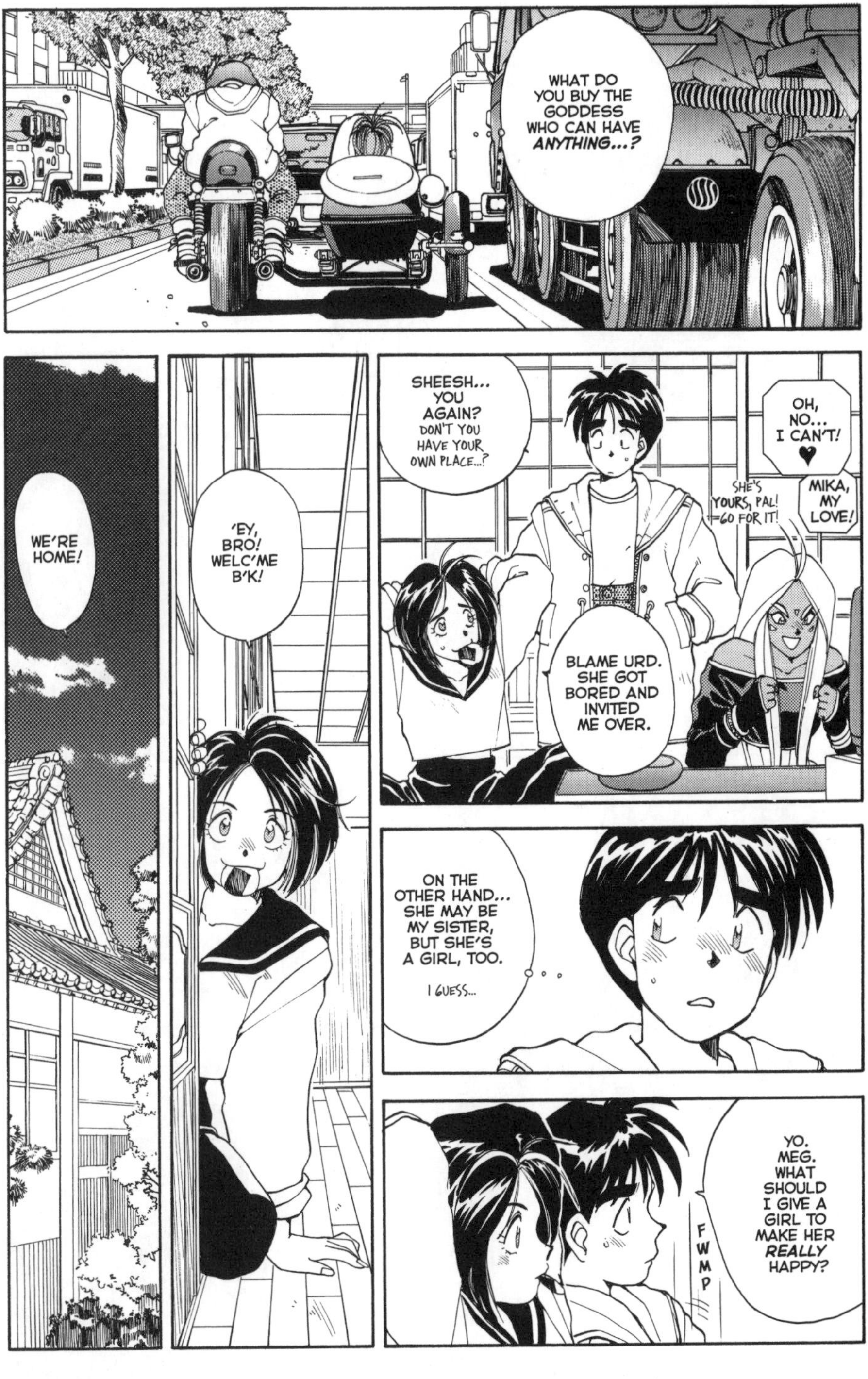
WHAT DO YOU BUY THE GODDESS WHO CAN HAVE *ANYTHING...?*
WE'RE HOME!
'EY, BRO! WELC'ME B'K!
SHEESH... YOU AGAIN? DON'T YOU HAVE YOUR OWN PLACE...?
OH, NO... I CAN'T! ♥
SHE'S YOURS, PAL! ¥60 FOR IT!
MIKA, MY LOVE!
BLAME URD. SHE GOT BORED AND INVITED ME OVER.
ON THE OTHER HAND... SHE MAY BE MY SISTER, BUT SHE'S A GIRL, TOO.
I GUESS...
YO. MEG. WHAT SHOULD I GIVE A GIRL TO MAKE HER *REALLY* HAPPY?
FWMP

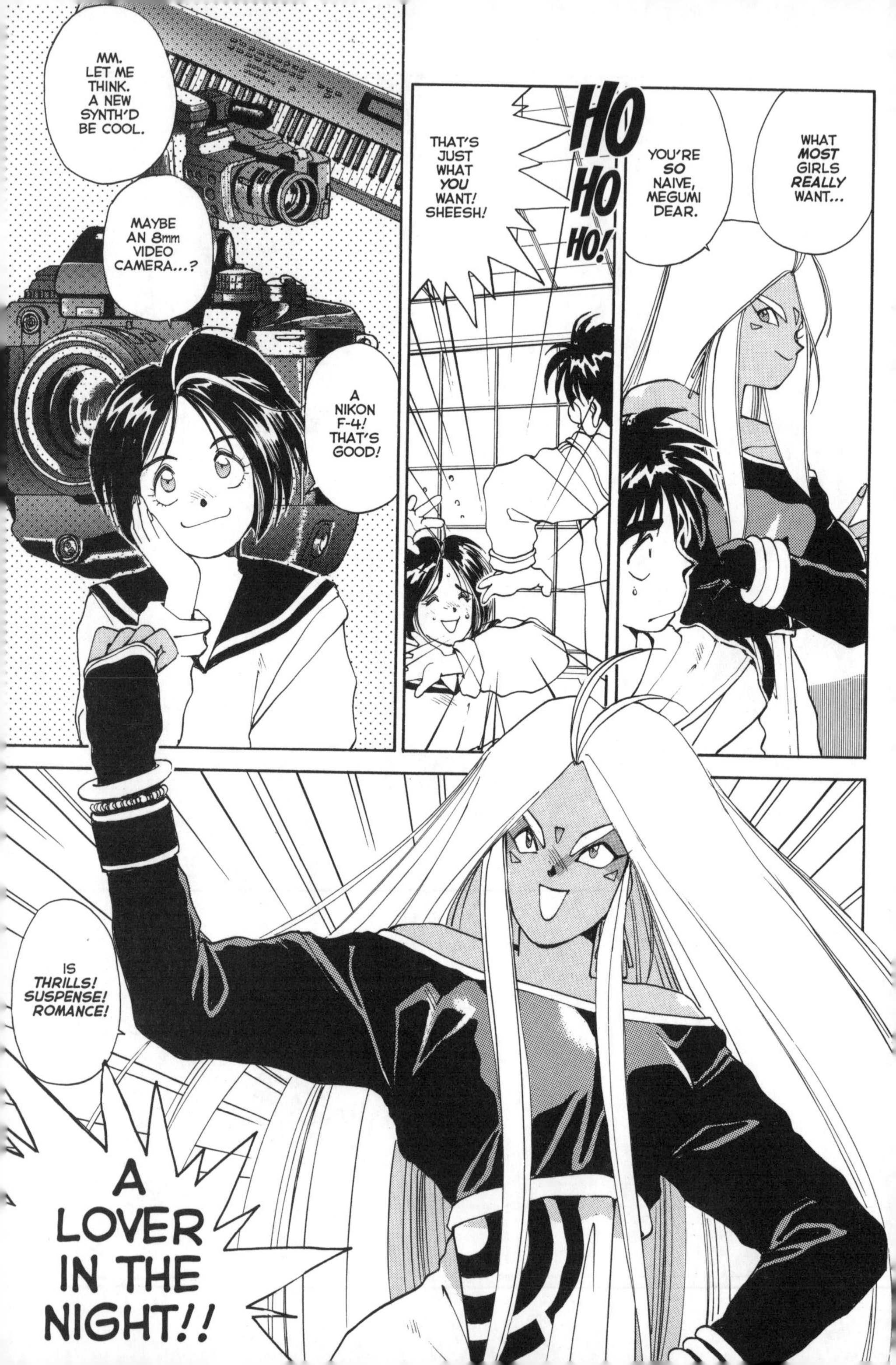
MM. LET ME THINK. A NEW SYNTH'D BE COOL.
MAYBE AN 8mm VIDEO CAMERA...?
A NIKON F-4! THAT'S GOOD!
THAT'S JUST WHAT YOU WANT! SHEESH!
HO HO HO!
YOU'RE SO NAIVE, MEGUMI DEAR.
WHAT MOST GIRLS REALLY WANT...
IS THRILLS! SUSPENSE! ROMANCE!
A LOVER IN THE NIGHT!!

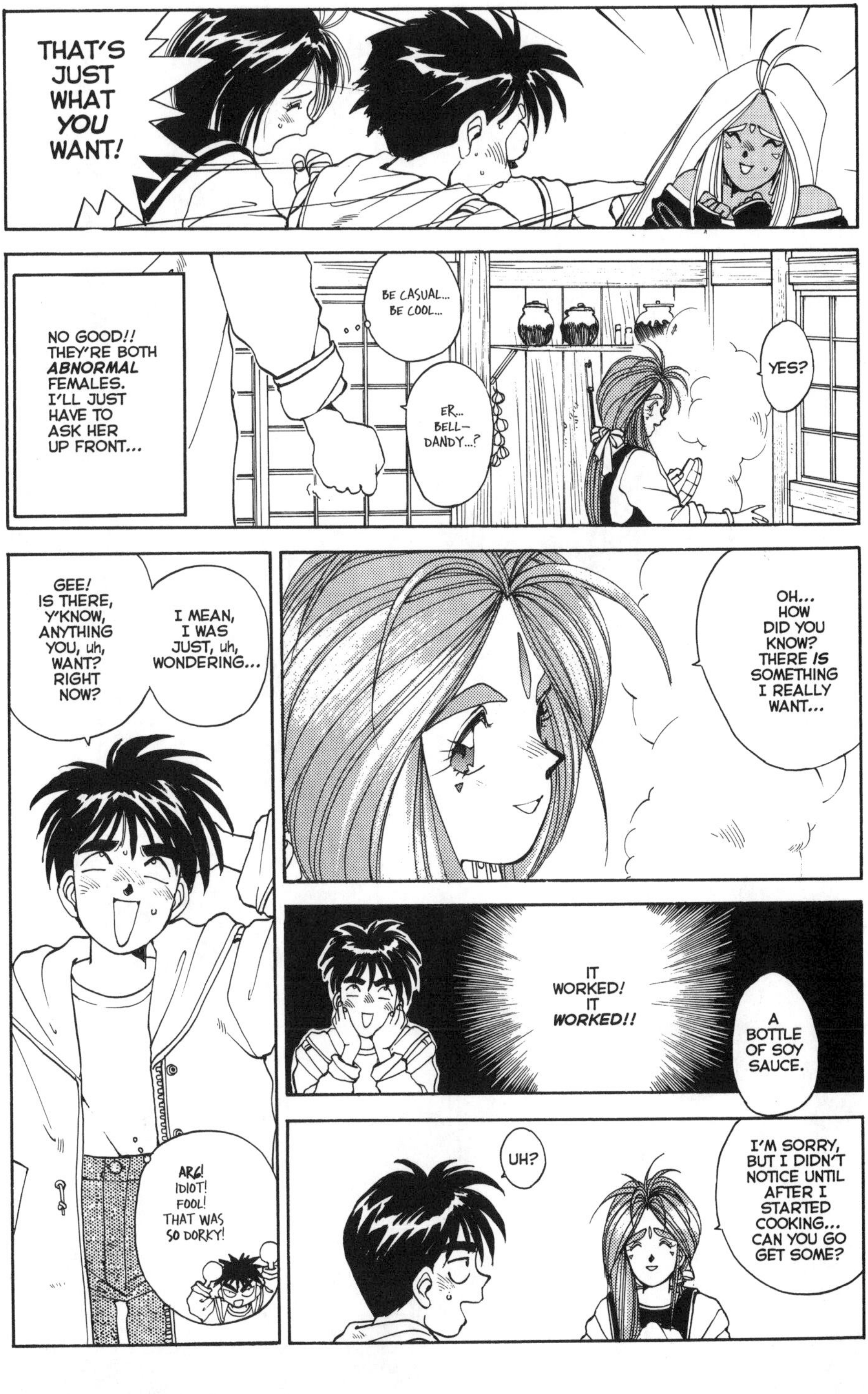
THAT'S JUST WHAT *YOU* WANT!
NO GOOD!! THEY'RE BOTH ***ABNORMAL*** FEMALES. I'LL JUST HAVE TO ASK HER UP FRONT...
BE CASUAL... BE COOL...
ER... BELL-DANDY...?
YES?
GEE! IS THERE, Y'KNOW, ANYTHING YOU, uh, WANT? RIGHT NOW?
I MEAN, I WAS JUST, uh, WONDERING...
ARG! IDIOT! FOOL! THAT WAS SO DORKY!
OH... HOW DID YOU KNOW? THERE *IS* SOMETHING I REALLY WANT...
IT WORKED! IT ***WORKED!!***
A BOTTLE OF SOY SAUCE.
UH?
I'M SORRY, BUT I DIDN'T NOTICE UNTIL AFTER I STARTED COOKING... CAN YOU GO GET SOME?

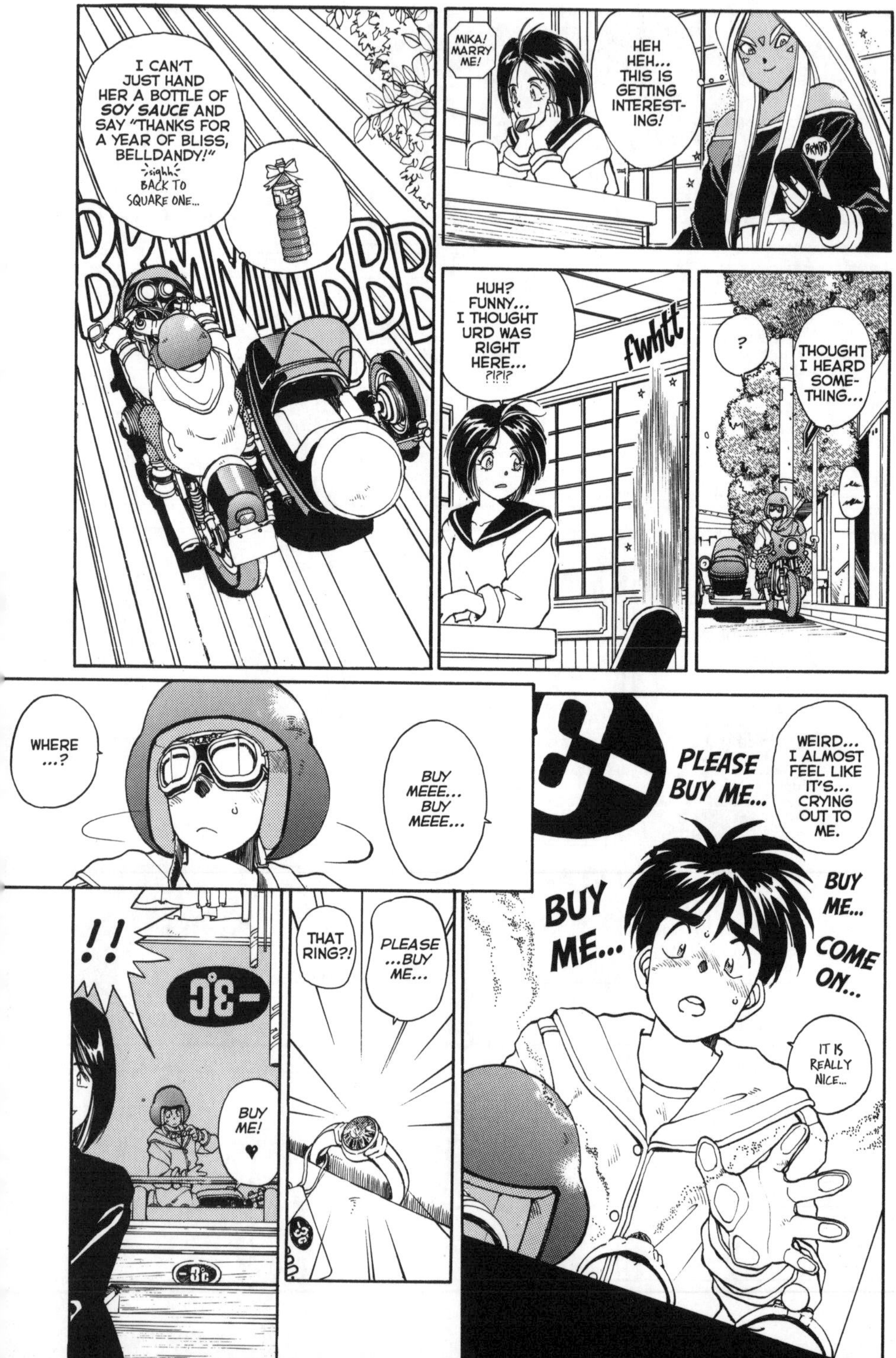

I CAN'T JUST HAND HER A BOTTLE OF SOY SAUCE AND SAY "THANKS FOR A YEAR OF BLISS, BELLDANDY!"
sighh
BACK TO SQUARE ONE...
BRMMMBBB
MIKA! MARRY ME!
HEH HEH... THIS IS GETTING INTEREST-ING!
BRMBB
HUH? FUNNY... I THOUGHT URD WAS RIGHT HERE... ?!?!?
fwhtt
?
THOUGHT I HEARD SOME-THING...
WHERE ...?
BUY MEEE... BUY MEEE...
!!
BUY ME! ♥
THAT RING?!
PLEASE ...BUY ME...
PLEASE BUY ME...
WEIRD... I ALMOST FEEL LIKE IT'S... CRYING OUT TO ME.
BUY ME...
BUY ME...
COME ON...
IT IS REALLY NICE...

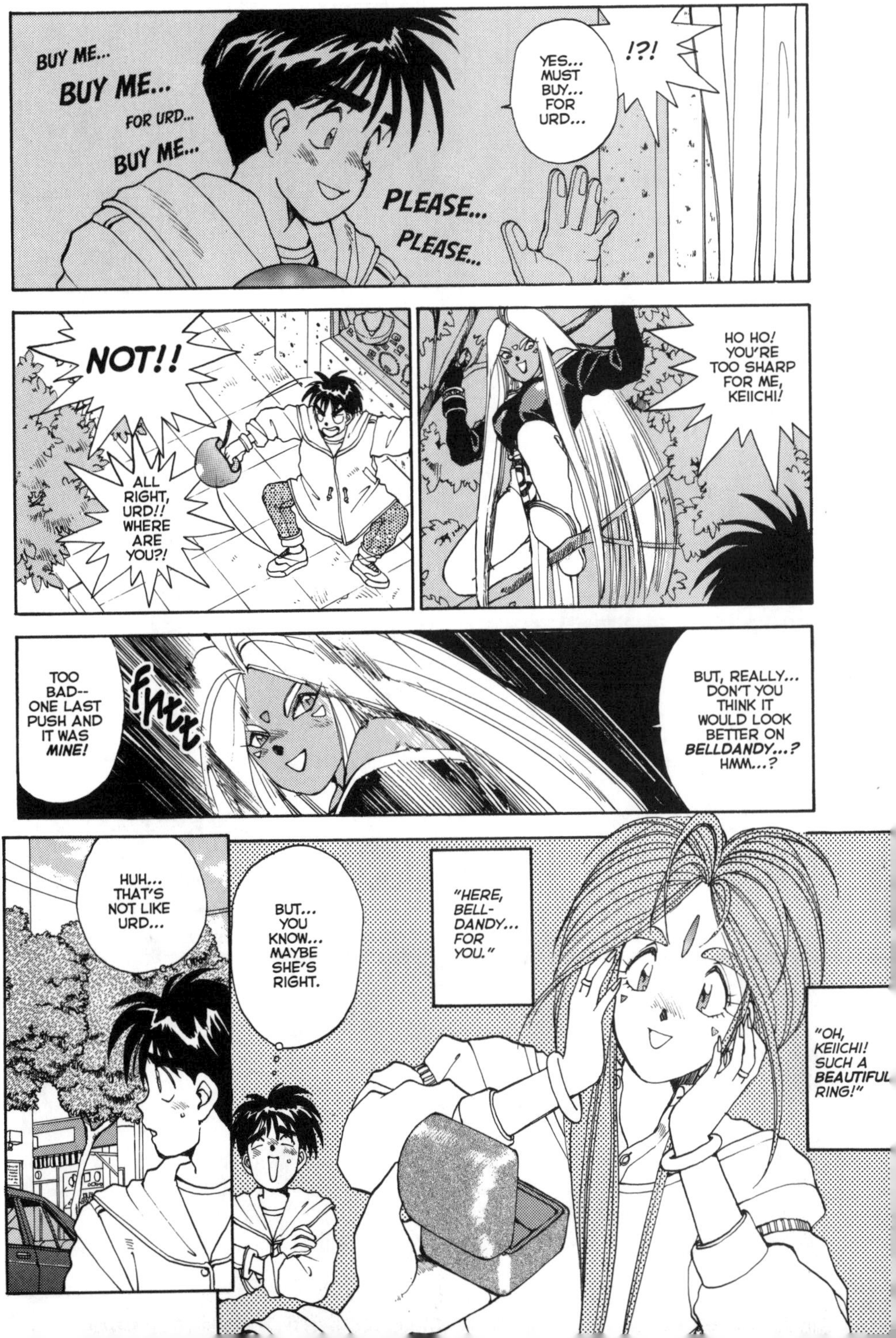
BUY ME...
BUY ME...
FOR URD...
BUY ME...
YES... MUST BUY... FOR URD...
PLEASE...
PLEASE...
!?!
NOT!!
ALL RIGHT, URD!! WHERE ARE YOU?!
HO HO! YOU'RE TOO SHARP FOR ME, KEIICHI!
TOO BAD-- ONE LAST PUSH AND IT WAS MINE!
fyttt
BUT, REALLY... DON'T YOU THINK IT WOULD LOOK BETTER ON BELLDANDY...? HMM...?
HUH... THAT'S NOT LIKE URD...
BUT... YOU KNOW... MAYBE SHE'S RIGHT.
"HERE, BELL-DANDY... FOR YOU."
"OH, KEIICHI! SUCH A BEAUTIFUL RING!"

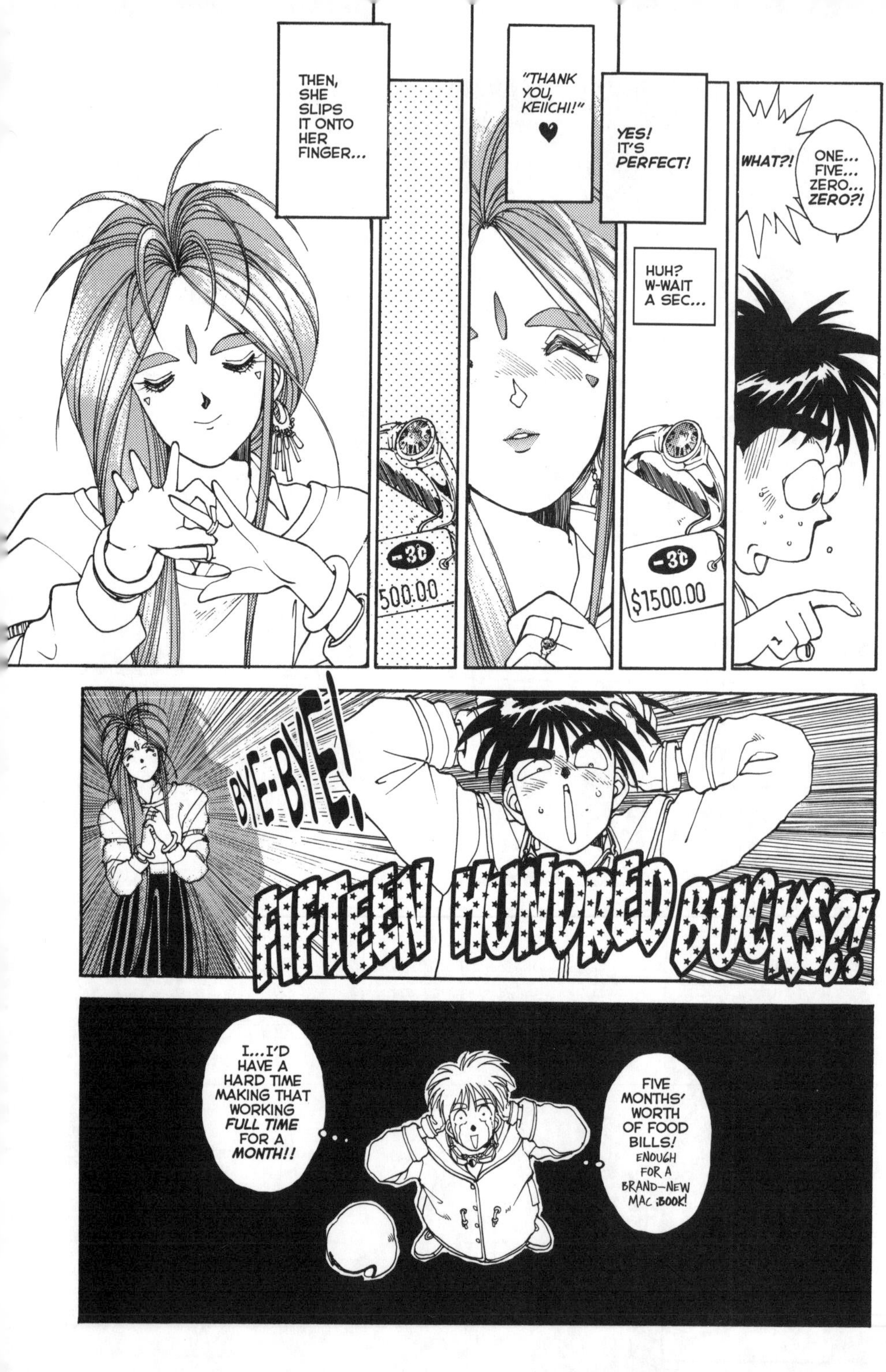
THEN, SHE SLIPS IT ONTO HER FINGER...
-3¢
500.00
"THANK YOU, KEIICHI!" ♥
YES! IT'S PERFECT!
HUH? W-WAIT A SEC...
-3¢
$1500.00
WHAT?!
ONE... FIVE... ZERO... ZERO?!
BYE-BYE!
FIFTEEN HUNDRED BUCKS?!
I...I'D HAVE A HARD TIME MAKING THAT WORKING FULL TIME FOR A MONTH!!
FIVE MONTHS' WORTH OF FOOD BILLS! ENOUGH FOR A BRAND-NEW MAC iBOOK!

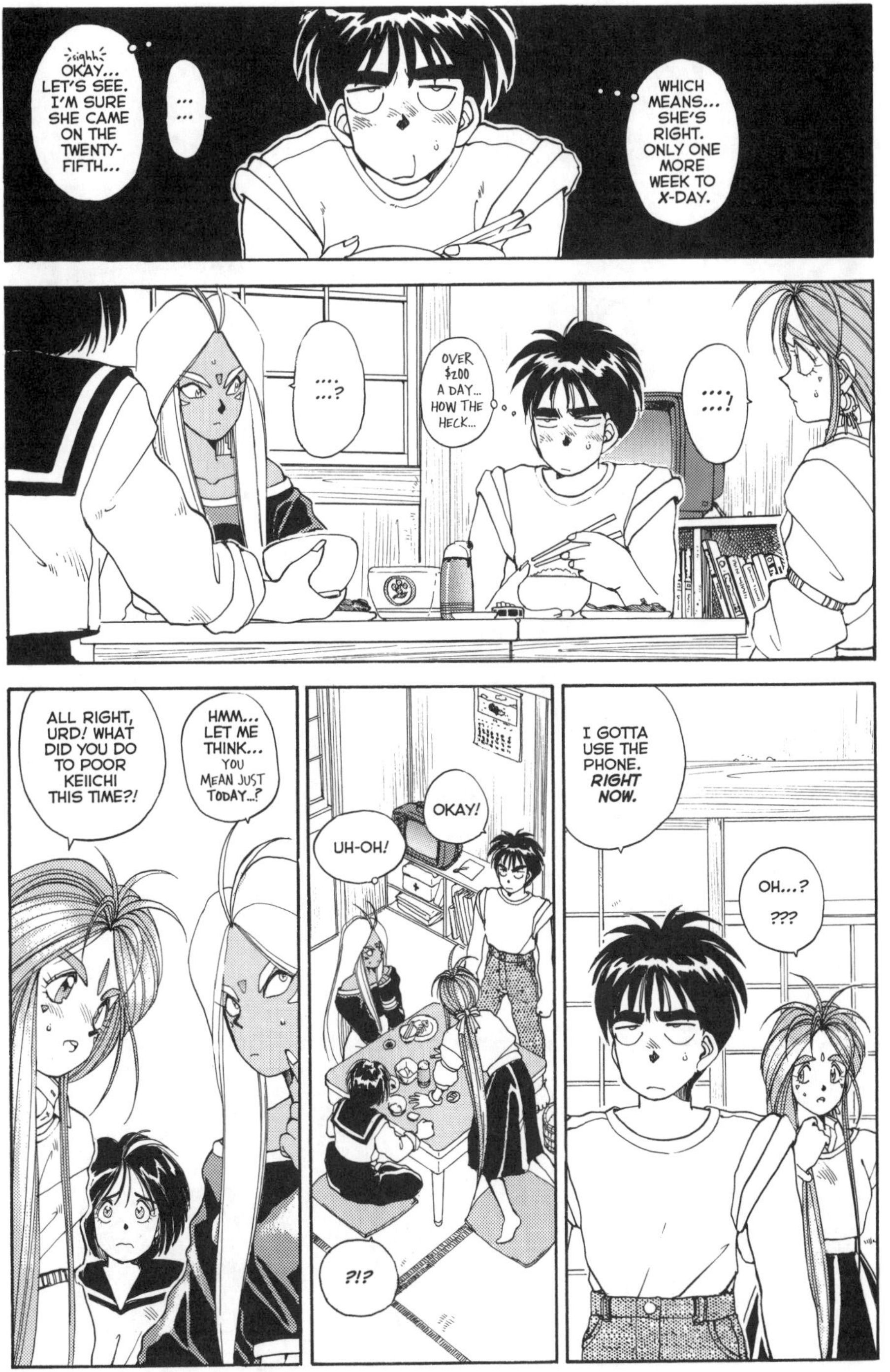
sighh
OKAY... LET'S SEE. I'M SURE SHE CAME ON THE TWENTY-FIFTH...
... ...
WHICH MEANS... SHE'S RIGHT. ONLY ONE MORE WEEK TO X-DAY.
.... ...?
OVER $200 A DAY... HOW THE HECK...
.... ...!
ALL RIGHT, URD! WHAT DID YOU DO TO POOR KEIICHI THIS TIME?!
HMM... LET ME THINK... YOU MEAN JUST TODAY...?
OKAY!
UH-OH!
?!?
I GOTTA USE THE PHONE. RIGHT NOW.
OH...?
???

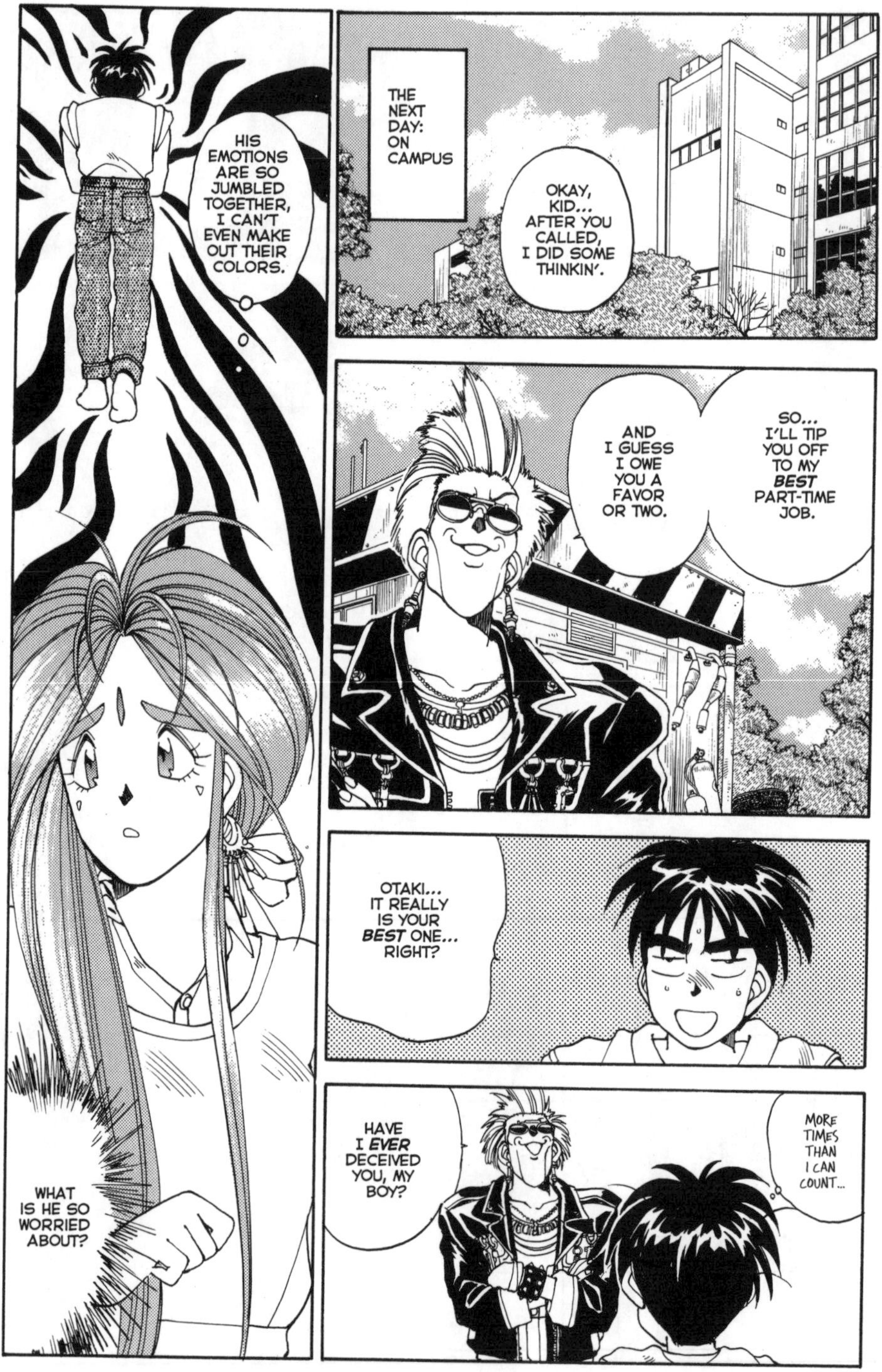
THE NEXT DAY: ON CAMPUS
OKAY, KID... AFTER YOU CALLED, I DID SOME THINKIN'.
HIS EMOTIONS ARE SO JUMBLED TOGETHER, I CAN'T EVEN MAKE OUT THEIR COLORS.
SO... I'LL TIP YOU OFF TO MY BEST PART-TIME JOB.
AND I GUESS I OWE YOU A FAVOR OR TWO.
OTAKI... IT REALLY IS YOUR BEST ONE... RIGHT?
MORE TIMES THAN I CAN COUNT...
HAVE I EVER DECEIVED YOU, MY BOY?
WHAT IS HE SO WORRIED ABOUT?

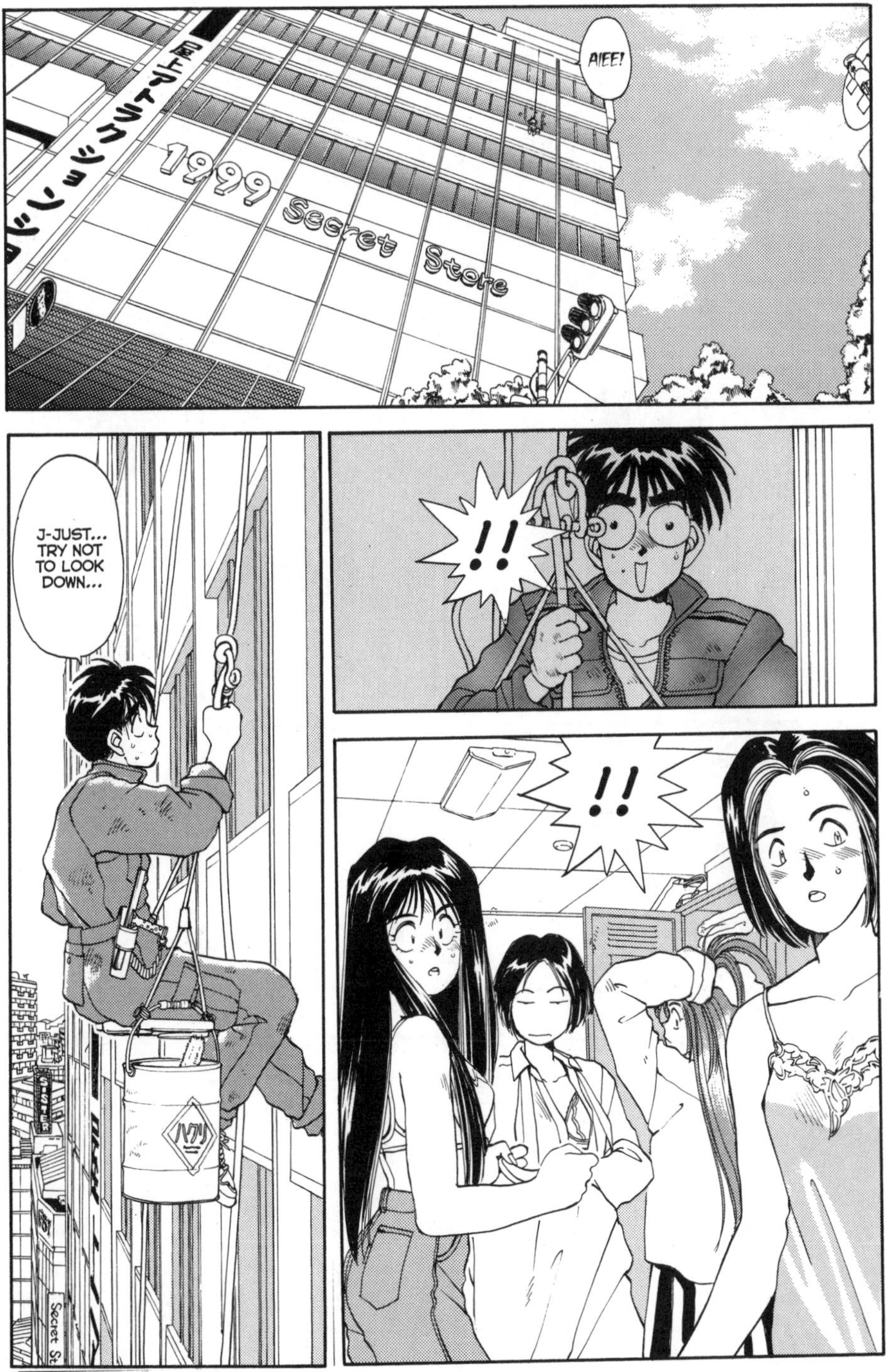
AIEE!
1999 Secret Store
J-JUST... TRY NOT TO LOOK DOWN...
ハクリ
Secret St
!!
!!

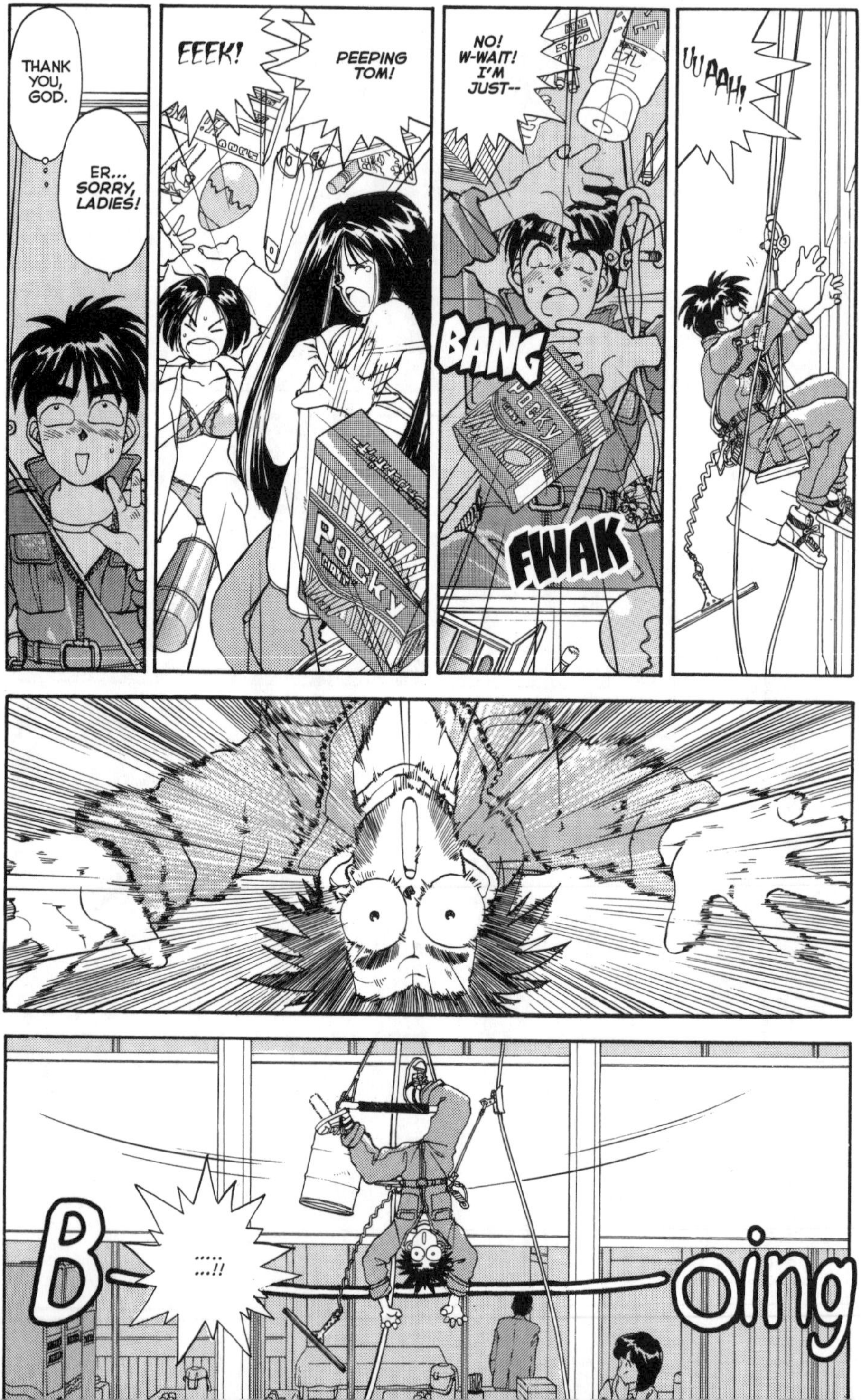
THANK YOU, GOD.
ER... SORRY, LADIES!
EEEK!
PEEPING TOM!
NO! W-WAIT! I'M JUST--
BANG
FWAK
UUAAH!
B-
.....
...!!
oing

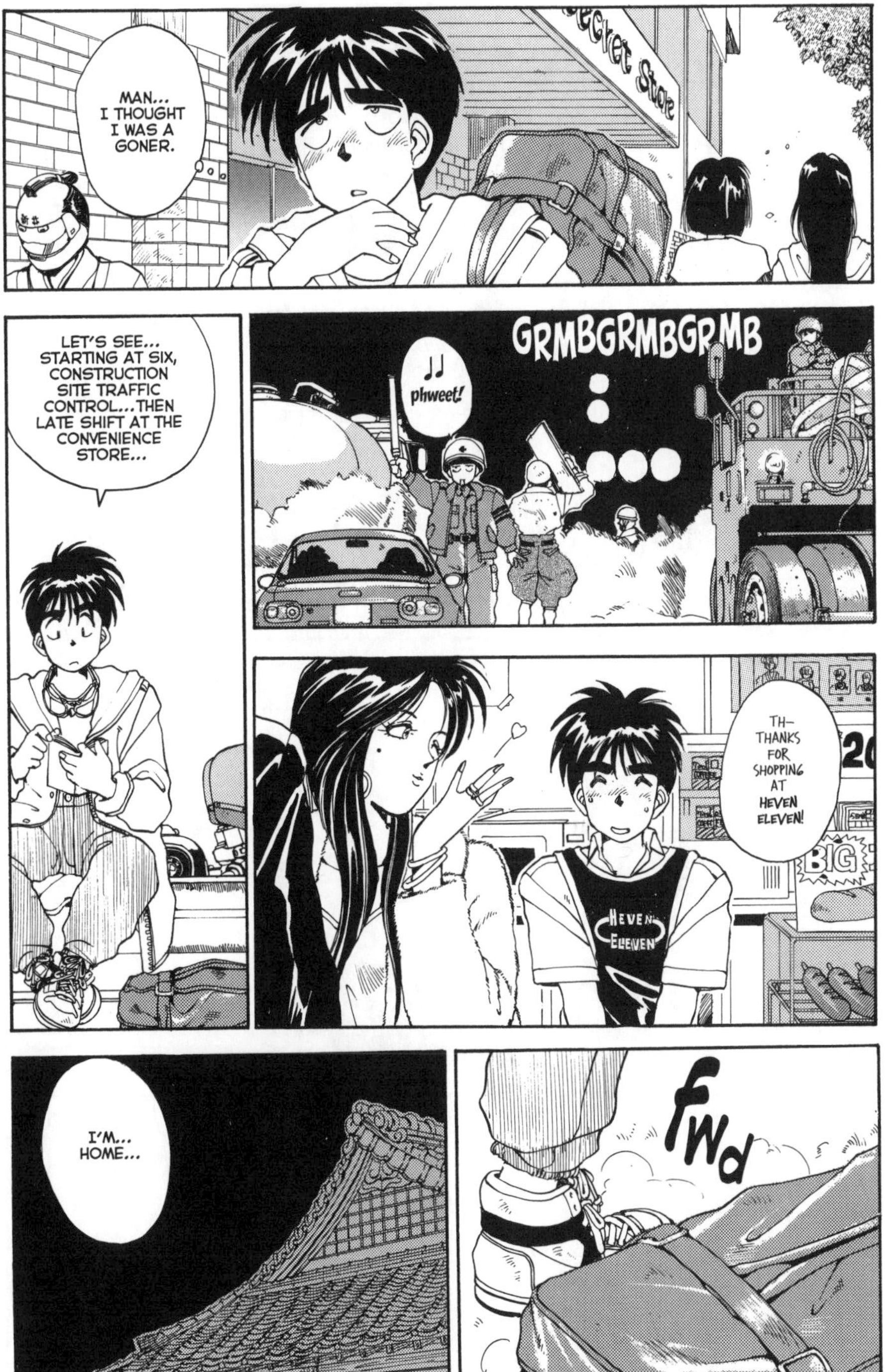
MAN... I THOUGHT I WAS A GONER.
ecret Store
LET'S SEE... STARTING AT SIX, CONSTRUCTION SITE TRAFFIC CONTROL...THEN LATE SHIFT AT THE CONVENIENCE STORE...
GRMBGRMBGRMB
♩♩ phweet!
TH— THANKS FOR SHOPPING AT HEVEN ELEVEN!
HEVEN ELEVEN
BIG
I'M... HOME...
fwd

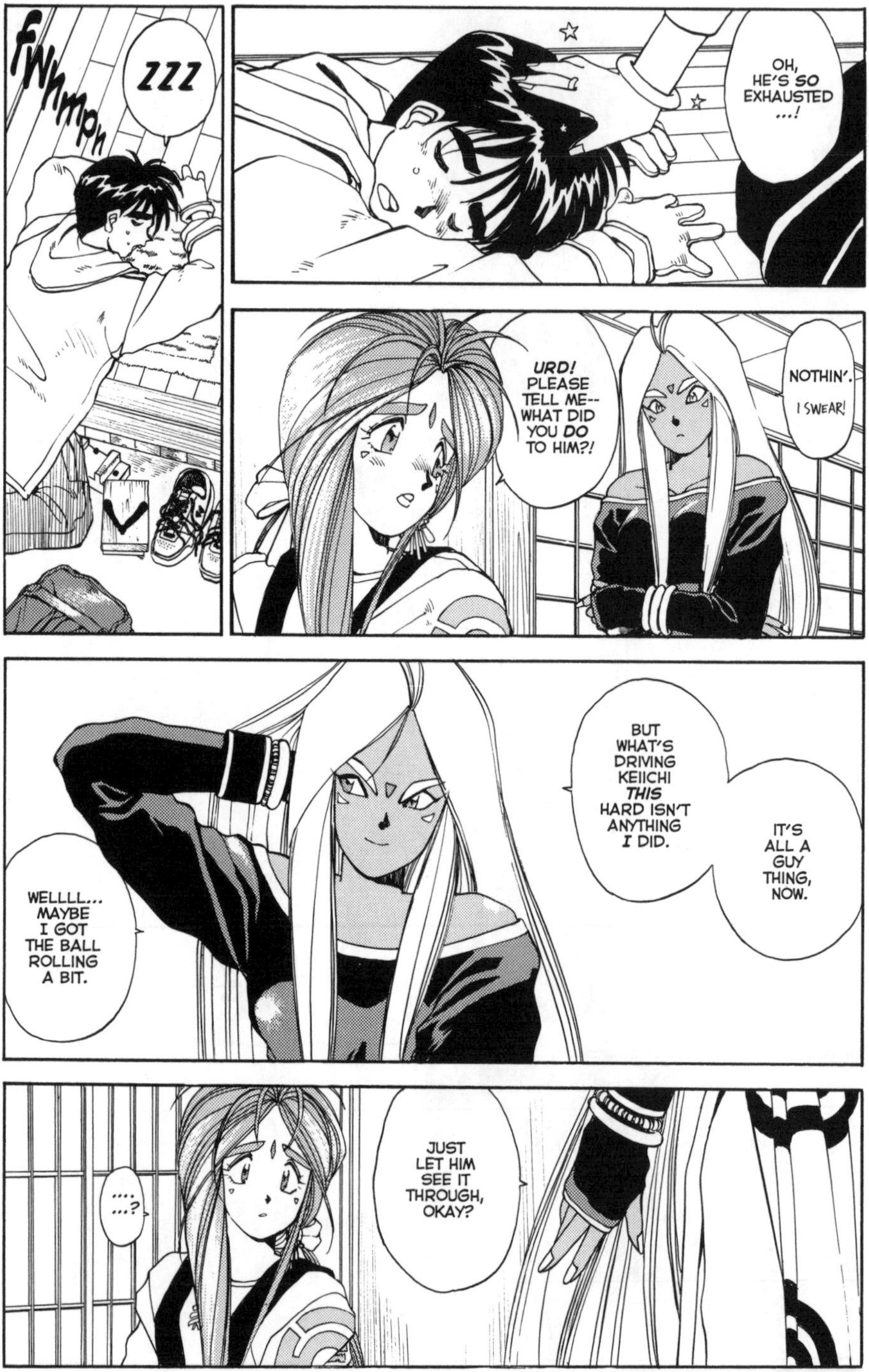

FWHMPH
ZZZ
OH, HE'S SO EXHAUSTED ...!
URD! PLEASE TELL ME-- WHAT DID YOU DO TO HIM?!
NOTHIN'.
I SWEAR!
WELLLL... MAYBE I GOT THE BALL ROLLING A BIT.
BUT WHAT'S DRIVING KEIICHI THIS HARD ISN'T ANYTHING I DID.
IT'S ALL A GUY THING, NOW.
....
...?
JUST LET HIM SEE IT THROUGH, OKAY?

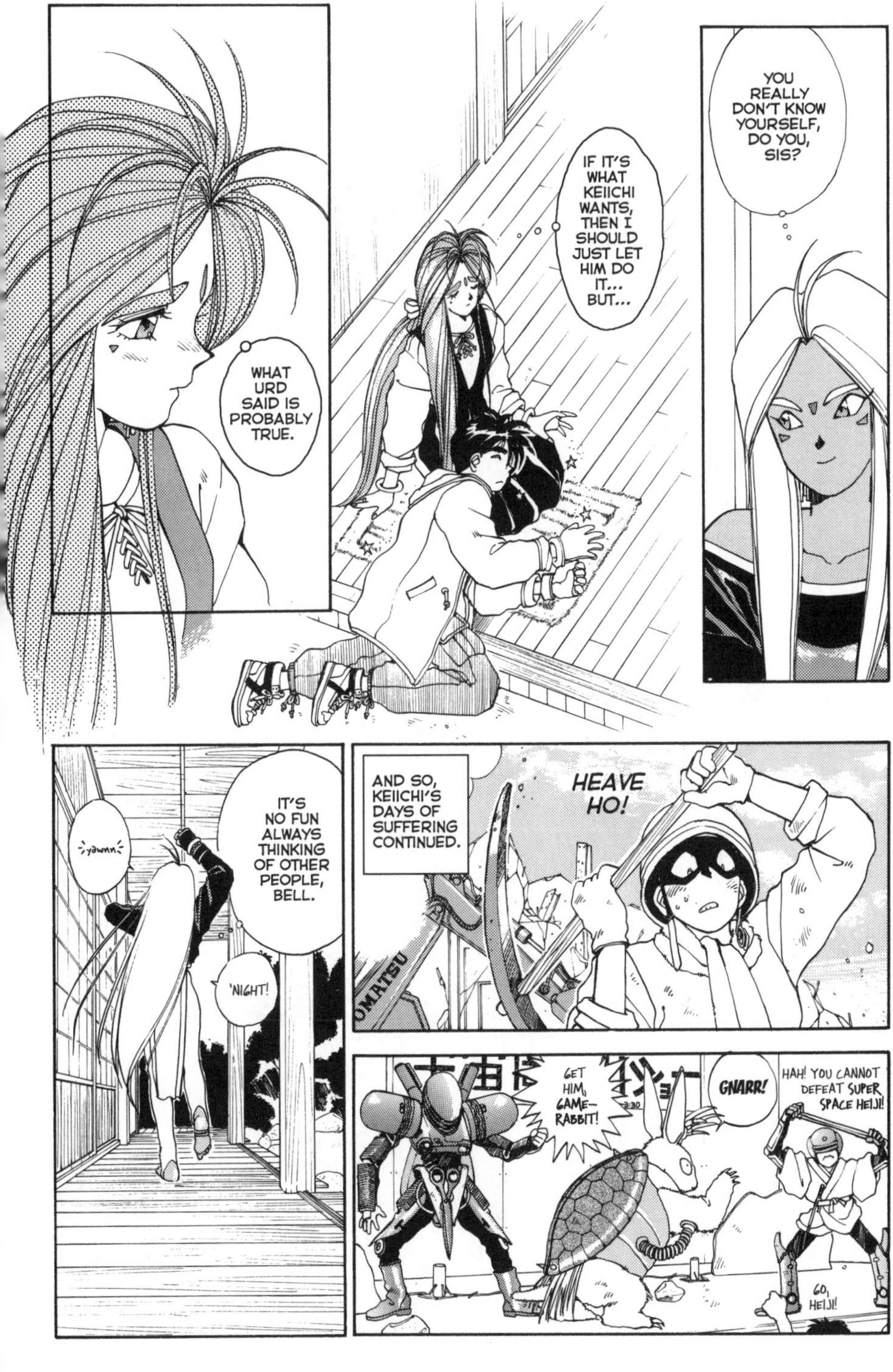
WHAT URD SAID IS PROBABLY TRUE.
IF IT'S WHAT KEIICHI WANTS, THEN I SHOULD JUST LET HIM DO IT... BUT...
YOU REALLY DON'T KNOW YOURSELF, DO YOU, SIS?
IT'S NO FUN ALWAYS THINKING OF OTHER PEOPLE, BELL.
yawnn
'NIGHT!
AND SO, KEIICHI'S DAYS OF SUFFERING CONTINUED.
HEAVE HO!
GET HIM, GAME-RABBIT!
GNARR!
HAH! YOU CANNOT DEFEAT SUPER SPACE HEIJI!
GO, HEIJI!

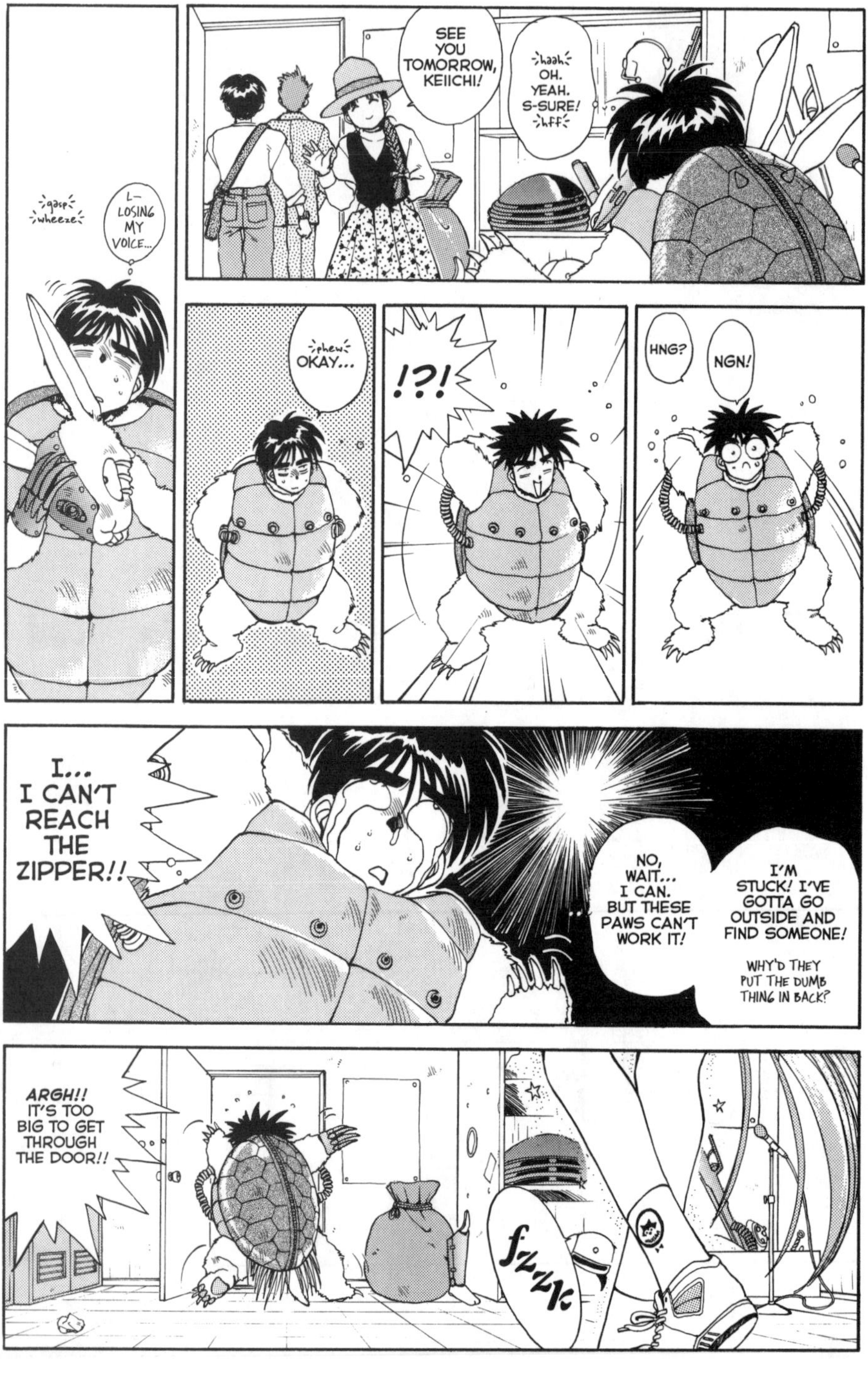

gasp
wheeze
L-LOSING MY VOICE...
SEE YOU TOMORROW, KEIICHI!
haah
OH. YEAH. S-SURE!
hff
phew
OKAY...
!?!
HNG?
NGN!
I... I CAN'T REACH THE ZIPPER!!
NO, WAIT... I CAN. BUT THESE PAWS CAN'T WORK IT!
I'M STUCK! I'VE GOTTA GO OUTSIDE AND FIND SOMEONE!
WHY'D THEY PUT THE DUMB THING IN BACK?
ARGH!! IT'S TOO BIG TO GET THROUGH THE DOOR!!
fzzzk

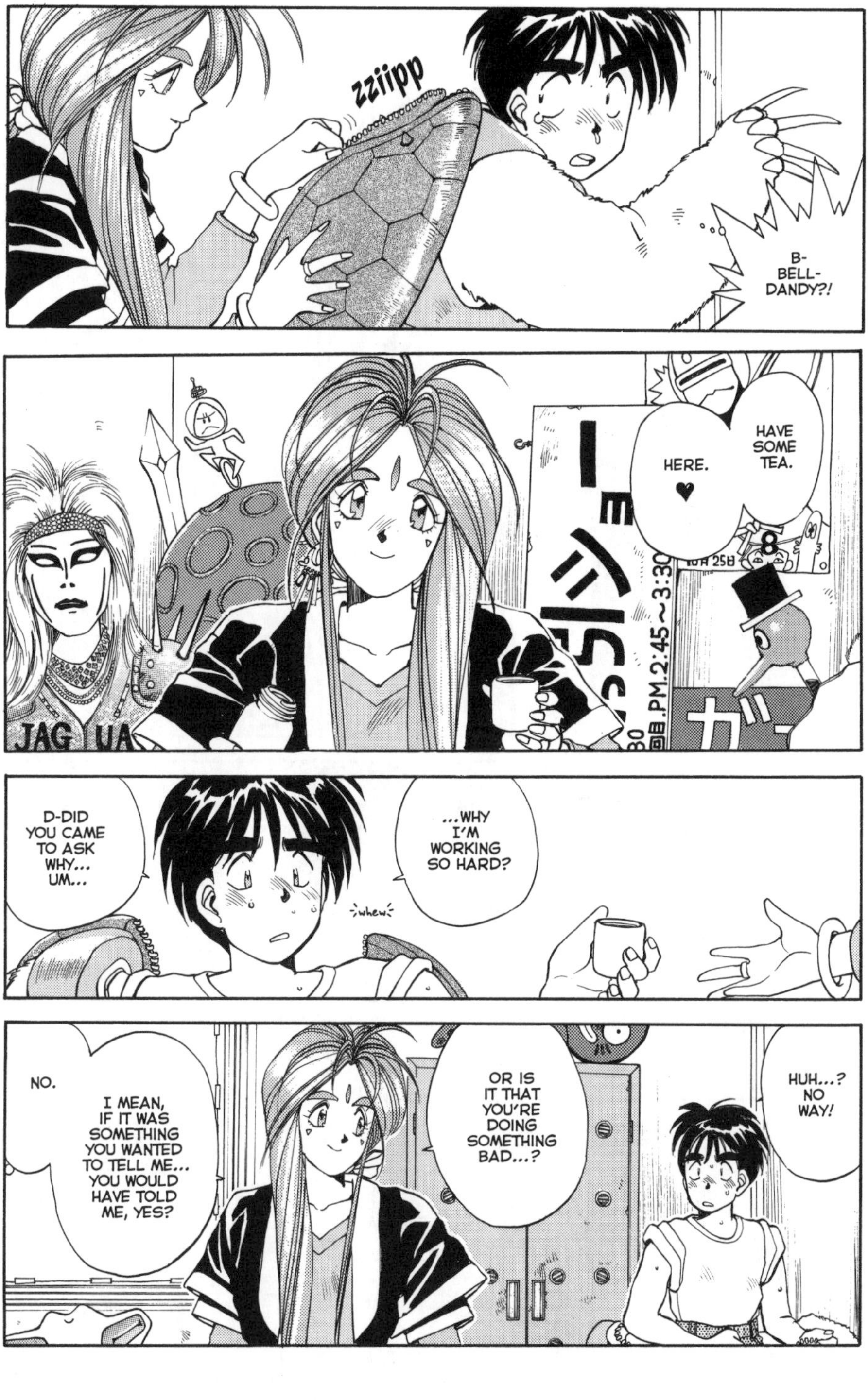
zziipp
B- BELL- DANDY?!
HAVE SOME TEA.
HERE. ♥
JAG UA
D-DID YOU CAME TO ASK WHY... UM...
whew
...WHY I'M WORKING SO HARD?
NO.
I MEAN, IF IT WAS SOMETHING YOU WANTED TO TELL ME... YOU WOULD HAVE TOLD ME, YES?
OR IS IT THAT YOU'RE DOING SOMETHING BAD...?
HUH...? NO WAY!

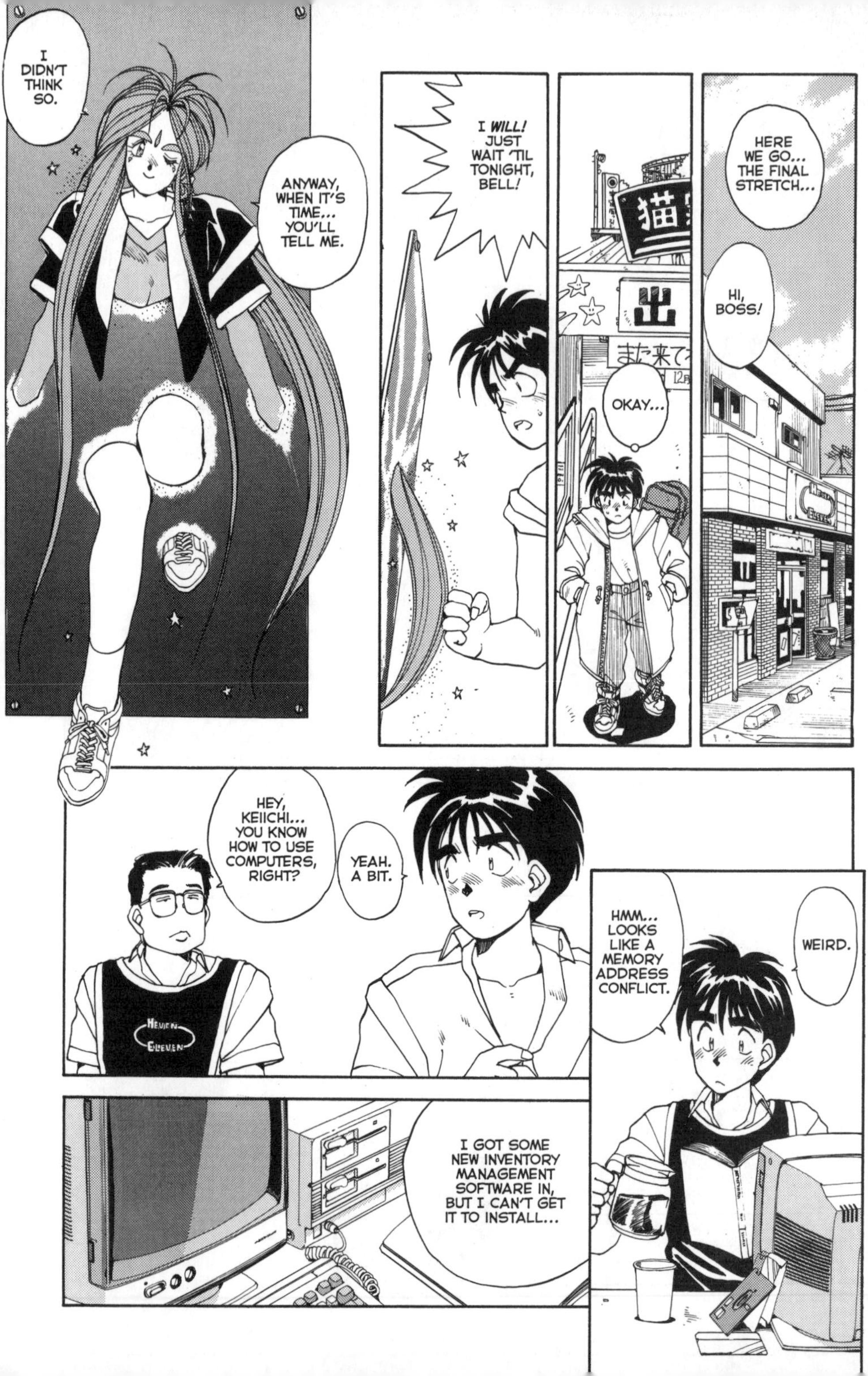
I DIDN'T THINK SO.
ANYWAY, WHEN IT'S TIME... YOU'LL TELL ME.
I *WILL!* JUST WAIT 'TIL TONIGHT, BELL!
OKAY...
HERE WE GO... THE FINAL STRETCH...
HI, BOSS!
HEY, KEIICHI... YOU KNOW HOW TO USE COMPUTERS, RIGHT?
YEAH. A BIT.
I GOT SOME NEW INVENTORY MANAGEMENT SOFTWARE IN, BUT I CAN'T GET IT TO INSTALL...
HMM... LOOKS LIKE A MEMORY ADDRESS CONFLICT.
WEIRD.

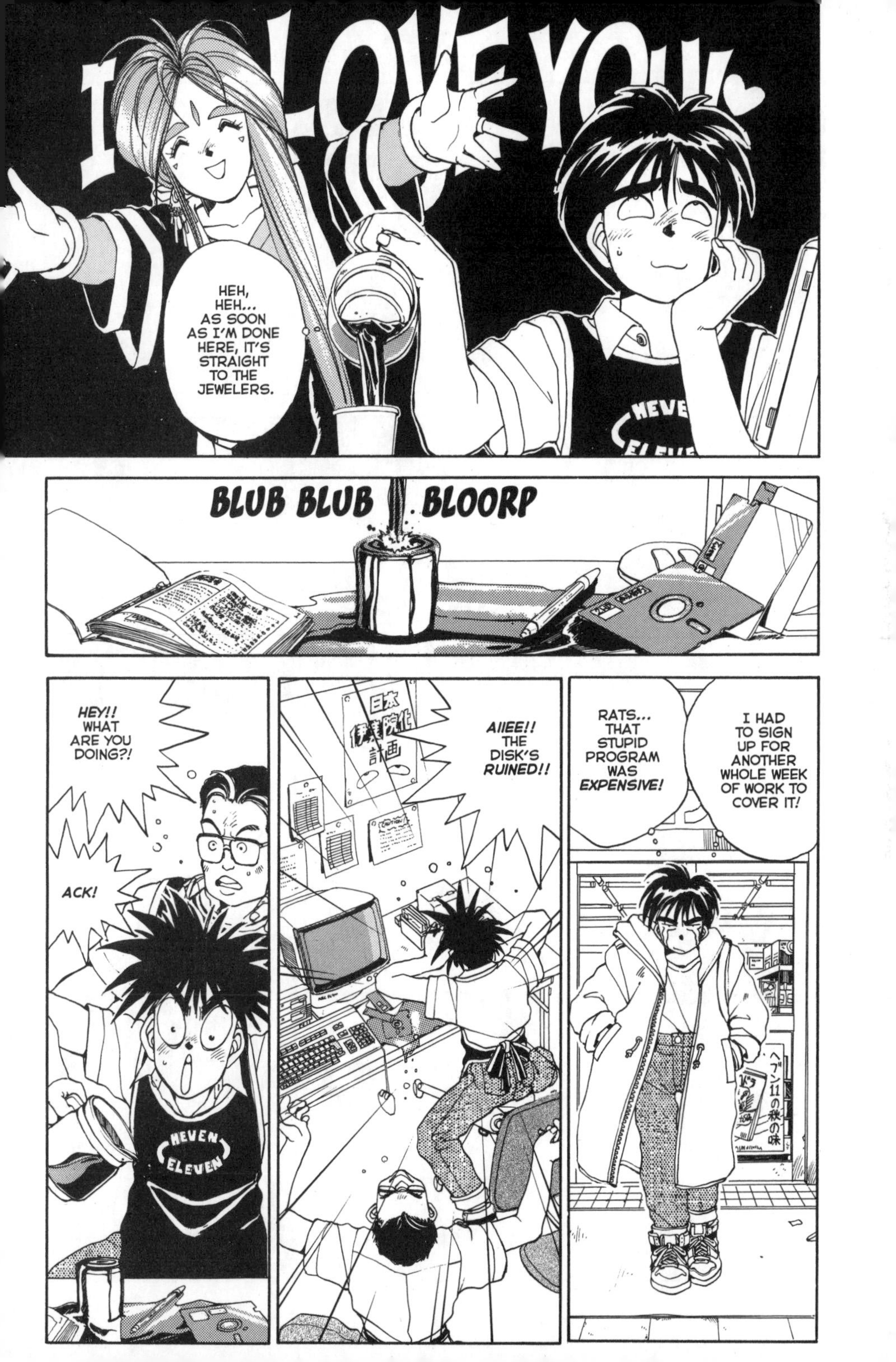
I LOVE YOU!♥
HEH, HEH... AS SOON AS I'M DONE HERE, IT'S STRAIGHT TO THE JEWELERS.
BLUB BLUB
BLOORP
HEY!! WHAT ARE YOU DOING?!
ACK!
HEVEN ELEVEN
AIIEE!! THE DISK'S RUINED!!
RATS... THAT STUPID PROGRAM WAS EXPENSIVE!
I HAD TO SIGN UP FOR ANOTHER WHOLE WEEK OF WORK TO COVER IT!

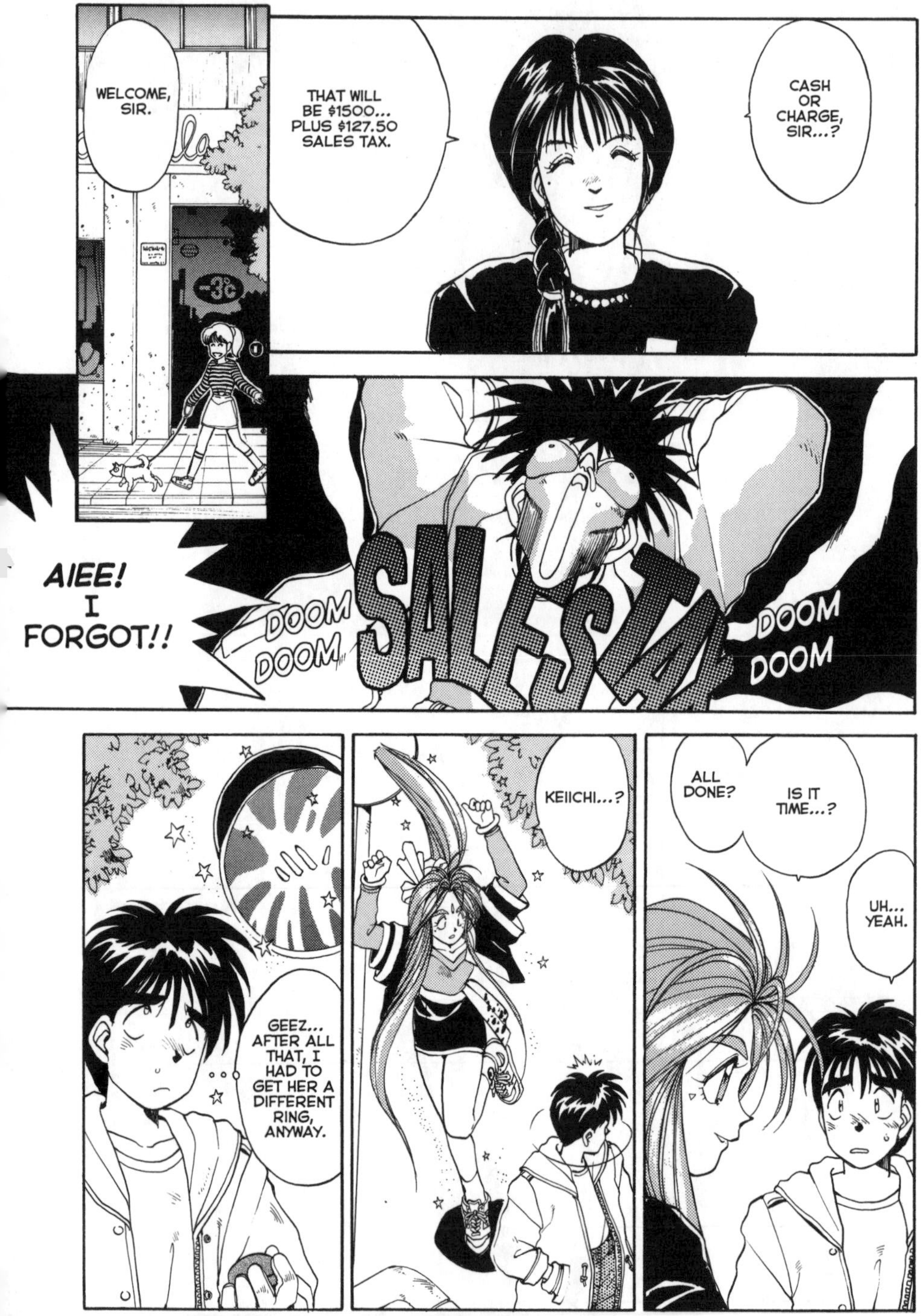

WELCOME, SIR.
THAT WILL BE $1500... PLUS $127.50 SALES TAX.
CASH OR CHARGE, SIR...?
AIEE! I FORGOT!!
DOOM DOOM
SALES TA
DOOM DOOM
GEEZ... AFTER ALL THAT, I HAD TO GET HER A DIFFERENT RING, ANYWAY.
KEIICHI...?
ALL DONE?
IS IT TIME...?
UH... YEAH.

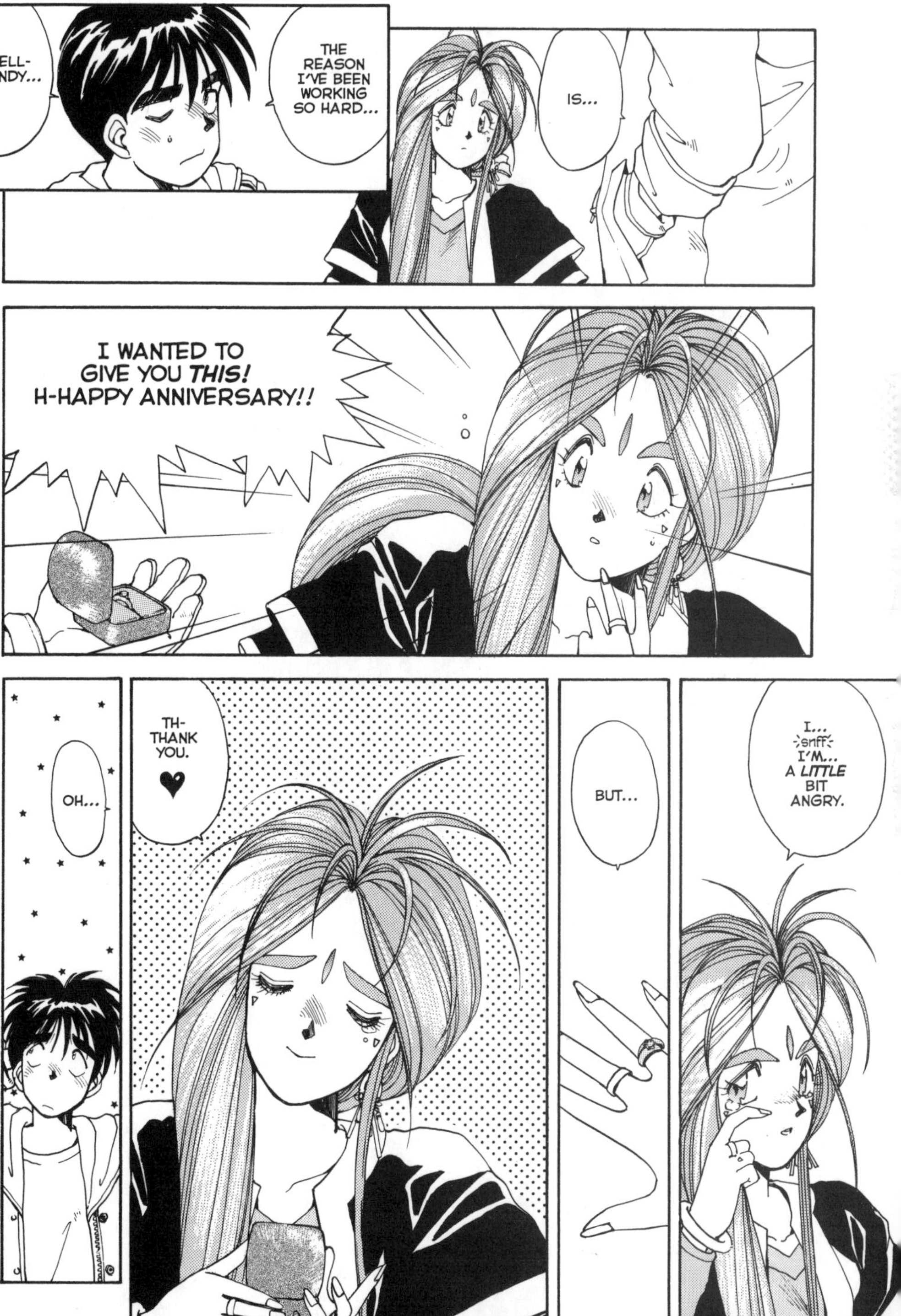
BELL-DANDY...
THE REASON I'VE BEEN WORKING SO HARD...
IS...
I WANTED TO GIVE YOU *THIS!* H-HAPPY ANNIVERSARY!!
OH...
TH-THANK YOU. ♥
BUT...
I... -SNIFF- I'M... A *LITTLE* BIT ANGRY.

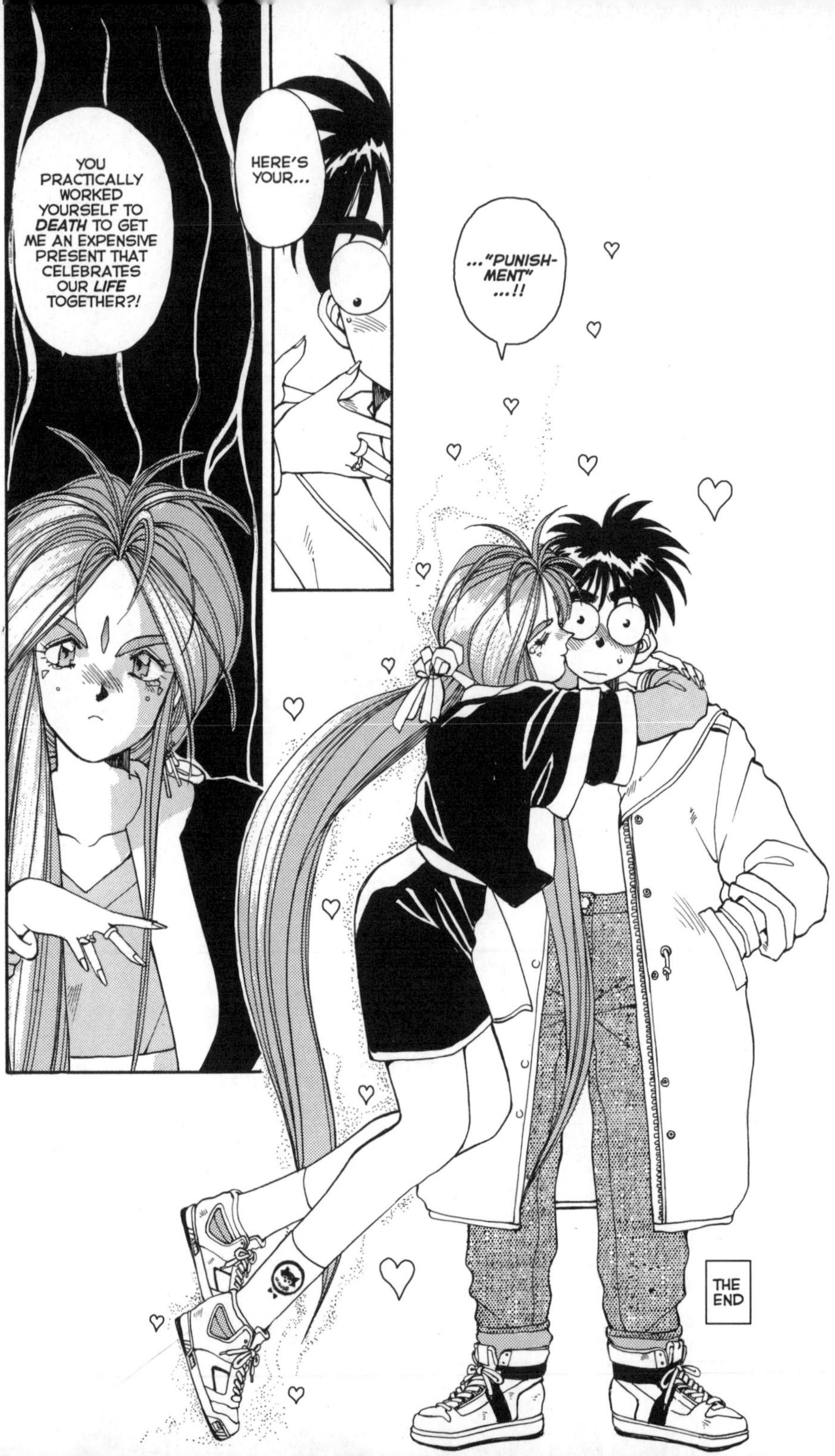
YOU PRACTICALLY WORKED YOURSELF TO *DEATH* TO GET ME AN EXPENSIVE PRESENT THAT CELEBRATES OUR *LIFE* TOGETHER?!
HERE'S YOUR...
..."PUNISH-MENT" ...!!
THE END

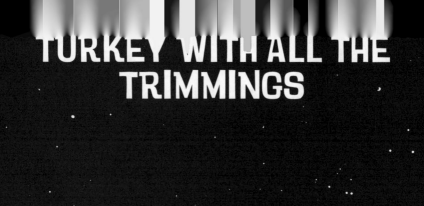

# TURKEY WITH ALL THE TRIMMINGS

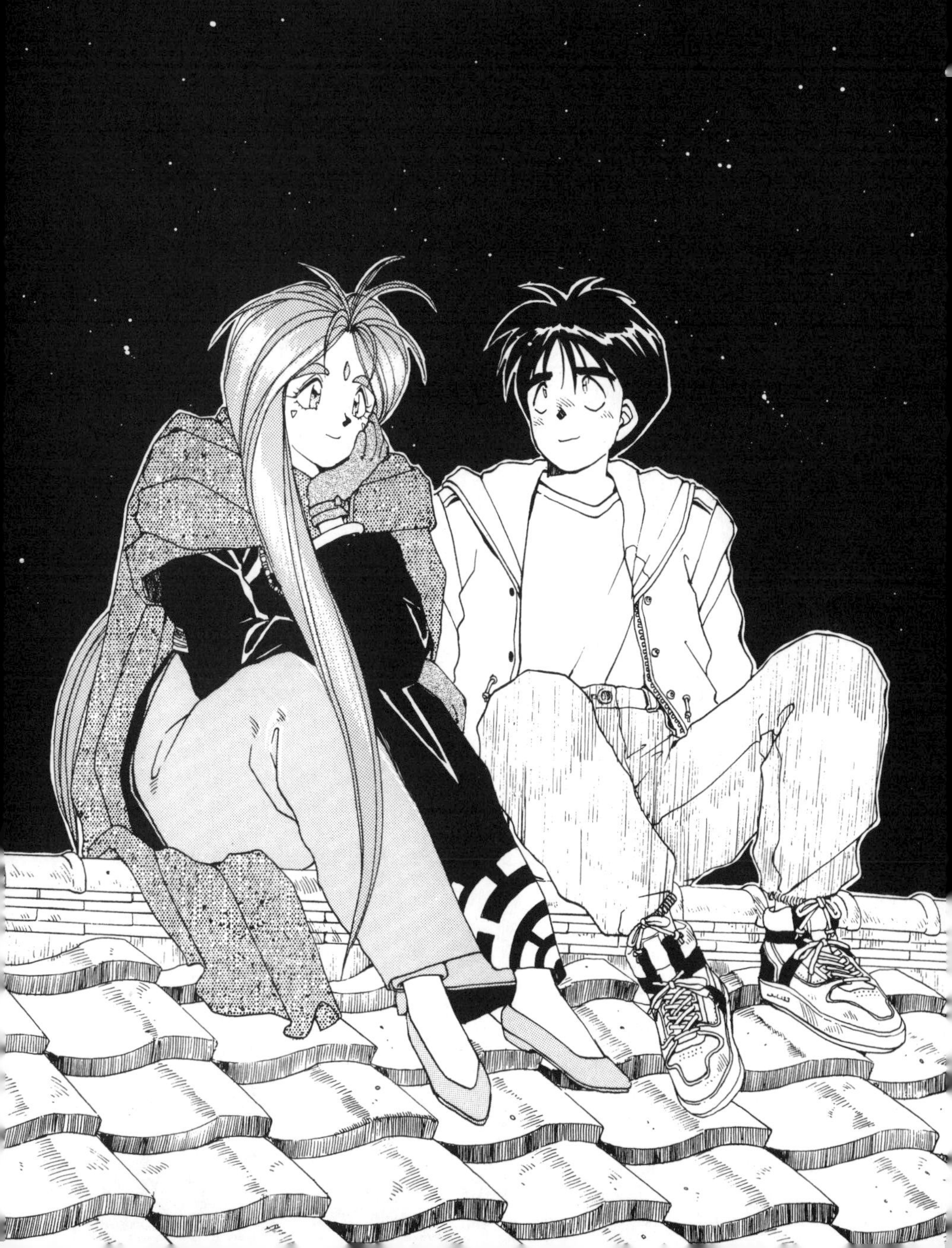

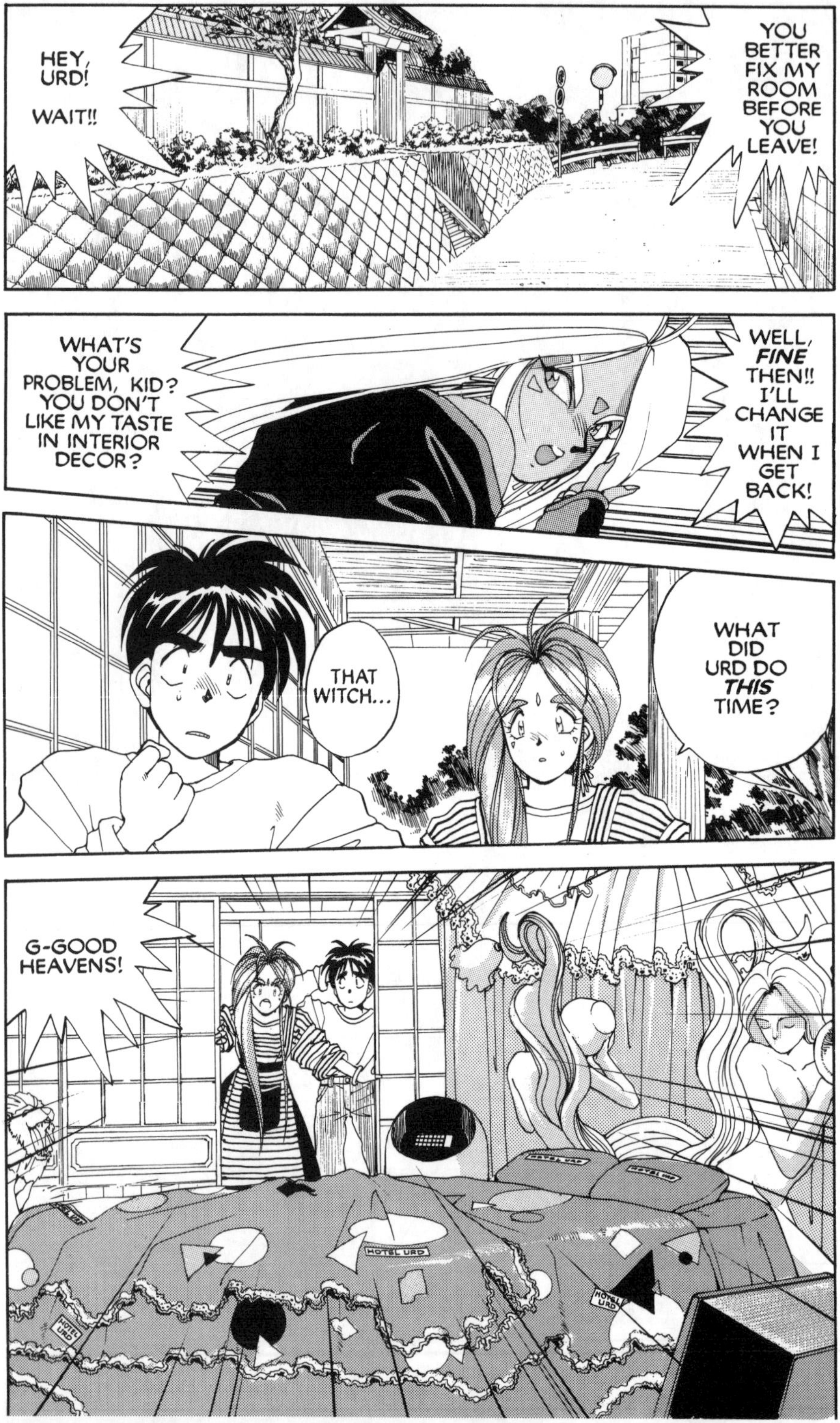
HEY, URD!
WAIT!!
YOU BETTER FIX MY ROOM BEFORE YOU LEAVE!
WHAT'S YOUR PROBLEM, KID? YOU DON'T LIKE MY TASTE IN INTERIOR DECOR?
WELL, *FINE* THEN!! I'LL CHANGE IT WHEN I GET BACK!
THAT WITCH...
WHAT DID URD DO *THIS* TIME?
G-GOOD HEAVENS!
HOTEL URD

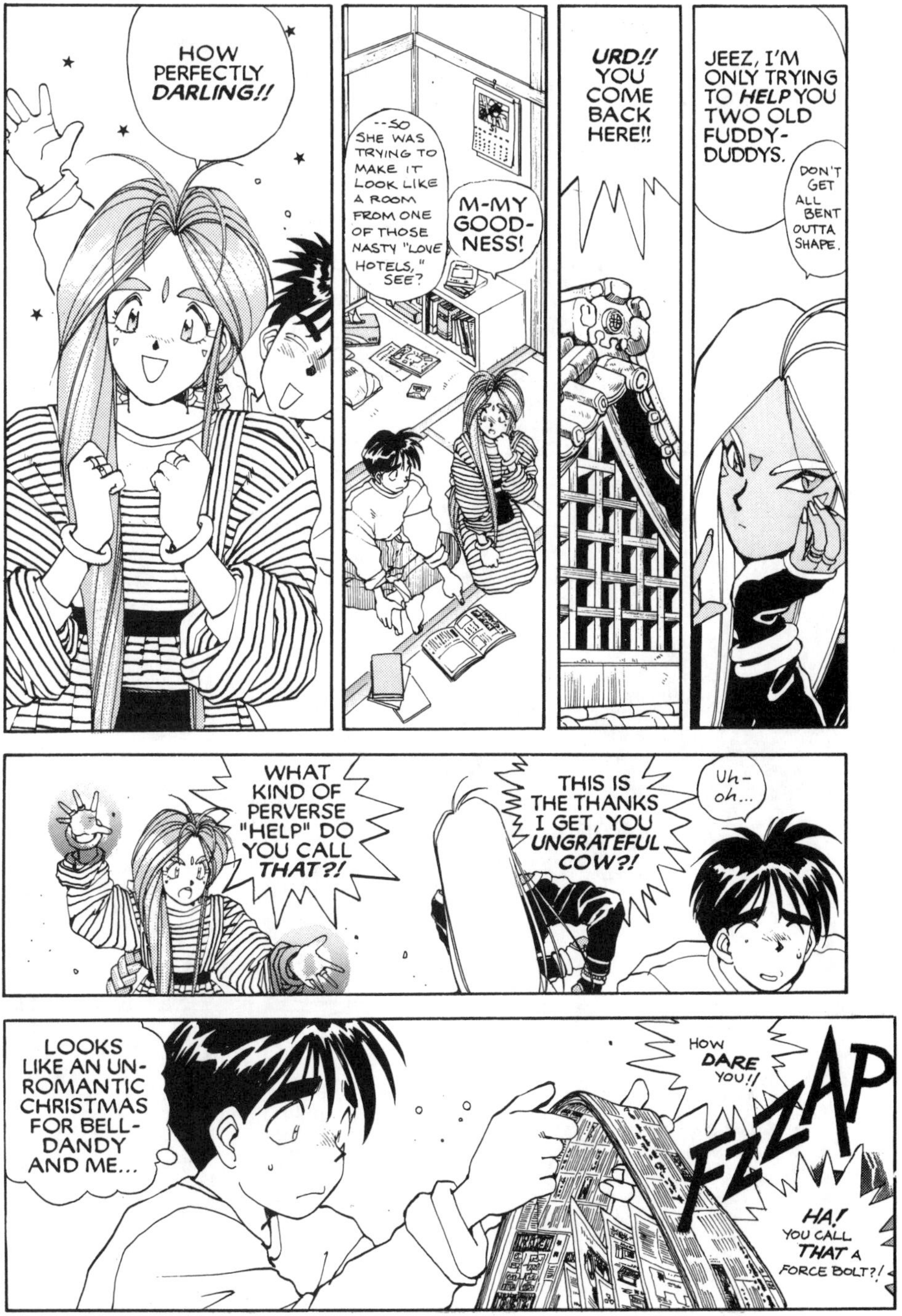
HOW PERFECTLY DARLING!!
--SO SHE WAS TRYING TO MAKE IT LOOK LIKE A ROOM FROM ONE OF THOSE NASTY "LOVE HOTELS," SEE?
M-MY GOODNESS!
URD!! YOU COME BACK HERE!!
JEEZ, I'M ONLY TRYING TO HELP YOU TWO OLD FUDDY-DUDDYS.
DON'T GET ALL BENT OUTTA SHAPE.
WHAT KIND OF PERVERSE "HELP" DO YOU CALL THAT?!
THIS IS THE THANKS I GET, YOU UNGRATEFUL COW?!
Uh-oh...
LOOKS LIKE AN UN-ROMANTIC CHRISTMAS FOR BELL-DANDY AND ME...
HOW DARE YOU!!
FZZZAP
HA! YOU CALL THAT A FORCE BOLT?!

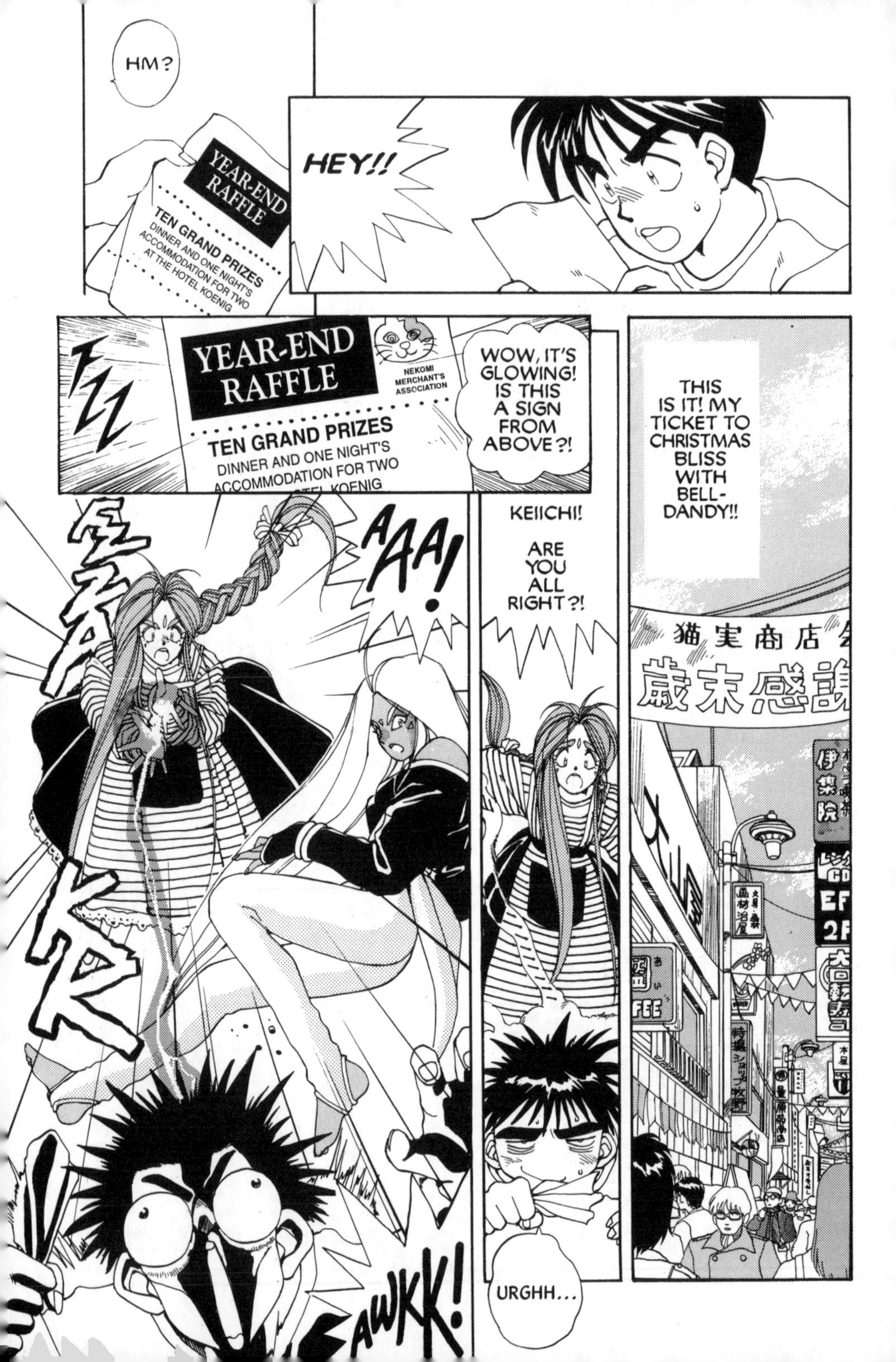

HM?
YEAR-END RAFFLE
TEN GRAND PRIZES
DINNER AND ONE NIGHT'S ACCOMMODATION FOR TWO AT THE HOTEL KOENIG
HEY!!
FZZ
YEAR-END RAFFLE
NEKOMI MERCHANT'S ASSOCIATION
TEN GRAND PRIZES
DINNER AND ONE NIGHT'S ACCOMMODATION FOR TWO
WOW, IT'S GLOWING! IS THIS A SIGN FROM ABOVE?!
FZZAP
AAAI!
SKWAWK!
KEIICHI!
ARE YOU ALL RIGHT?!
URGHH...
THIS IS IT! MY TICKET TO CHRISTMAS BLISS WITH BELL-DANDY!!

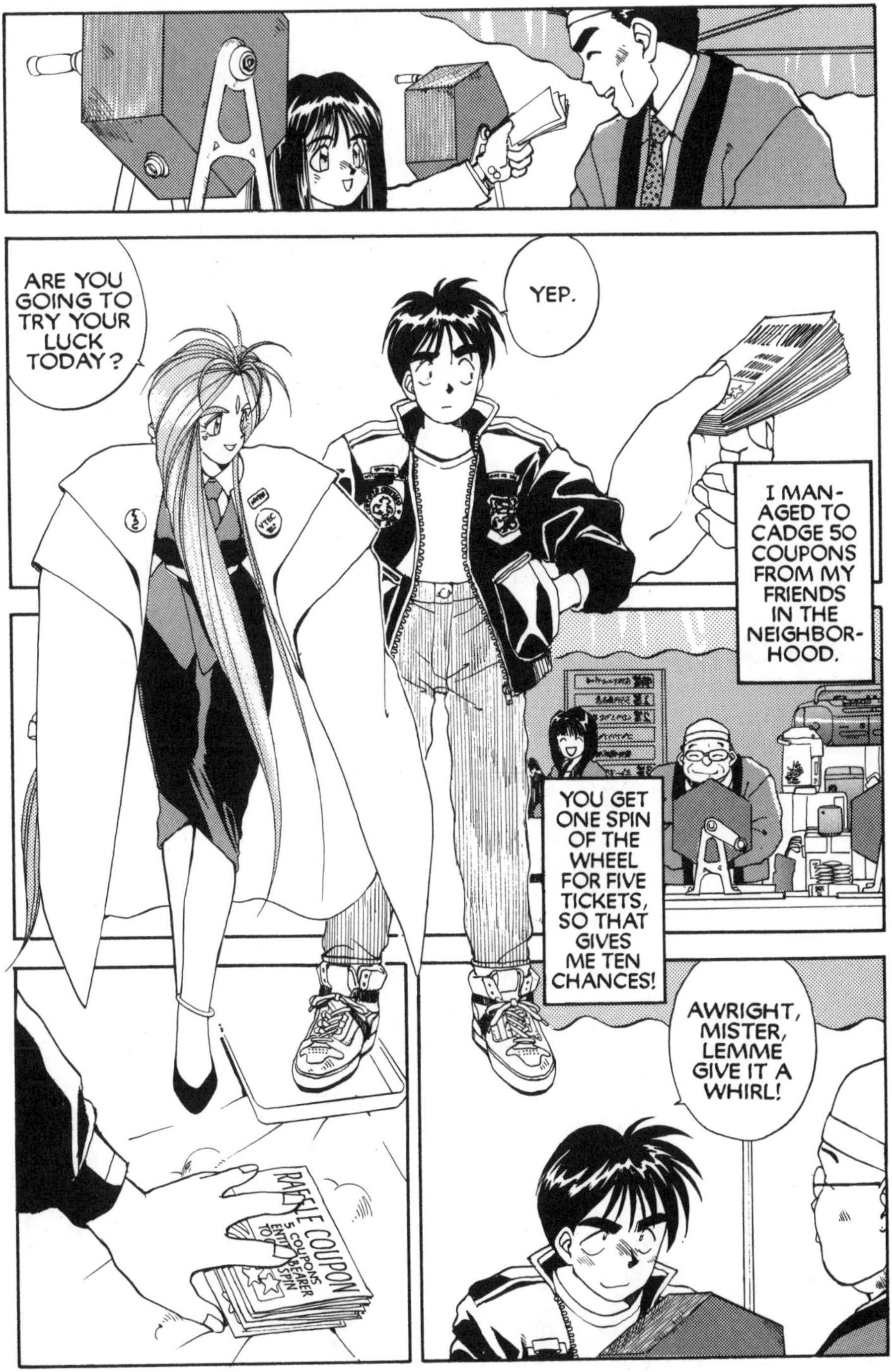
ARE YOU GOING TO TRY YOUR LUCK TODAY?
YEP.
I MANAGED TO CADGE 50 COUPONS FROM MY FRIENDS IN THE NEIGHBORHOOD.
YOU GET ONE SPIN OF THE WHEEL FOR FIVE TICKETS, SO THAT GIVES ME TEN CHANCES!
AWRIGHT, MISTER, LEMME GIVE IT A WHIRL!

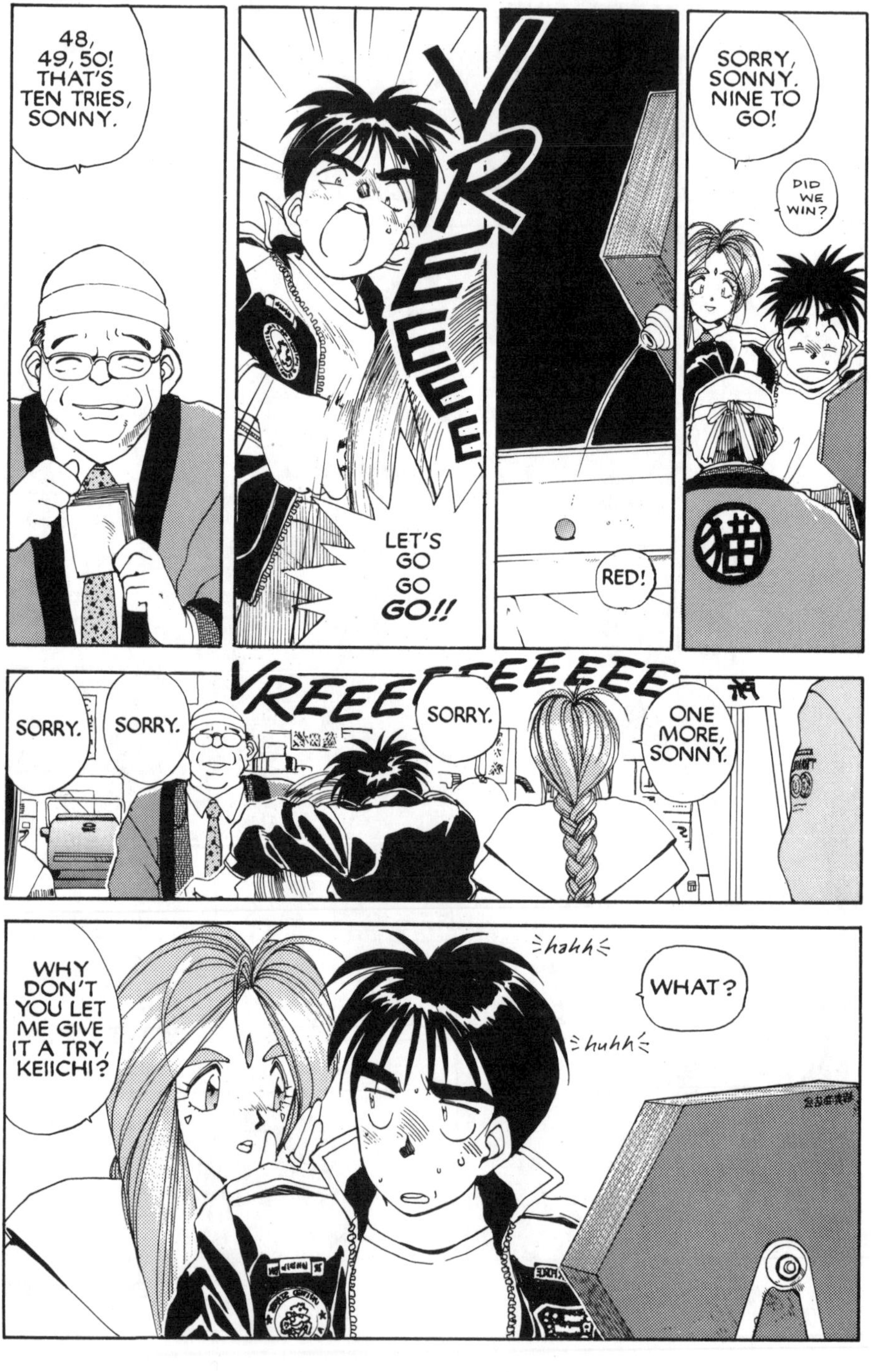
48, 49, 50! THAT'S TEN TRIES, SONNY.
VREEEE
LET'S GO GO GO!!
RED!
SORRY, SONNY. NINE TO GO!
DID WE WIN?
VREEEEEEEEEEE
SORRY.
SORRY.
SORRY.
ONE MORE, SONNY.
WHY DON'T YOU LET ME GIVE IT A TRY, KEIICHI?
hahh
WHAT?
huhh

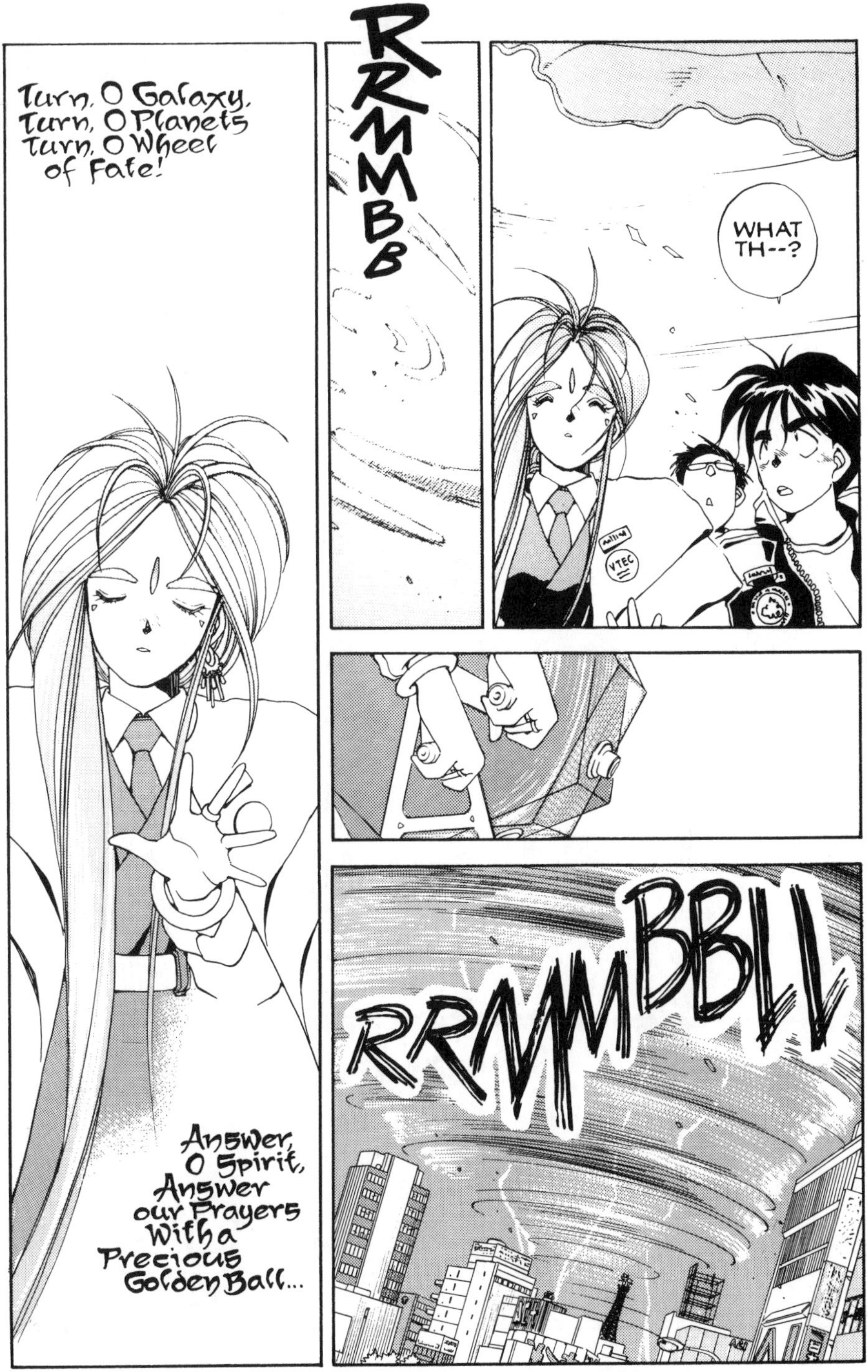
Turn, O Galaxy, Turn, O Planets Turn, O Wheel of Fate!
Answer, O Spirit, Answer our Prayers With a Precious Golden Ball...
RRMMBB
WHAT TH--?
RRMMBBLL

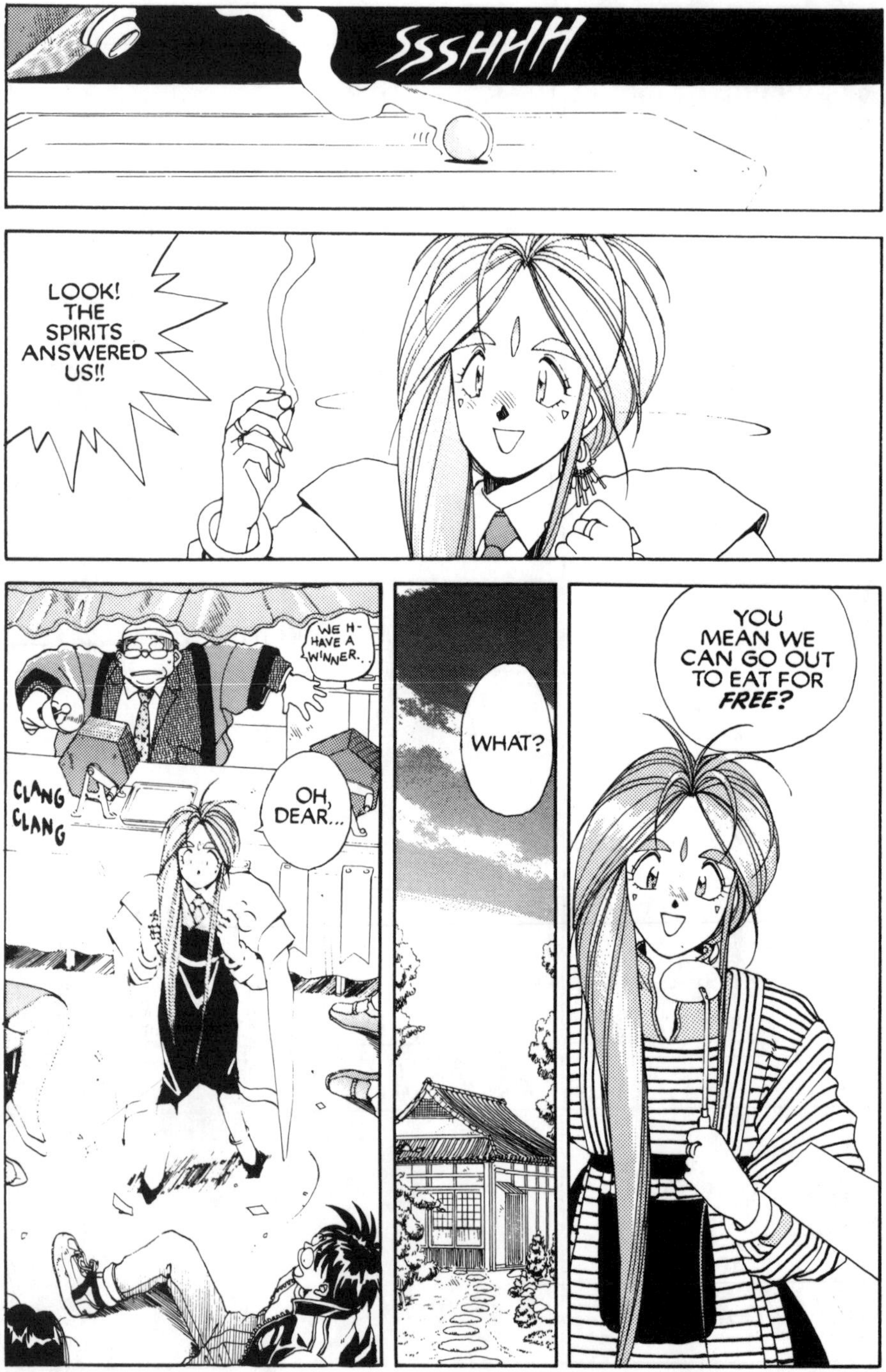
SSSHHH
LOOK! THE SPIRITS ANSWERED US!!
WE H-HAVE A WINNER...
CLANG CLANG
OH, DEAR...
WHAT?
YOU MEAN WE CAN GO OUT TO EAT FOR *FREE?*

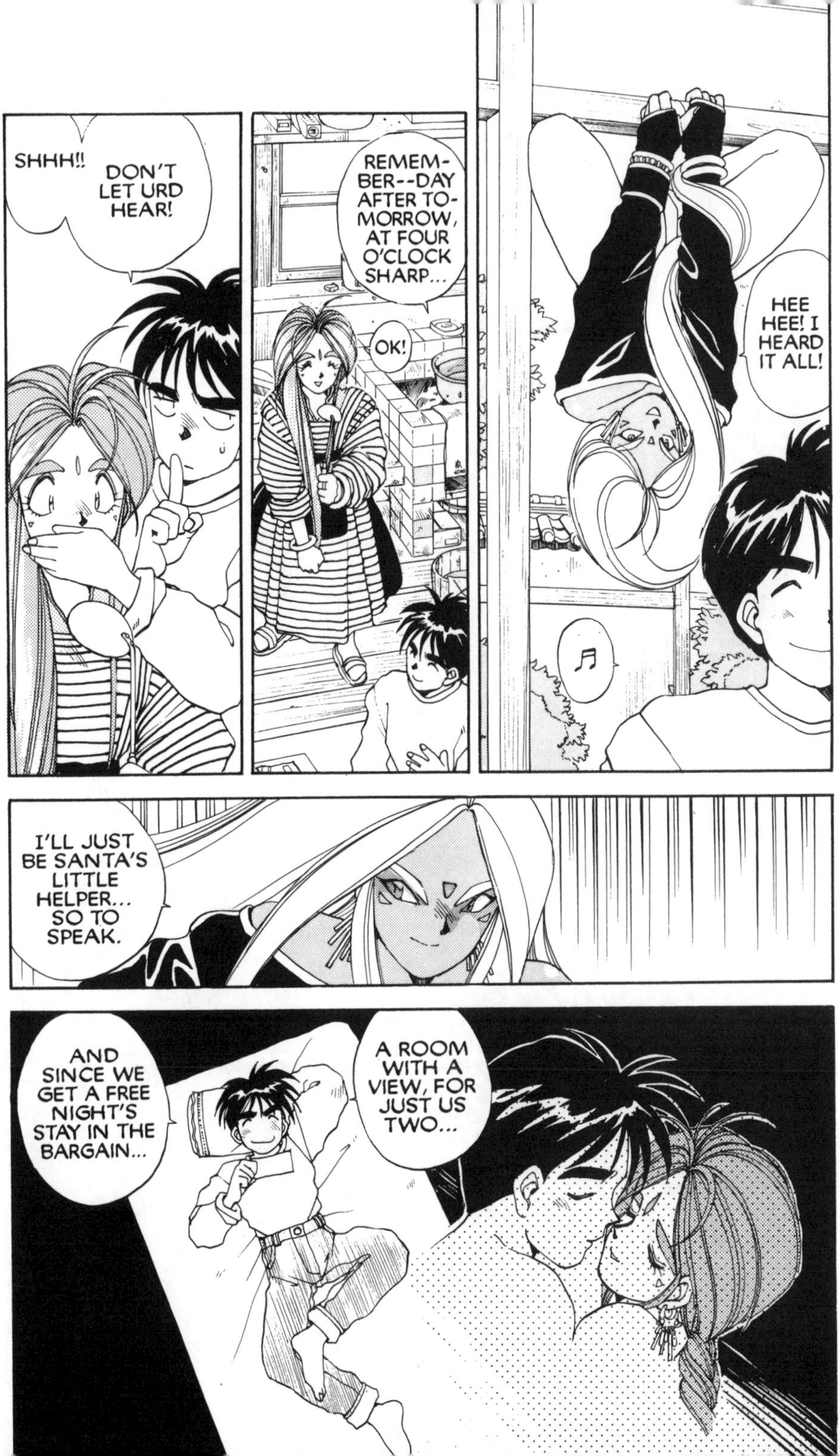
SHHH!!
DON'T LET URD HEAR!
REMEM-BER--DAY AFTER TO-MORROW, AT FOUR O'CLOCK SHARP...
OK!
HEE HEE! I HEARD IT ALL!
♫
I'LL JUST BE SANTA'S LITTLE HELPER... SO TO SPEAK.
AND SINCE WE GET A FREE NIGHT'S STAY IN THE BARGAIN...
A ROOM WITH A VIEW, FOR JUST US TWO...

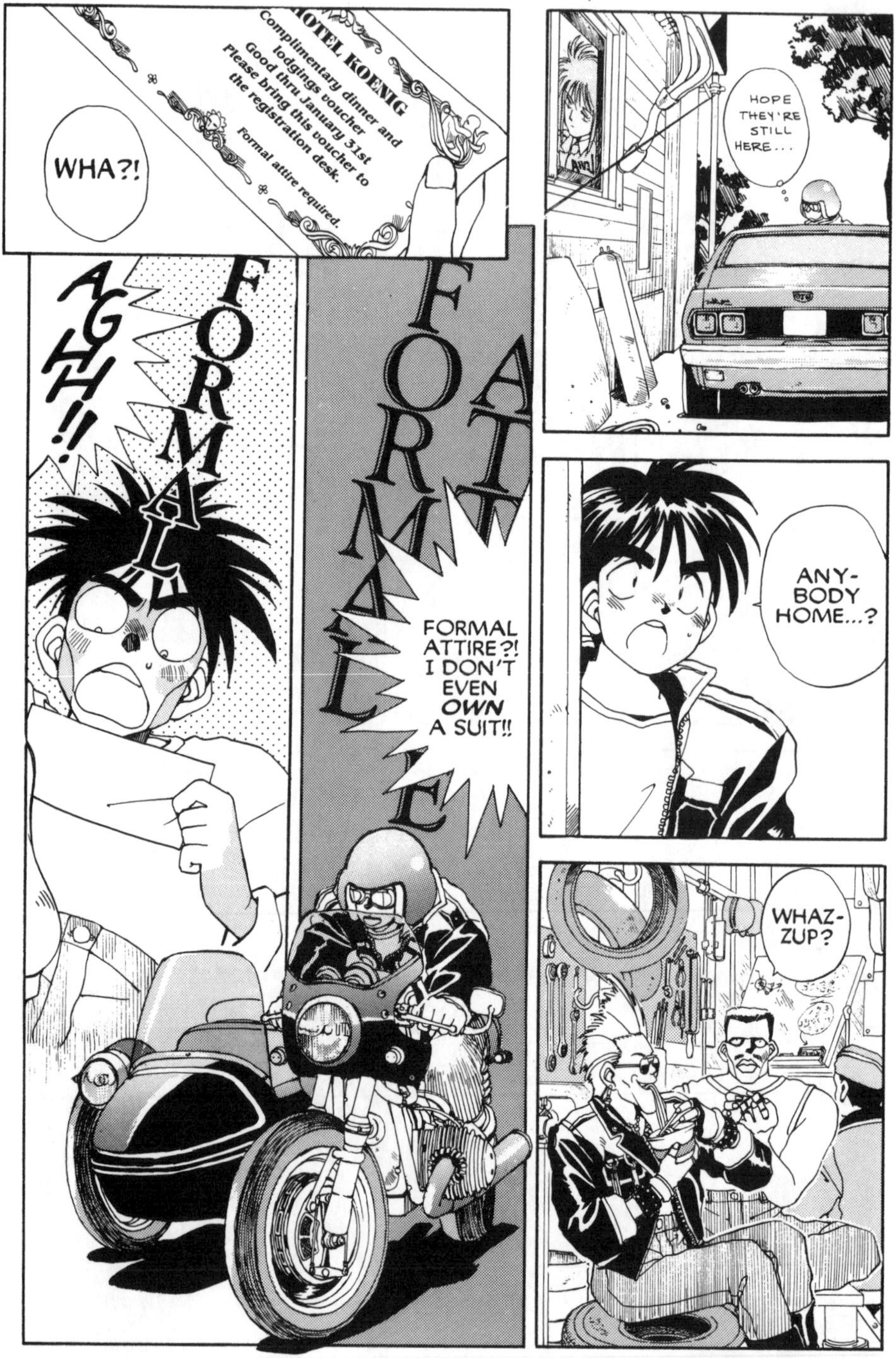
HOTEL KOENIG
Complimentary dinner and lodgings voucher
Good thru January 31st
Please bring this voucher to the registration desk.
Formal attire required.
WHA?!
HOPE THEY'RE STILL HERE...
AGHH!!
FORMAL
FORMAL ATTIRE
FORMAL ATTIRE?! I DON'T EVEN OWN A SUIT!!
ANY-BODY HOME...?
WHAZ-ZUP?

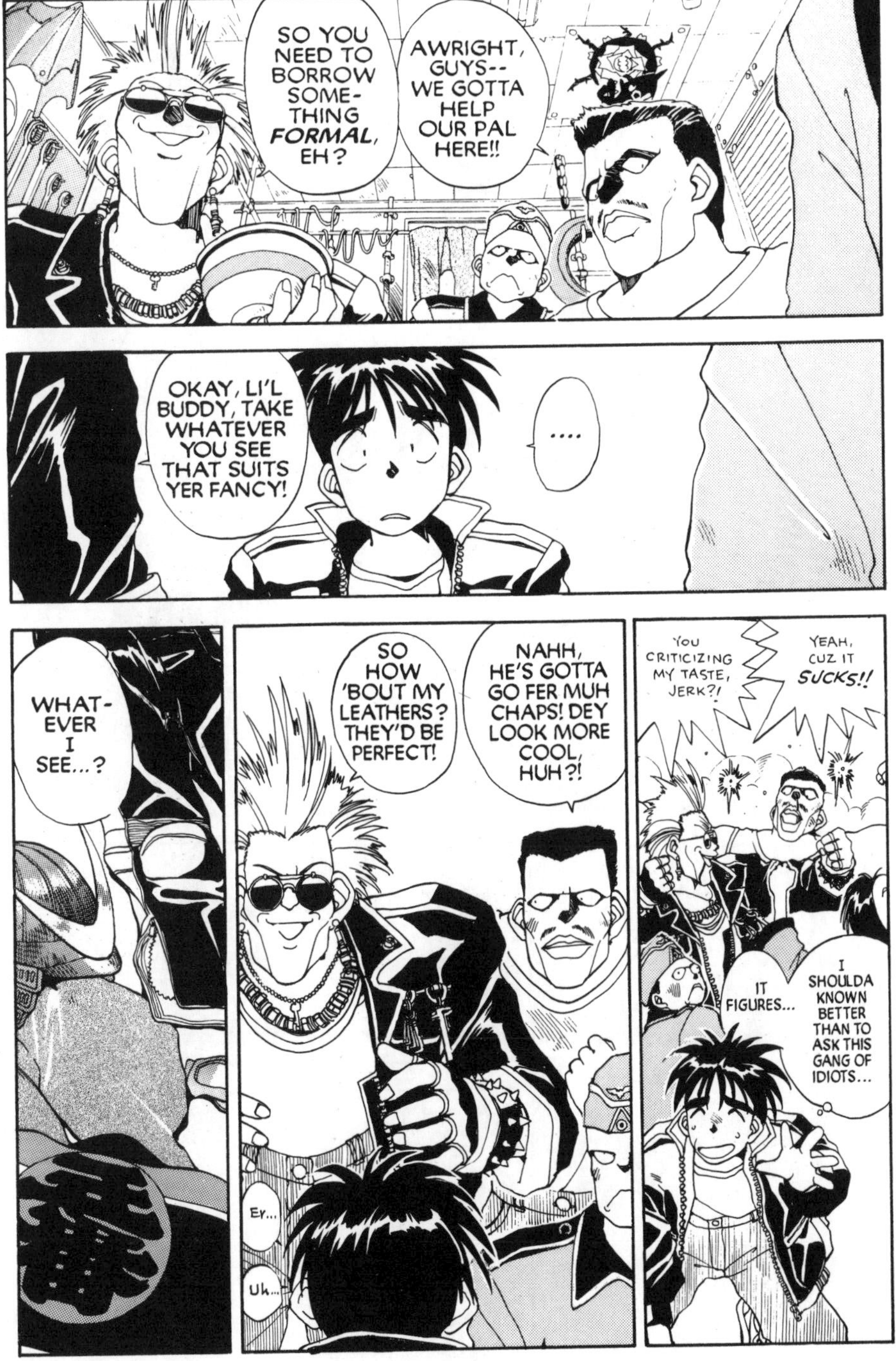
SO YOU NEED TO BORROW SOME-THING *FORMAL*, EH?
AWRIGHT, GUYS-- WE GOTTA HELP OUR PAL HERE!!
OKAY, LI'L BUDDY, TAKE WHATEVER YOU SEE THAT SUITS YER FANCY!
....
WHAT-EVER I SEE...?
SO HOW 'BOUT MY LEATHERS? THEY'D BE PERFECT!
NAHH, HE'S GOTTA GO FER MUH CHAPS! DEY LOOK MORE COOL, HUH?!
Er...
Uh...
YOU CRITICIZING MY TASTE, JERK?!
YEAH, CUZ IT *SUCKS!!*
IT FIGURES...
I SHOULDA KNOWN BETTER THAN TO ASK THIS GANG OF IDIOTS...

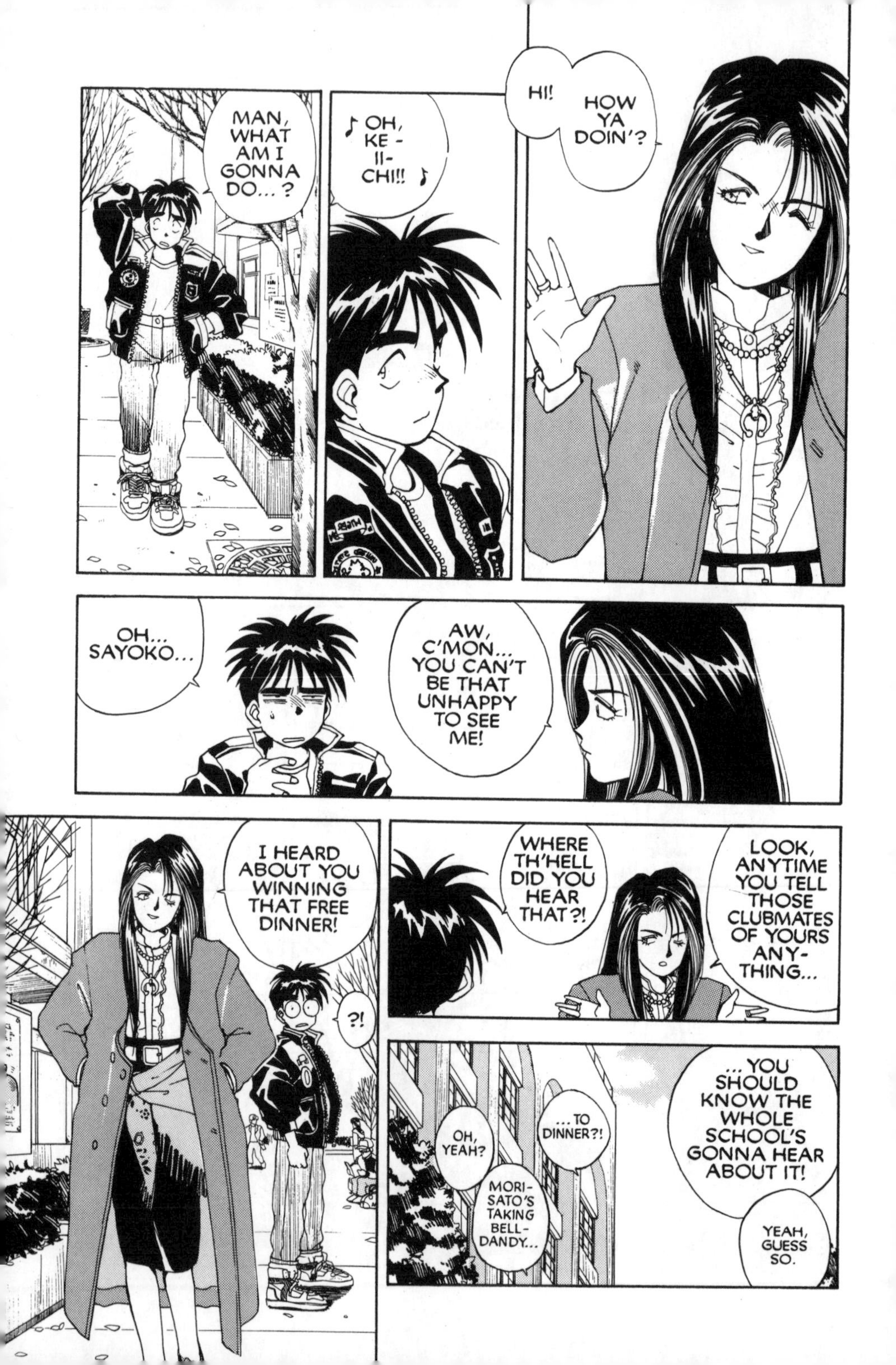
MAN, WHAT AM I GONNA DO...?
♪ OH, KE-II-CHI!! ♪
HI!
HOW YA DOIN'?
OH... SAYOKO...
AW, C'MON... YOU CAN'T BE THAT UNHAPPY TO SEE ME!
I HEARD ABOUT YOU WINNING THAT FREE DINNER!
?!
WHERE TH'HELL DID YOU HEAR THAT?!
LOOK, ANYTIME YOU TELL THOSE CLUBMATES OF YOURS ANY-THING...
...YOU SHOULD KNOW THE WHOLE SCHOOL'S GONNA HEAR ABOUT IT!
MORI-SATO'S TAKING BELL-DANDY...
...TO DINNER?!
OH, YEAH?
YEAH, GUESS SO.

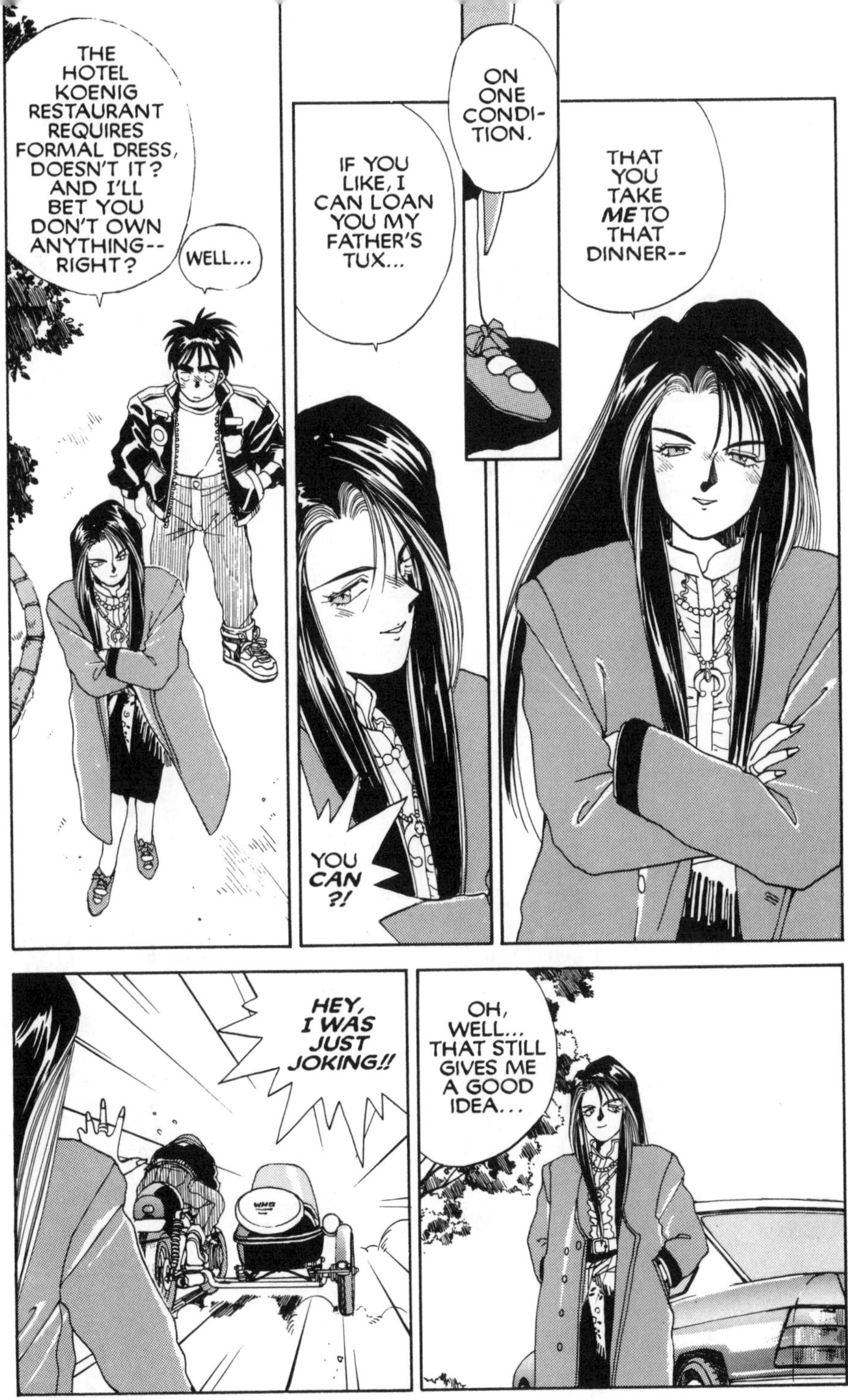
THE HOTEL KOENIG RESTAURANT REQUIRES FORMAL DRESS, DOESN'T IT? AND I'LL BET YOU DON'T OWN ANYTHING--RIGHT?
WELL...
IF YOU LIKE, I CAN LOAN YOU MY FATHER'S TUX...
YOU CAN?!
ON ONE CONDITION.
THAT YOU TAKE ME TO THAT DINNER--
HEY, I WAS JUST JOKING!!
OH, WELL... THAT STILL GIVES ME A GOOD IDEA...

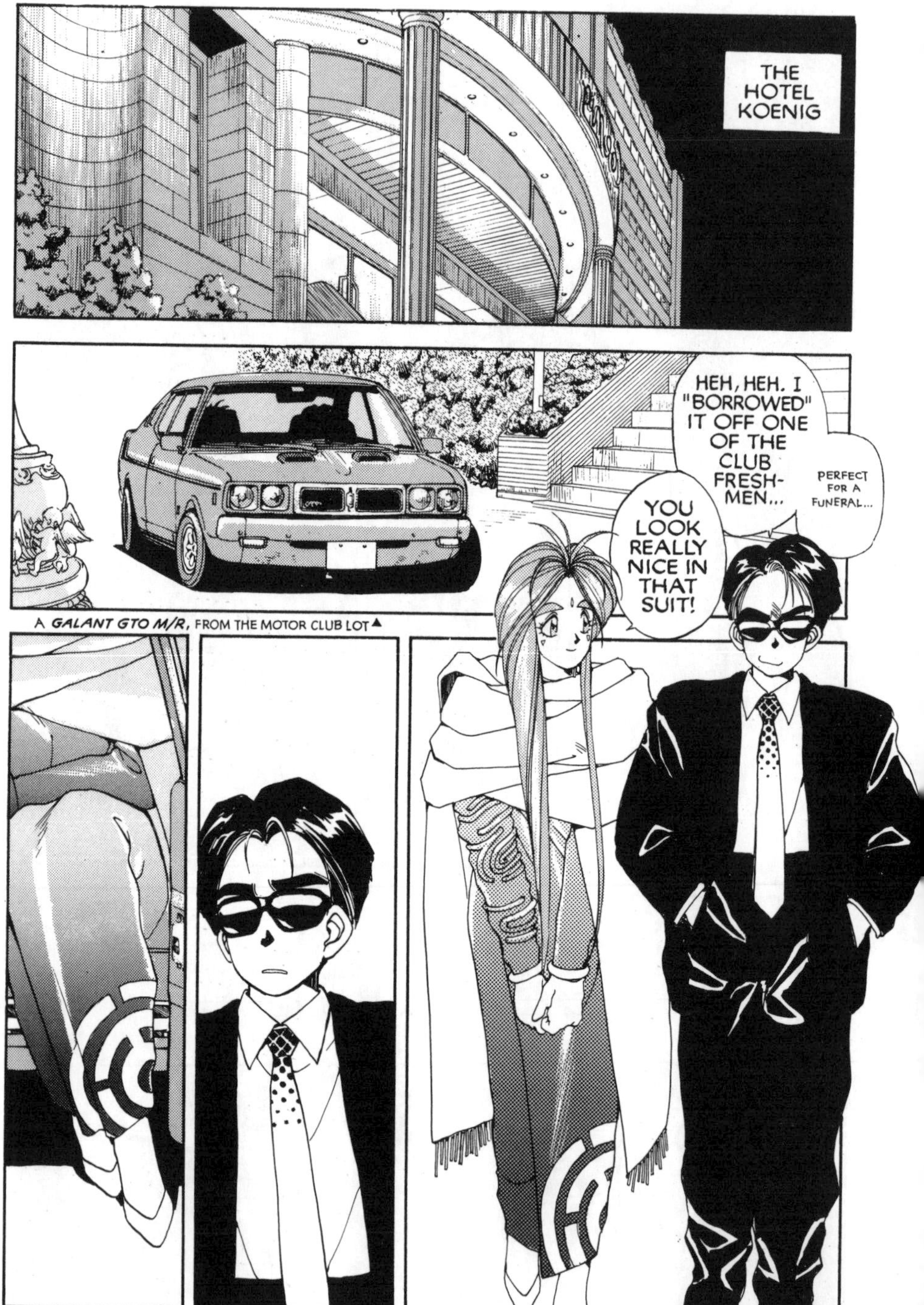
THE HOTEL KOENIG
HEH, HEH. I "BORROWED" IT OFF ONE OF THE CLUB FRESH-MEN...
PERFECT FOR A FUNERAL...
YOU LOOK REALLY NICE IN THAT SUIT!
A GALANT GTO M/R, FROM THE MOTOR CLUB LOT ▲

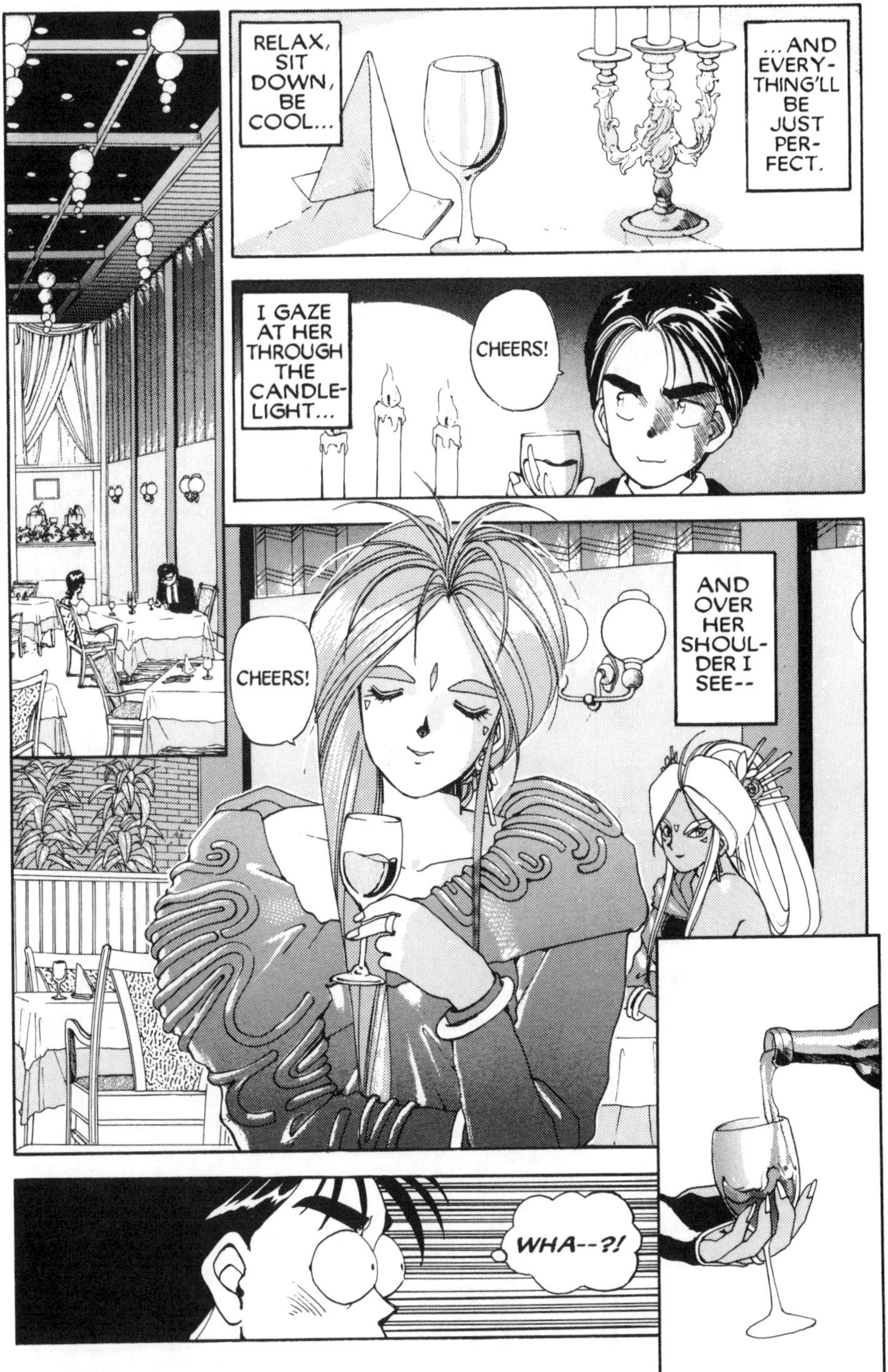
RELAX, SIT DOWN, BE COOL...
...AND EVERY-THING'LL BE JUST PER-FECT.
I GAZE AT HER THROUGH THE CANDLE-LIGHT...
CHEERS!
CHEERS!
AND OVER HER SHOUL-DER I SEE--
WHA--?!

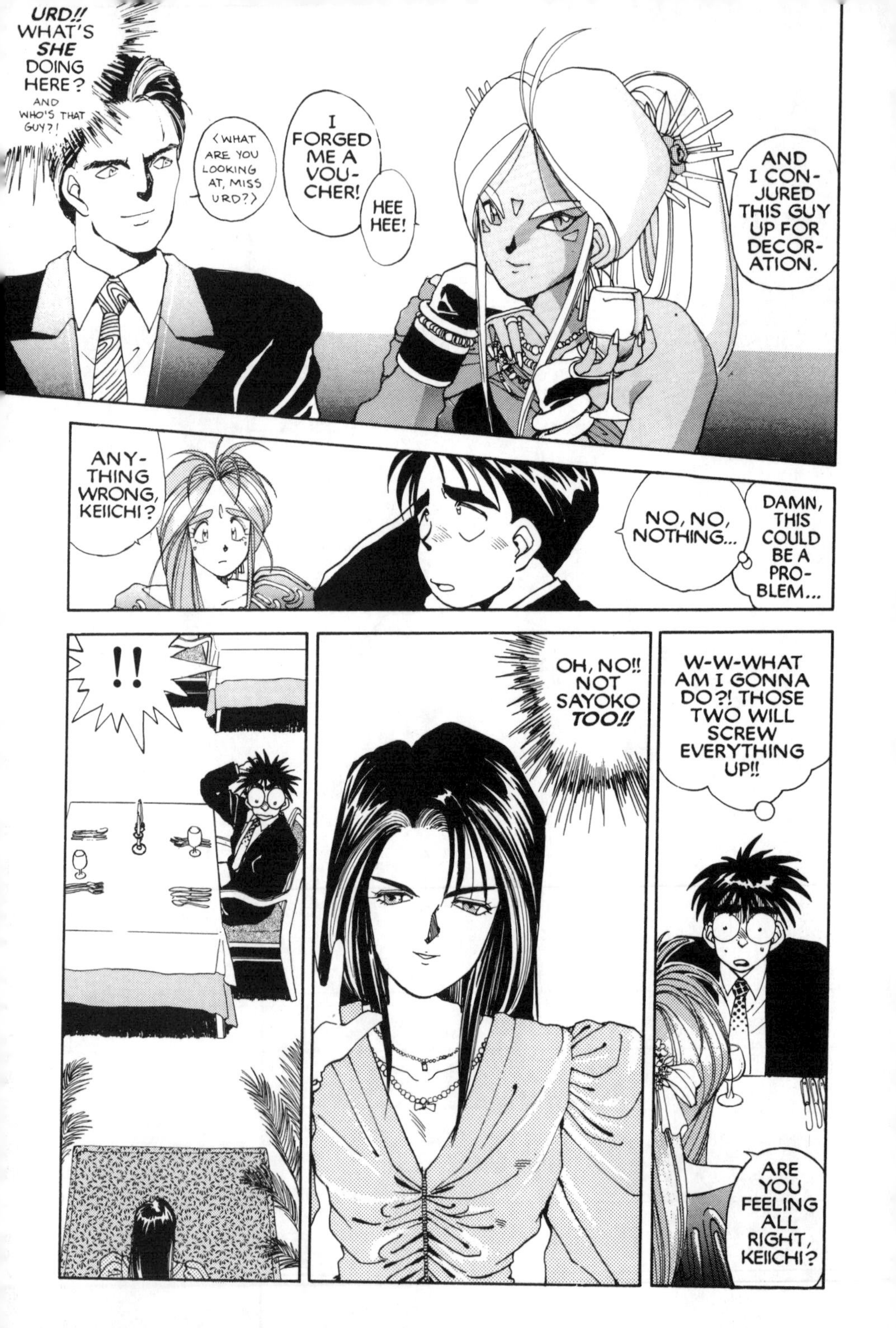
URD!! WHAT'S SHE DOING HERE?
AND WHO'S THAT GUY?!
<WHAT ARE YOU LOOKING AT, MISS URD?>
I FORGED ME A VOUCHER!
HEE HEE!
AND I CONJURED THIS GUY UP FOR DECORATION.
ANYTHING WRONG, KEIICHI?
NO, NO, NOTHING...
DAMN, THIS COULD BE A PROBLEM...
!!
OH, NO!! NOT SAYOKO TOO!!
W-W-WHAT AM I GONNA DO?! THOSE TWO WILL SCREW EVERYTHING UP!!
ARE YOU FEELING ALL RIGHT, KEIICHI?

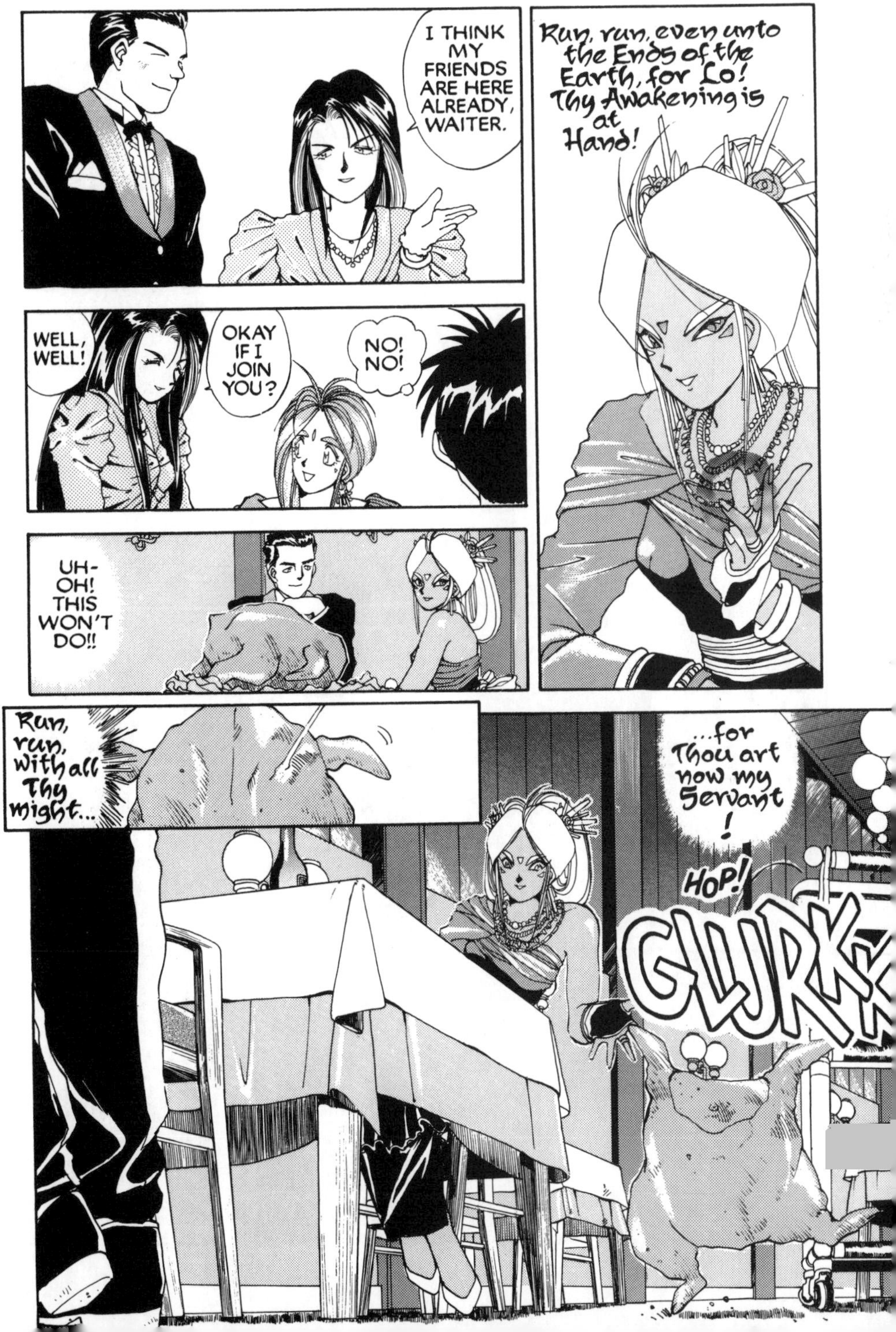
I THINK MY FRIENDS ARE HERE ALREADY, WAITER.
WELL, WELL!
OKAY IF I JOIN YOU?
NO! NO!
UH-OH! THIS WON'T DO!!
Run, run, even unto the Ends of the Earth, for Lo! Thy Awakening is at Hand!
Run, run, with all Thy might...
...for Thou art now my Servant!
HOP!
GLURK

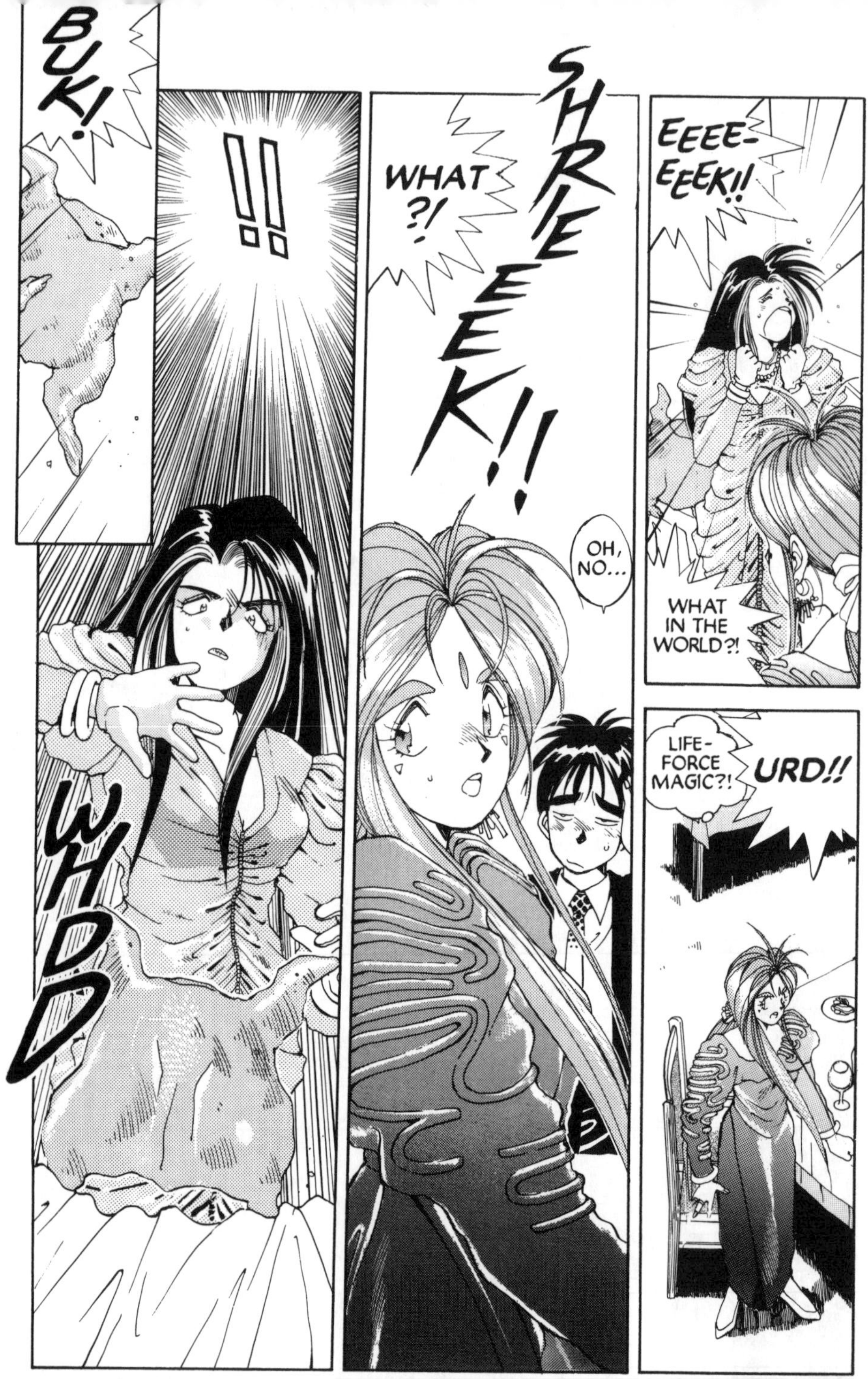
BUKI!
!!
WHDDD
WHAT?!
SHRIEEEEK!!
OH, NO...
EEEE-EEEK!!
WHAT IN THE WORLD?!
LIFE-FORCE MAGIC?!
URD!!

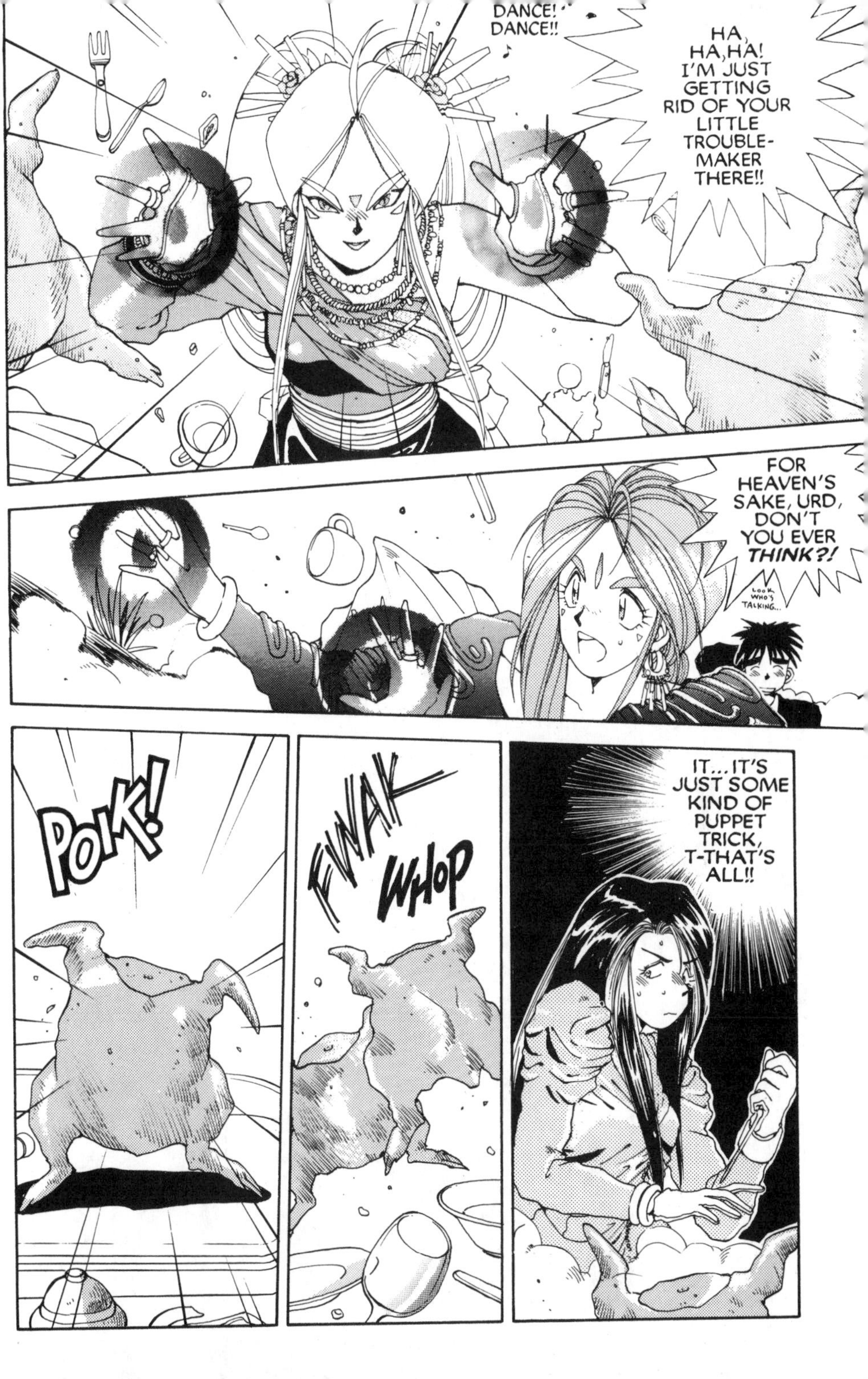
DANCE! DANCE!!
HA, HA,HA! I'M JUST GETTING RID OF YOUR LITTLE TROUBLE-MAKER THERE!!
FOR HEAVEN'S SAKE, URD, DON'T YOU EVER *THINK?!*
LOOK WHO'S TALKING...
POIK!
FWAK
WHOP
IT... IT'S JUST SOME KIND OF PUPPET TRICK, T-THAT'S ALL!!

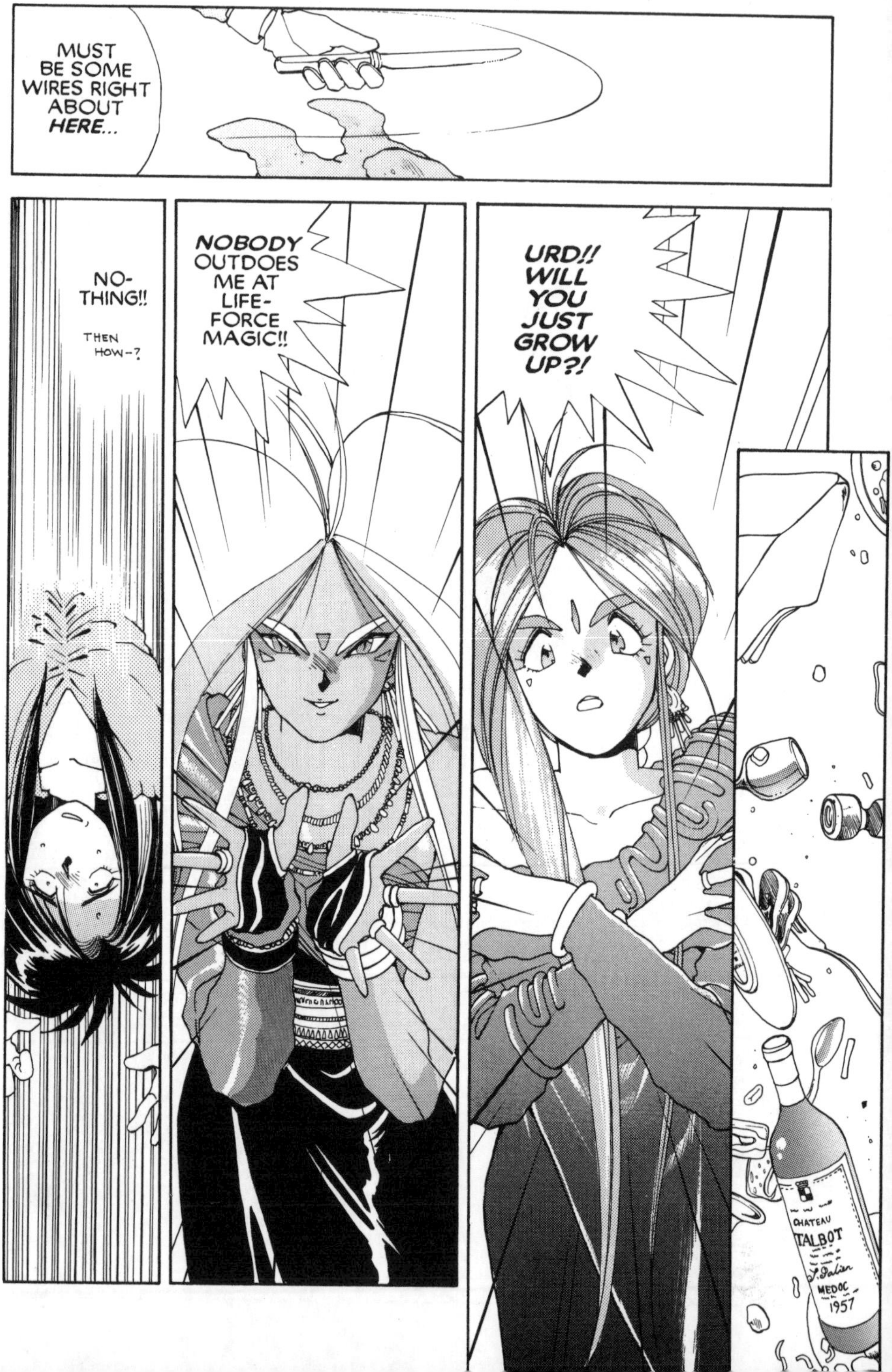
MUST BE SOME WIRES RIGHT ABOUT *HERE*...
NO-THING!!
THEN HOW-?
*NOBODY* OUTDOES ME AT LIFE-FORCE MAGIC!!
*URD!! WILL YOU JUST GROW UP?!*
CHATEAU TALBOT
MEDOC
1957

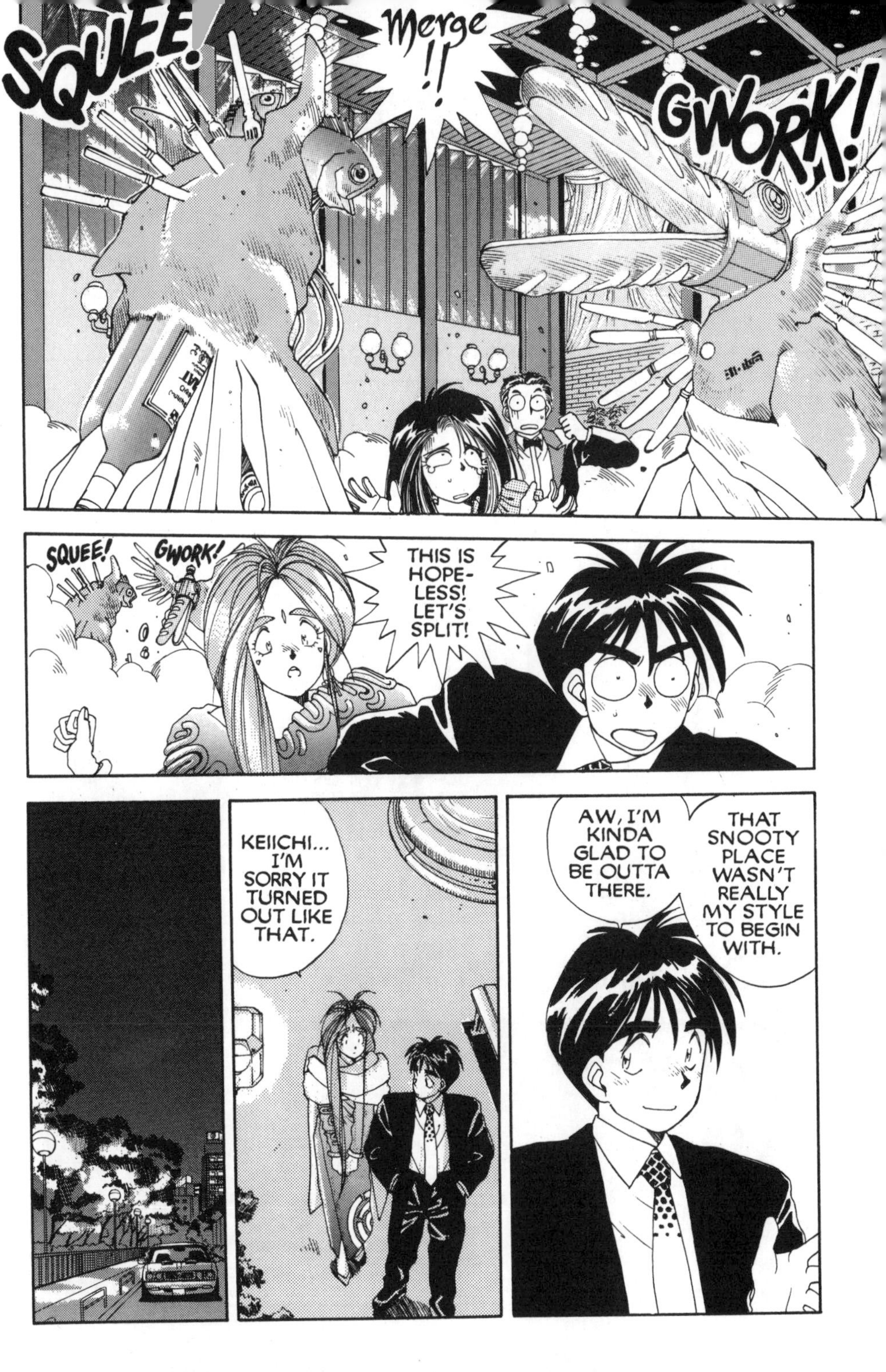
SQUEE!
Merge !!
GWORK!
SQUEE!
GWORK!
THIS IS HOPE-LESS! LET'S SPLIT!
KEIICHI... I'M SORRY IT TURNED OUT LIKE THAT.
AW, I'M KINDA GLAD TO BE OUTTA THERE.
THAT SNOOTY PLACE WASN'T REALLY MY STYLE TO BEGIN WITH.

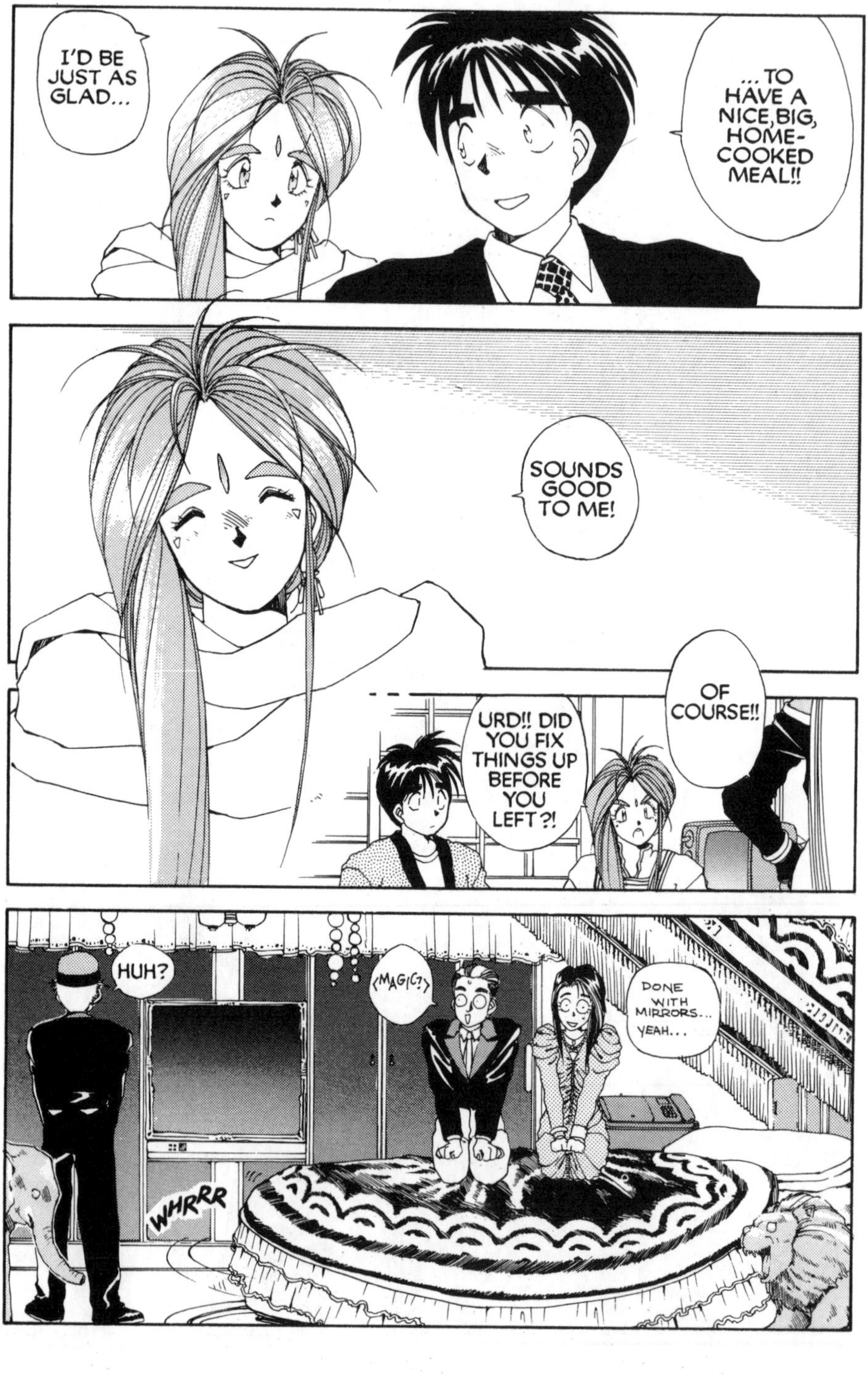
I'D BE JUST AS GLAD...
...TO HAVE A NICE,BIG, HOME-COOKED MEAL!!
SOUNDS GOOD TO ME!
URD!! DID YOU FIX THINGS UP BEFORE YOU LEFT?!
OF COURSE!!
HUH?
‹MAGIC?›
DONE WITH MIRRORS... YEAH...
WHRRR

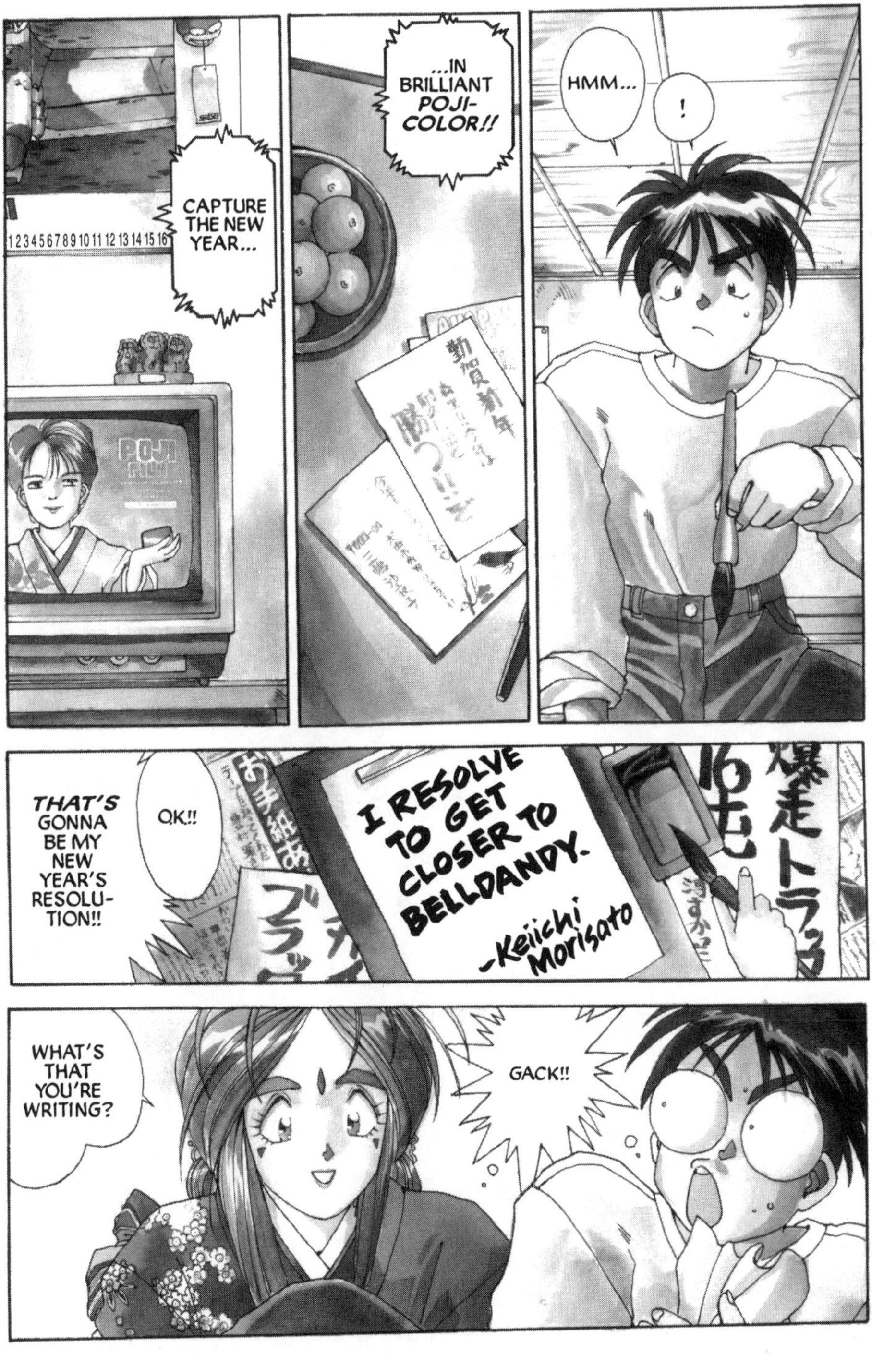
CAPTURE THE NEW YEAR...
...IN BRILLIANT POJI-COLOR!!
HMM...
!
THAT'S GONNA BE MY NEW YEAR'S RESOLUTION!!
O.K.!!
I RESOLVE TO GET CLOSER TO BELLDANDY.
-Keiichi Morisato
WHAT'S THAT YOU'RE WRITING?
GACK!!

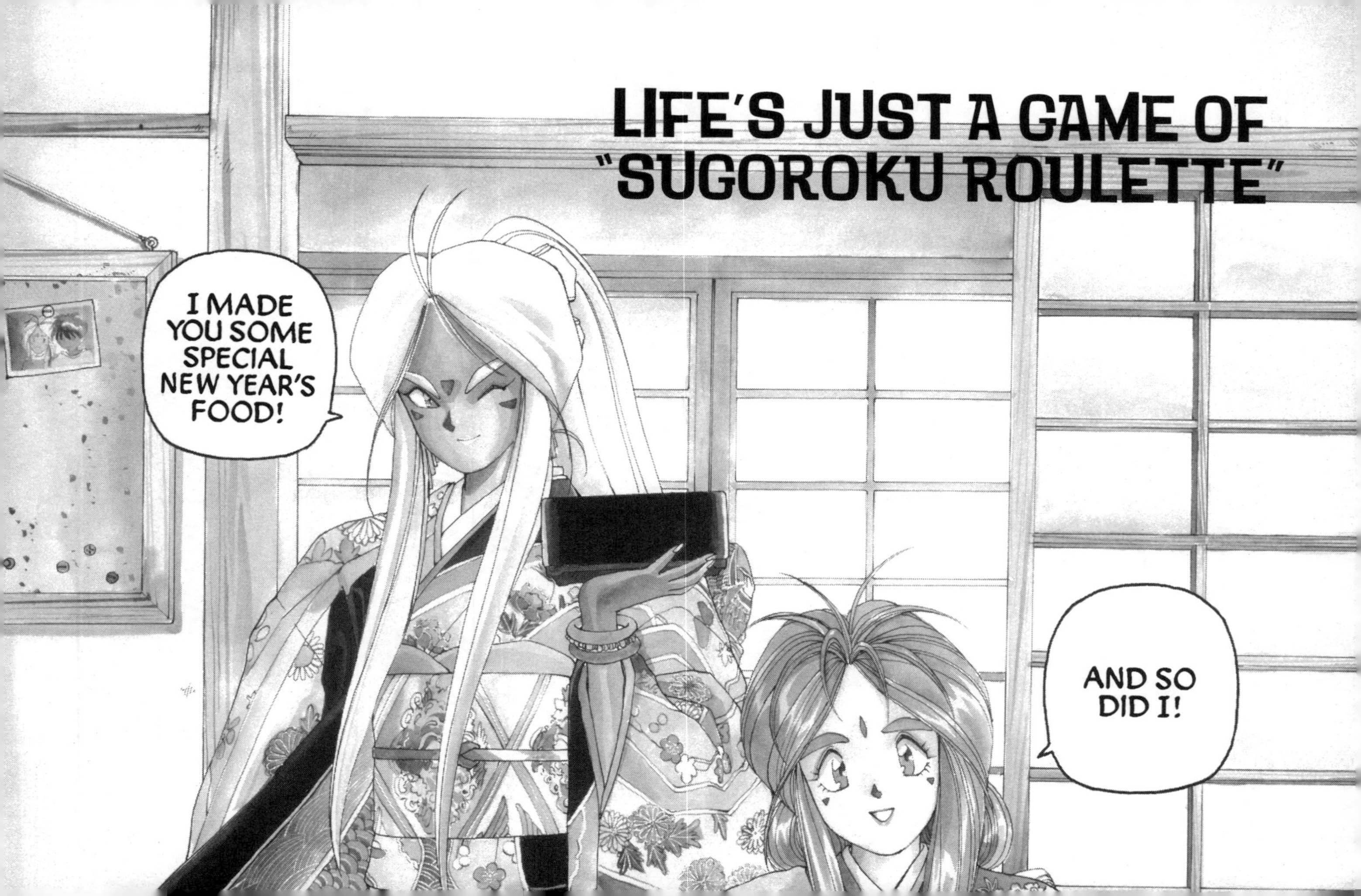
LIFE'S JUST A GAME OF "SUGOROKU ROULETTE"
I MADE YOU SOME SPECIAL NEW YEAR'S FOOD!
AND SO DID I!

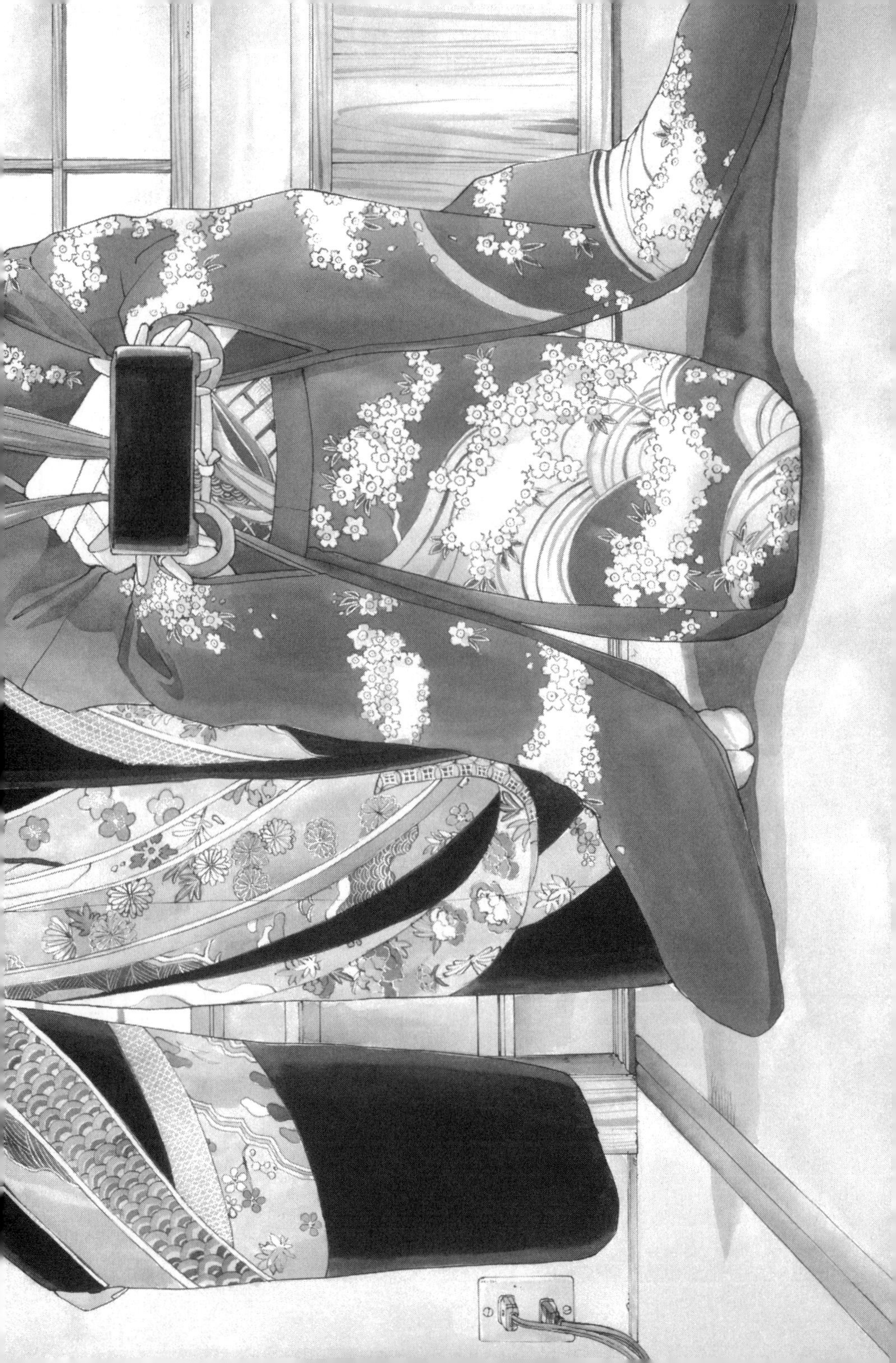

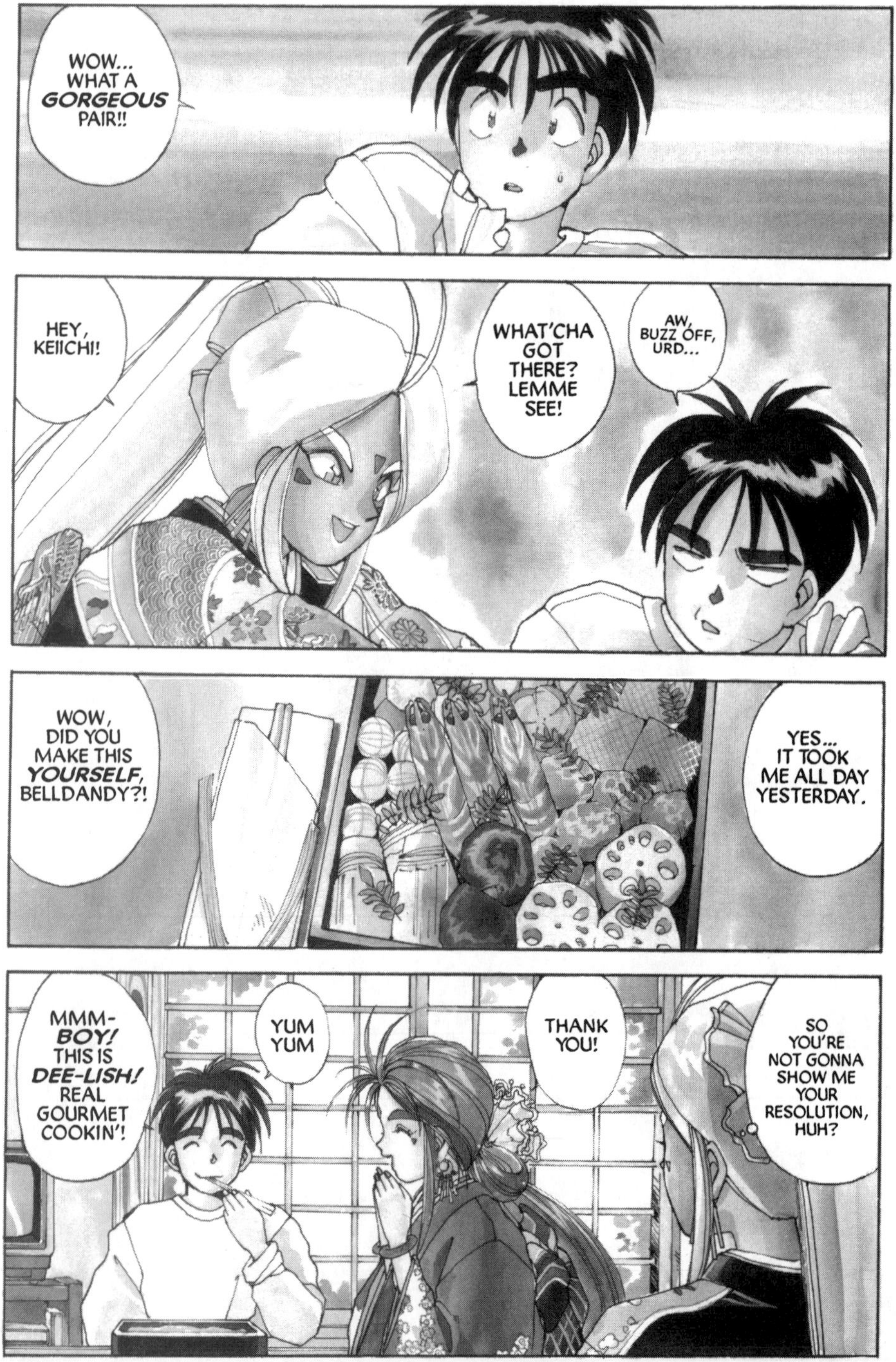
WOW... WHAT A *GORGEOUS* PAIR!!
HEY, KEIICHI!
WHAT'CHA GOT THERE? LEMME SEE!
AW, BUZZ OFF, URD...
WOW, DID YOU MAKE THIS *YOURSELF*, BELLDANDY?!
YES... IT TOOK ME ALL DAY YESTERDAY.
MMM-*BOY!* THIS IS *DEE-LISH!* REAL GOURMET COOKIN'!
YUM YUM
THANK YOU!
SO YOU'RE NOT GONNA SHOW ME YOUR RESOLUTION, HUH?

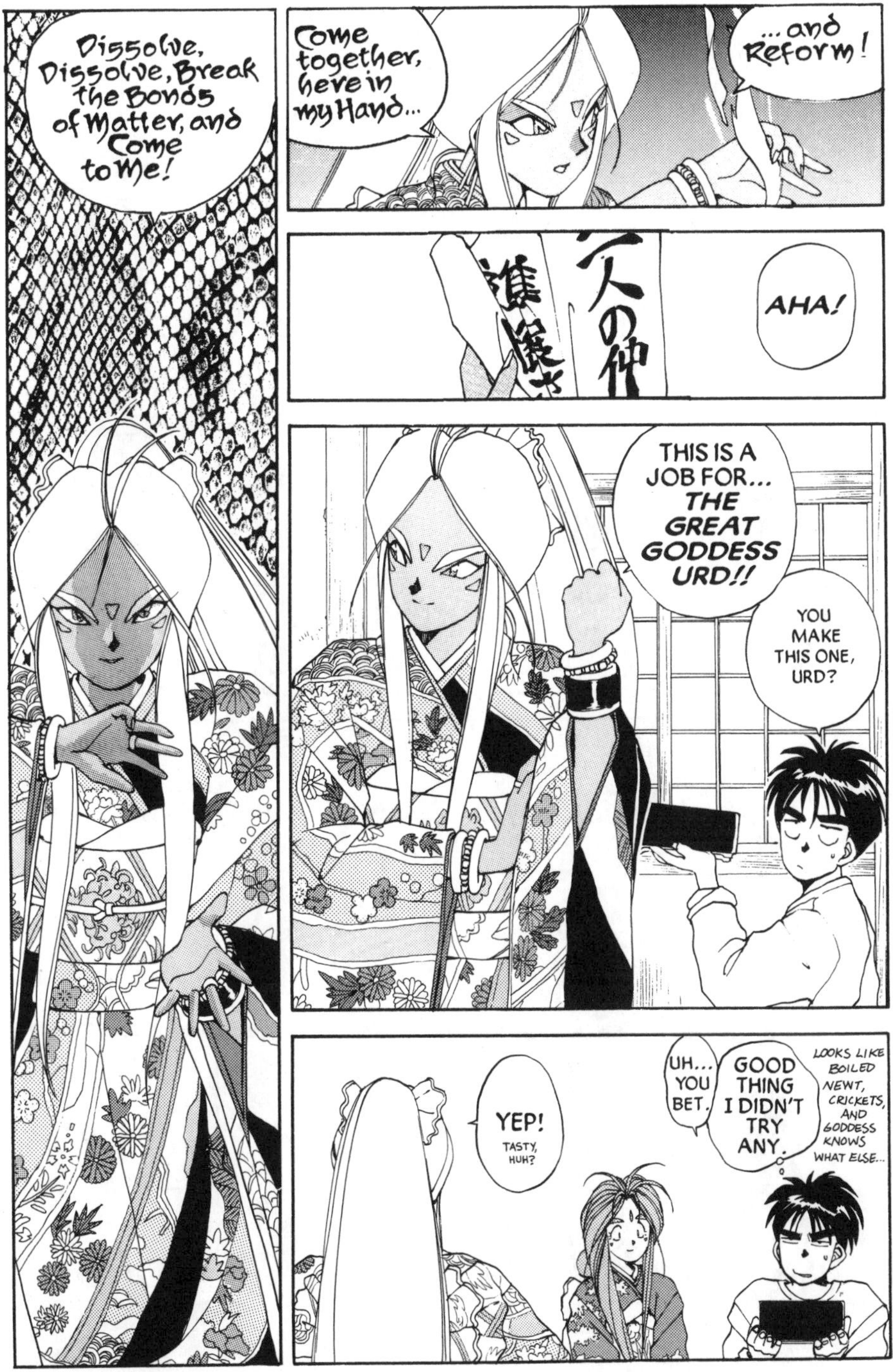

Dissolve, Dissolve, Break the Bonds of Matter, and Come to Me!
Come together, here in my Hand...
...and Reform!
AHA!
THIS IS A JOB FOR... ***THE GREAT GODDESS URD!!***
YOU MAKE THIS ONE, URD?
YEP! TASTY, HUH?
UH... YOU BET.
GOOD THING I DIDN'T TRY ANY.
LOOKS LIKE BOILED NEWT, CRICKETS, AND GODDESS KNOWS WHAT ELSE...

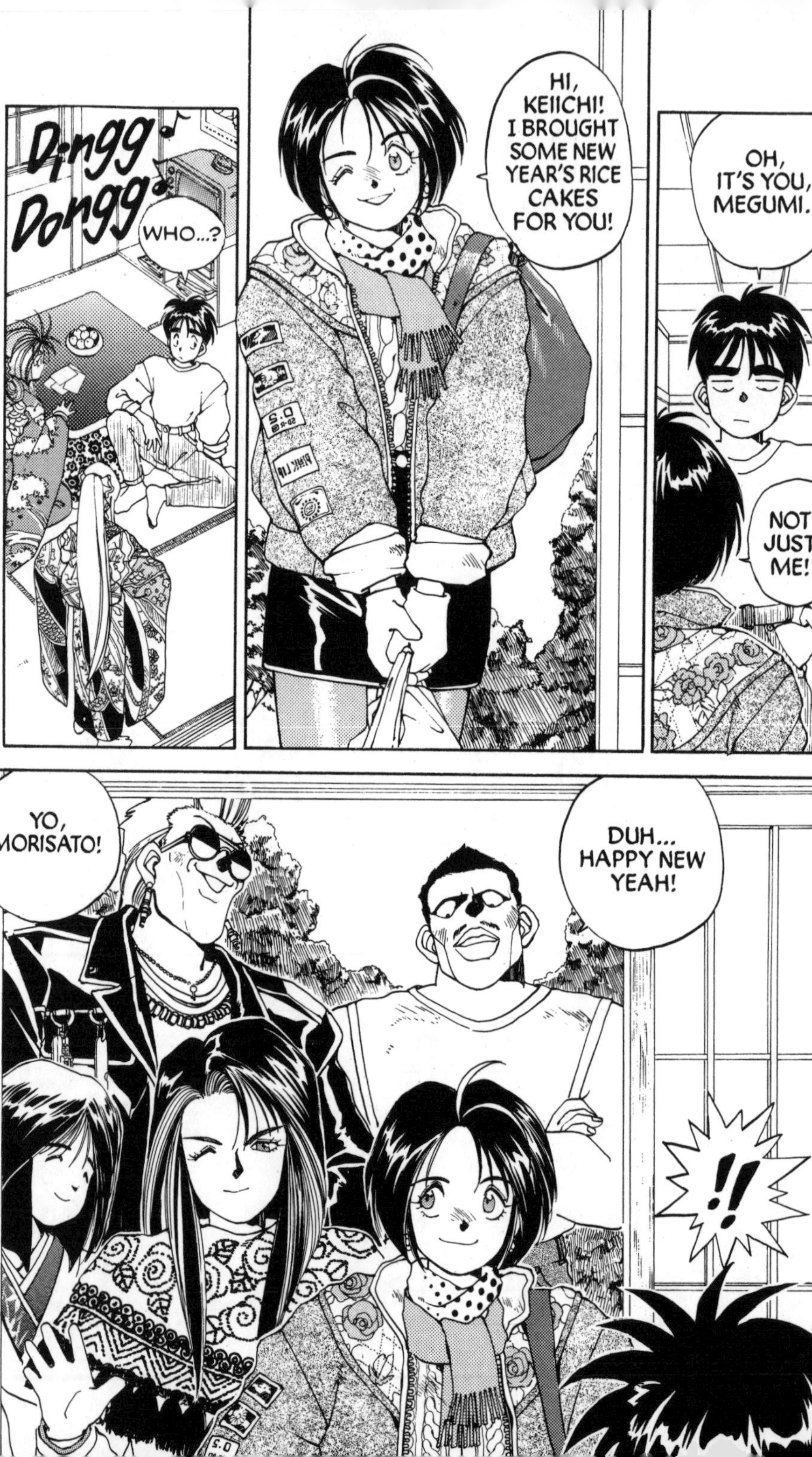
Dingg Dongg
WHO...?
HI, KEIICHI! I BROUGHT SOME NEW YEAR'S RICE CAKES FOR YOU!
OH, IT'S YOU, MEGUMI.
NOT JUST ME!
YO, MORISATO!
DUH... HAPPY NEW YEAH!
!!

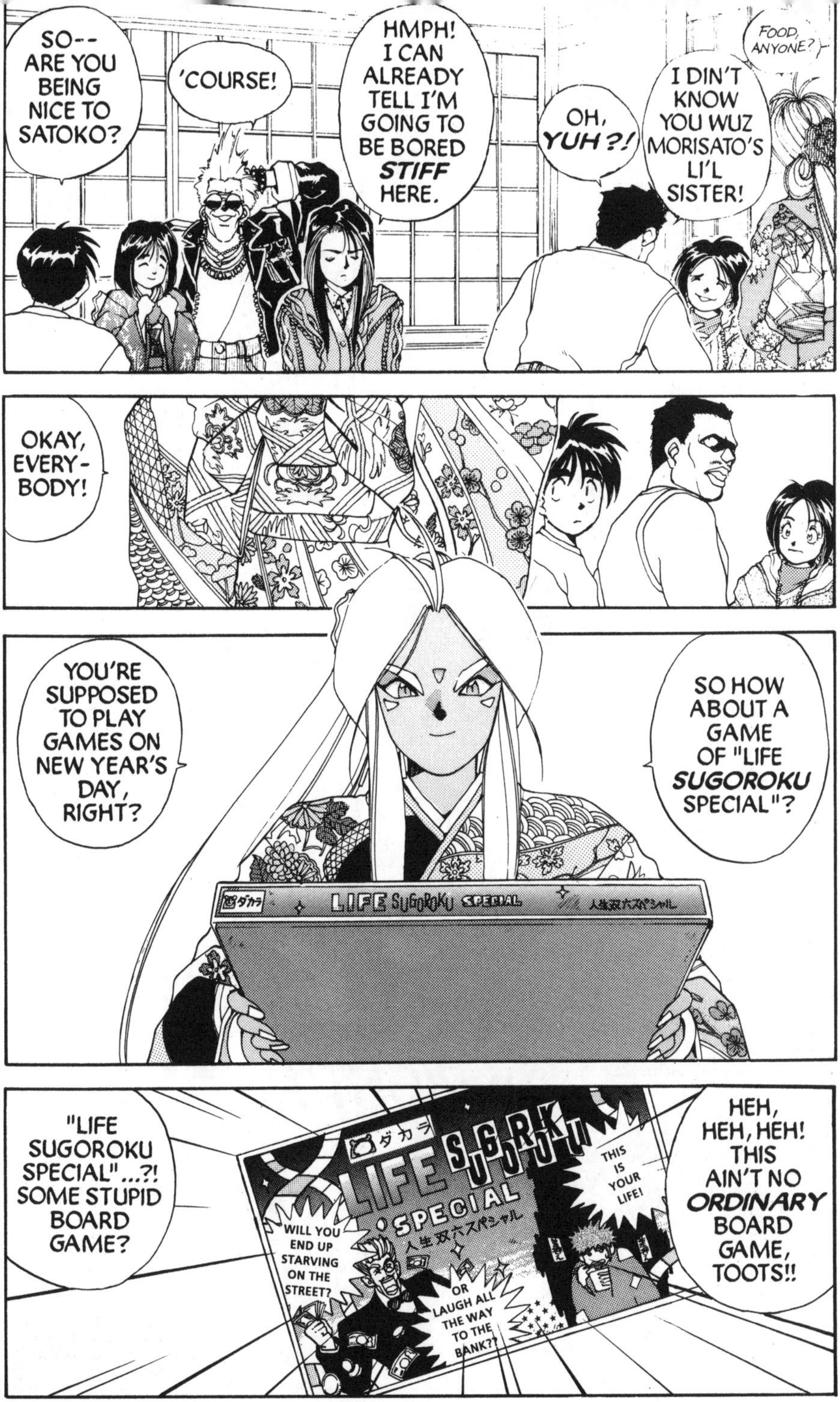
SO-- ARE YOU BEING NICE TO SATOKO?
'COURSE!
HMPH! I CAN ALREADY TELL I'M GOING TO BE BORED **STIFF** HERE.
OH, ***YUH?!***
FOOD, ANYONE?
I DIN'T KNOW YOU WUZ MORISATO'S LI'L SISTER!
OKAY, EVERY-BODY!
YOU'RE SUPPOSED TO PLAY GAMES ON NEW YEAR'S DAY, RIGHT?
SO HOW ABOUT A GAME OF "LIFE ***SUGOROKU*** SPECIAL"?
ダカラ
LIFE SUGOROKU SPECIAL
人生双六スペシャル
"LIFE SUGOROKU SPECIAL"...?! SOME STUPID BOARD GAME?
ダカラ
LIFE SUGOROKU SPECIAL
人生双六スペシャル
THIS IS YOUR LIFE!
WILL YOU END UP STARVING ON THE STREET?
OR LAUGH ALL THE WAY TO THE BANK??
HEH, HEH, HEH! THIS AIN'T NO ***ORDINARY*** BOARD GAME, TOOTS!!

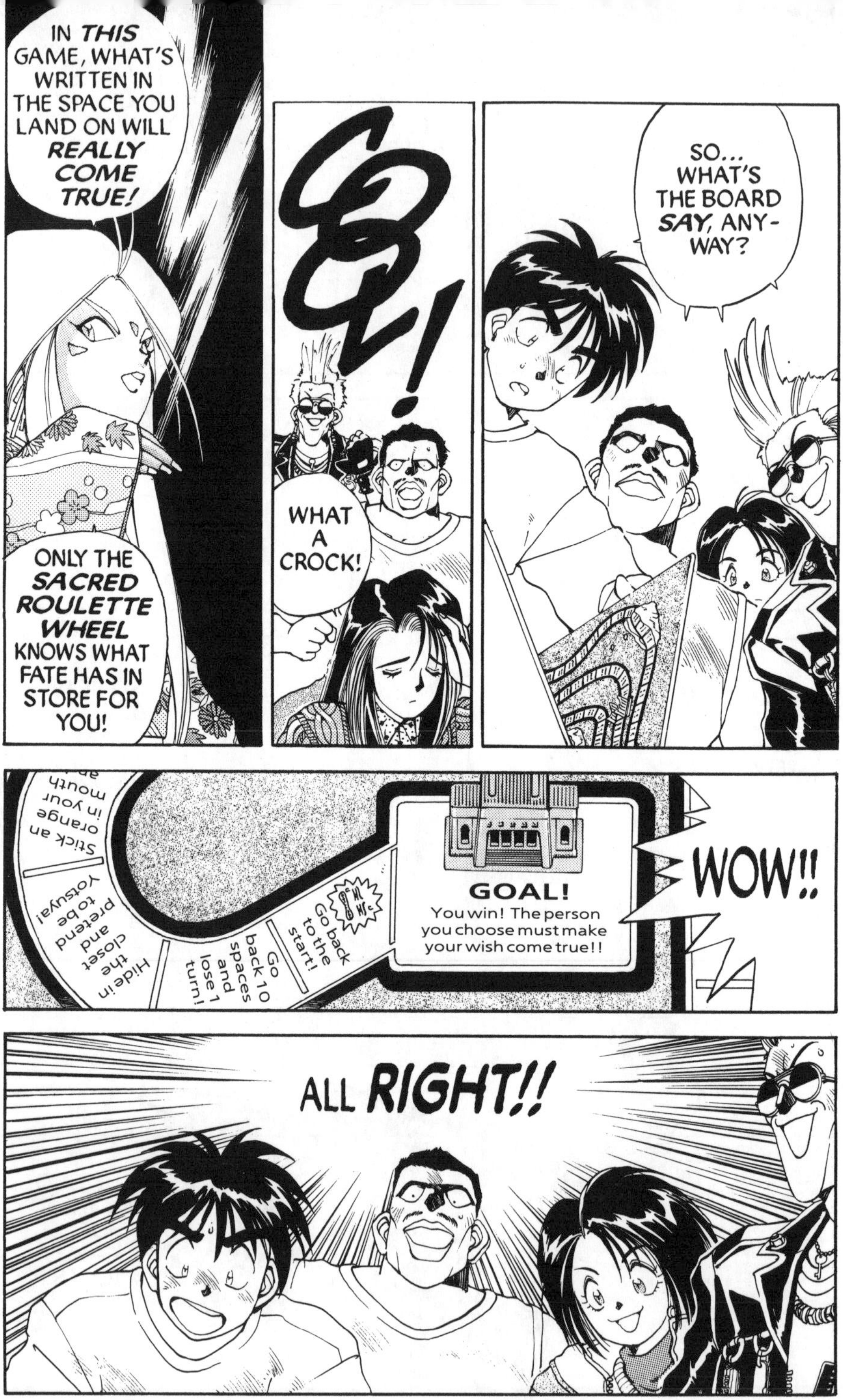
IN THIS GAME, WHAT'S WRITTEN IN THE SPACE YOU LAND ON WILL REALLY COME TRUE!
ONLY THE SACRED ROULETTE WHEEL KNOWS WHAT FATE HAS IN STORE FOR YOU!
WHAT A CROCK!
SO... WHAT'S THE BOARD SAY, ANYWAY?
Stick an orange in your mouth
Hide in the closet and pretend to be Yotsuya!
Go back 10 spaces and lose 1 turn!
Go back to the start!
GOAL!
You win! The person you choose must make your wish come true!!
WOW!!
ALL RIGHT!!

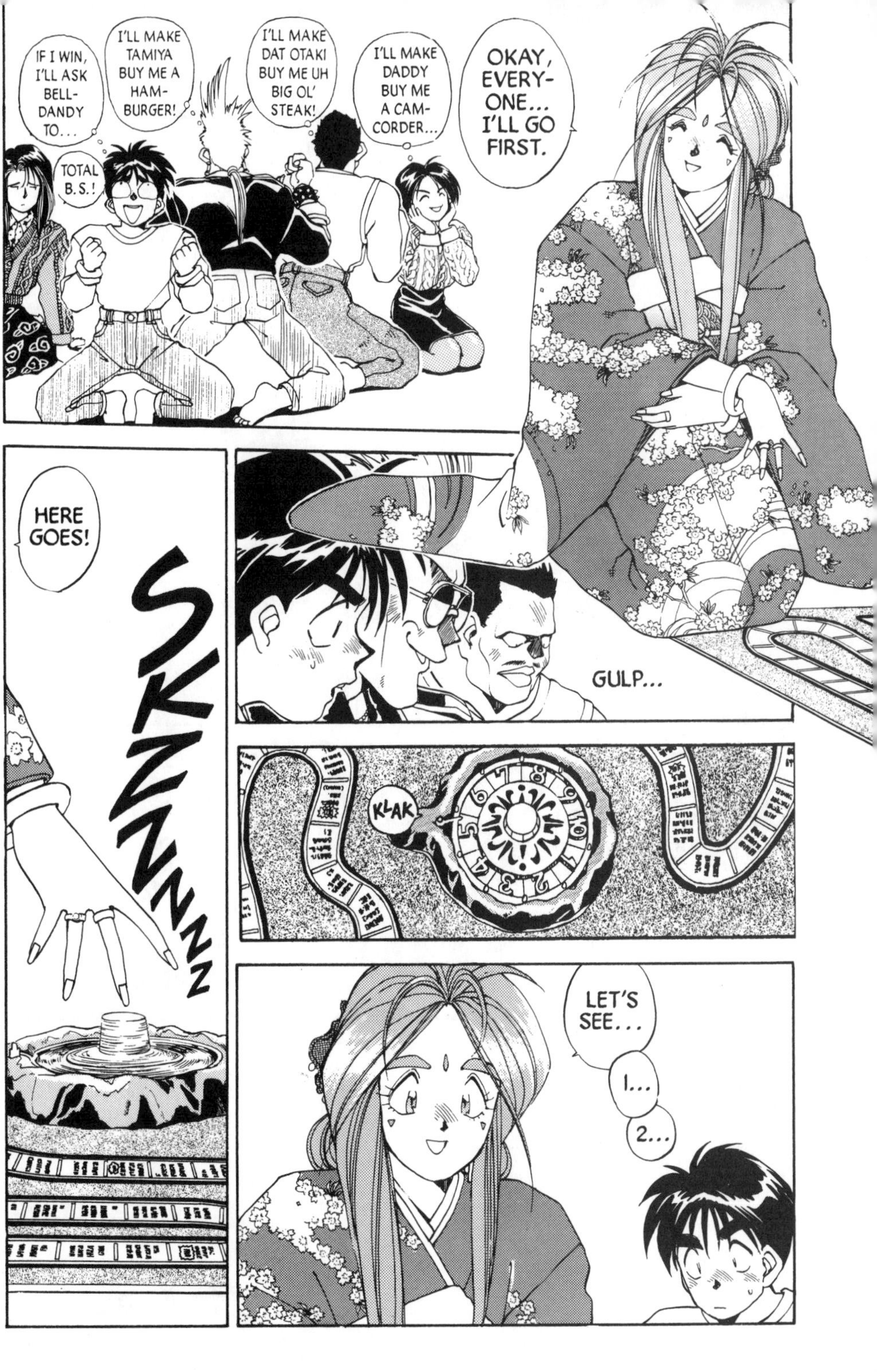
IF I WIN, I'LL ASK BELL-DANDY TO...
TOTAL B.S.!
I'LL MAKE TAMIYA BUY ME A HAM-BURGER!
I'LL MAKE DAT OTAKI BUY ME UH BIG OL' STEAK!
I'LL MAKE DADDY BUY ME A CAM-CORDER...
OKAY, EVERY-ONE... I'LL GO FIRST.
HERE GOES!
SKNNNNNN
GULP...
KLAK
LET'S SEE...
1...
2...

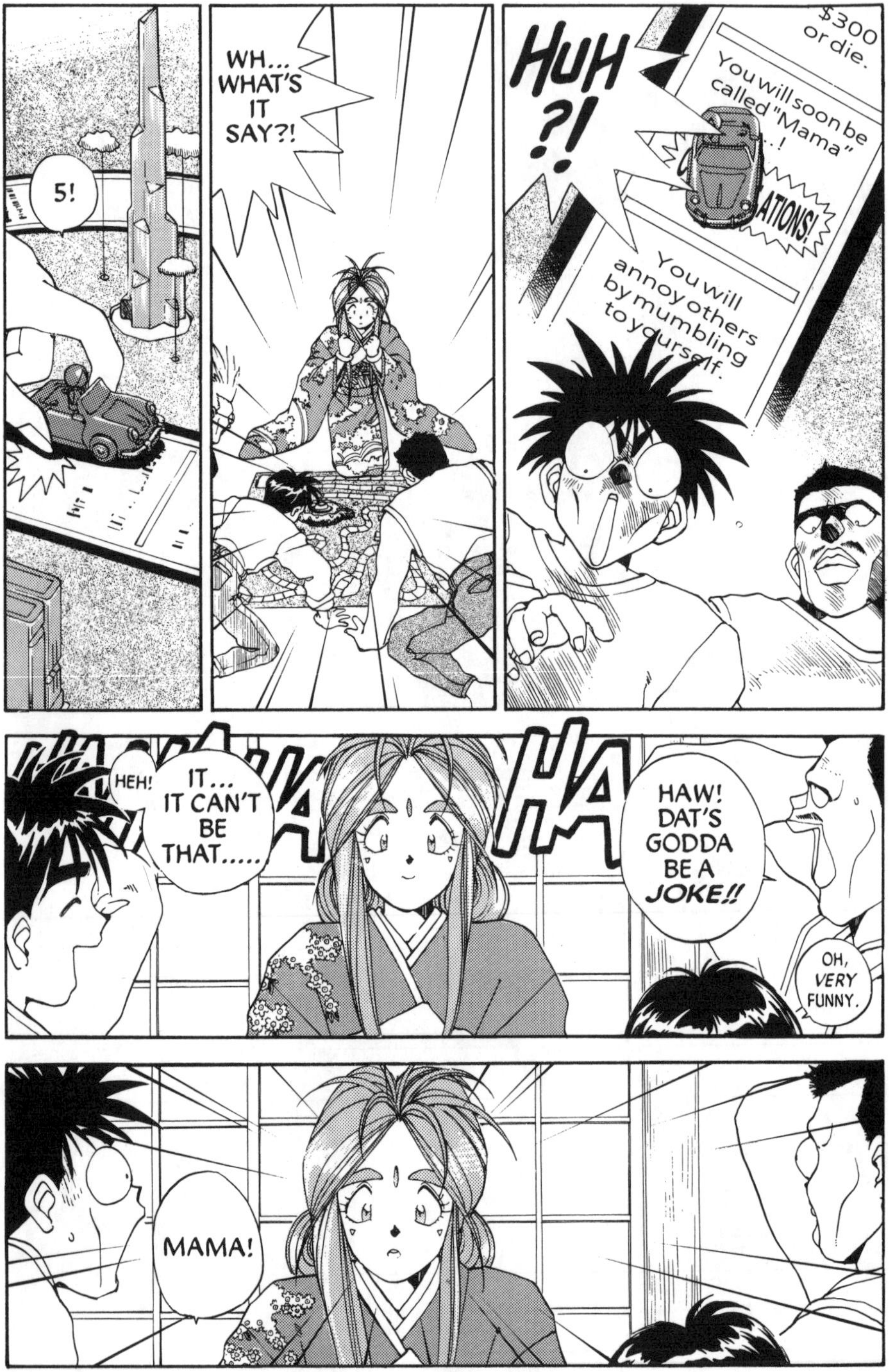
5!
WH... WHAT'S IT SAY?!
HUH ?!
$300 or die.
You will soon be called "Mama" ...!
You will annoy others by mumbling to yourself.
HA
HEH!
IT... IT CAN'T BE THAT.....
HAW! DAT'S GODDA BE A JOKE!!
OH, VERY FUNNY.
MAMA!

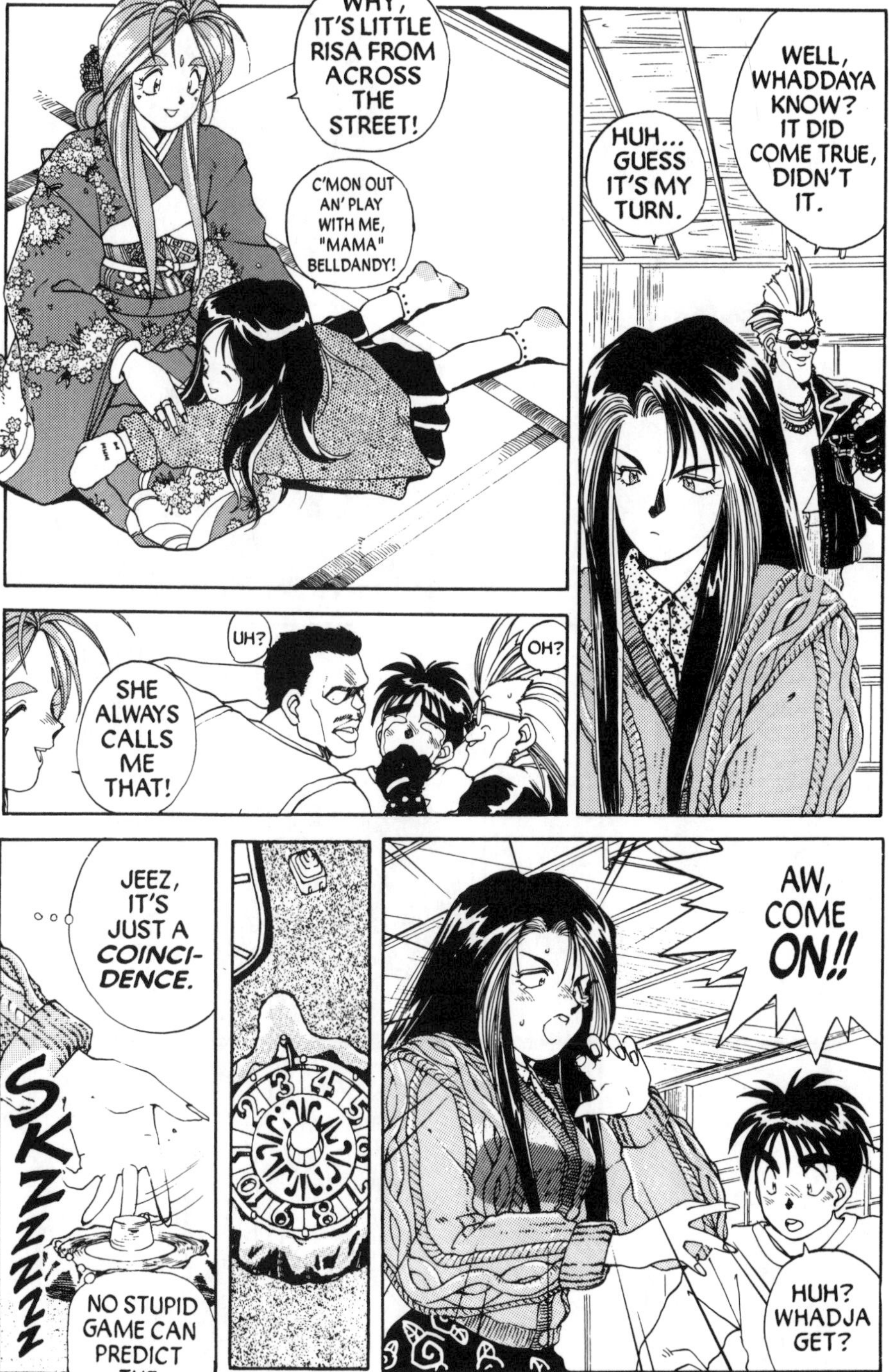
WHY, IT'S LITTLE RISA FROM ACROSS THE STREET!
C'MON OUT AN' PLAY WITH ME, "MAMA" BELLDANDY!
SHE ALWAYS CALLS ME THAT!
UH?
OH?
HUH... GUESS IT'S MY TURN.
WELL, WHADDAYA KNOW? IT DID COME TRUE, DIDN'T IT.
...
JEEZ, IT'S JUST A *COINCI-DENCE.*
SKZZZZZZ
NO STUPID GAME CAN PREDICT THE FUTURE!
AW, COME **ON!!**
HUH? WHADJA GET?

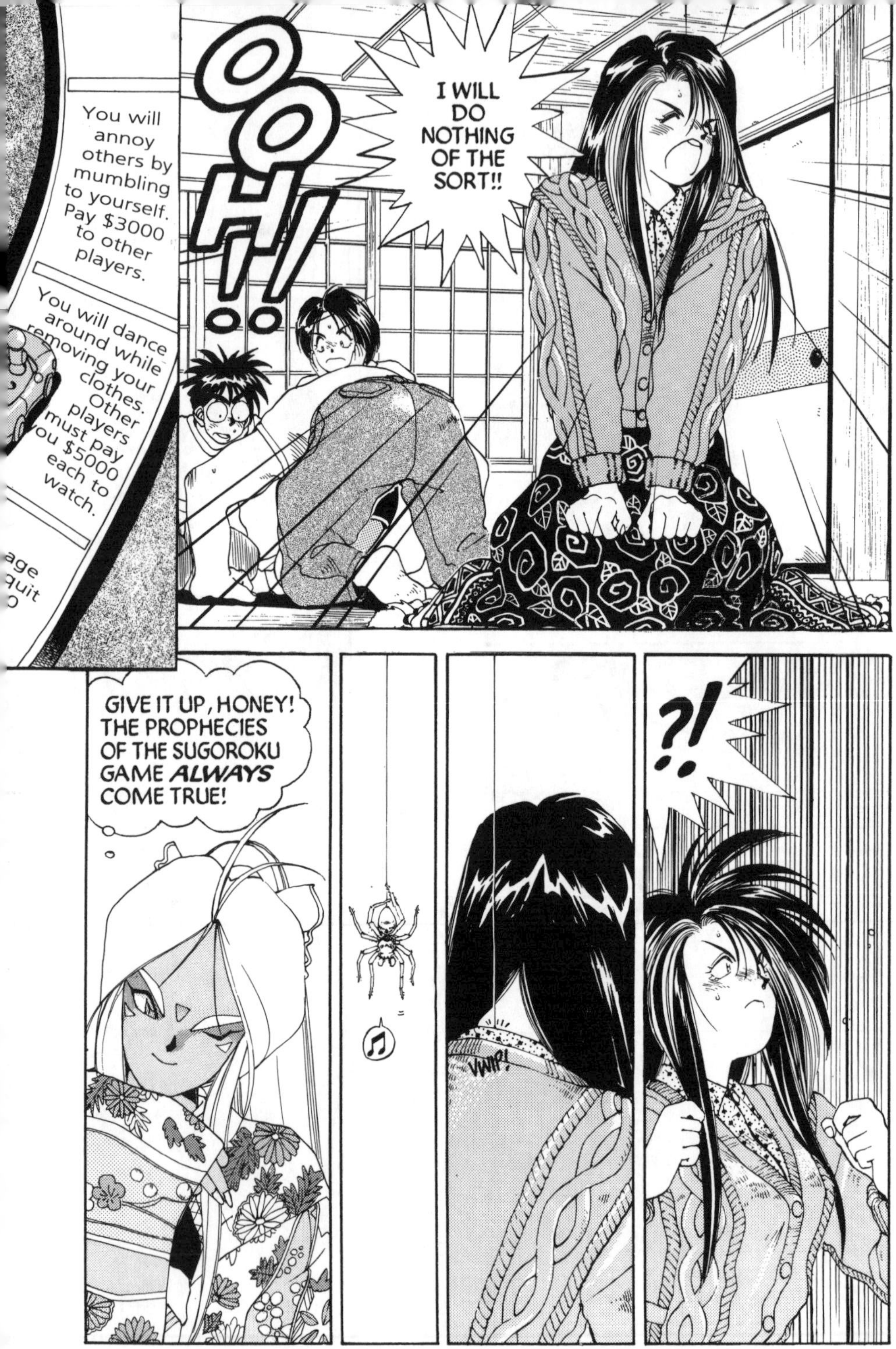
You will annoy others by mumbling to yourself. Pay $3000 to other players.
You will dance around while removing your clothes. Other players must pay you $5000 each to watch.
age
quit
OOH!!
I WILL DO NOTHING OF THE SORT!!
GIVE IT UP, HONEY! THE PROPHECIES OF THE SUGOROKU GAME *ALWAYS* COME TRUE!
♫
VWIP!
?!

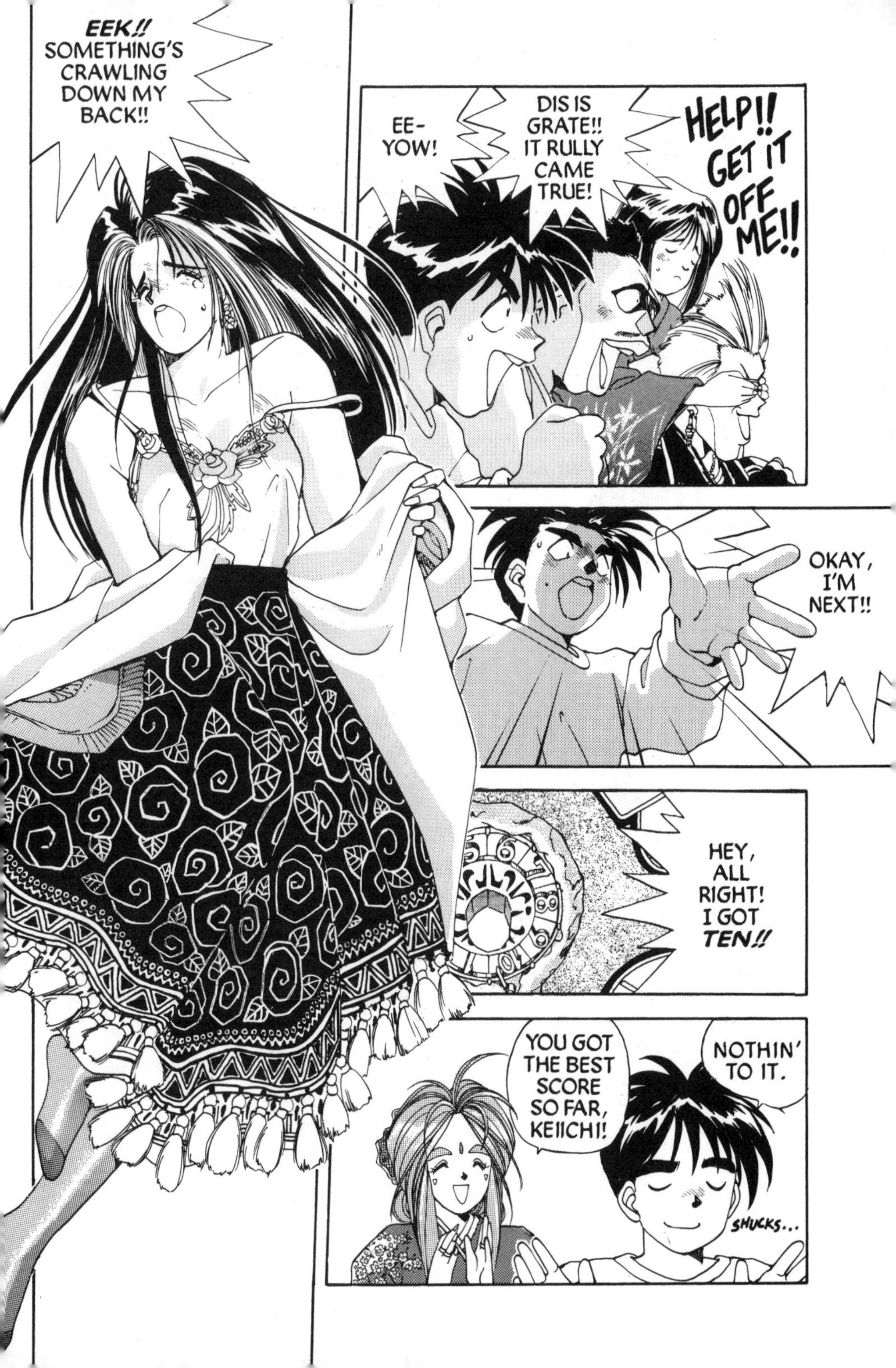
EEK!! SOMETHING'S CRAWLING DOWN MY BACK!!
EE-YOW!
DIS IS GRATE!! IT RULLY CAME TRUE!
HELP!! GET IT OFF ME!!
OKAY, I'M NEXT!!
HEY, ALL RIGHT! I GOT TEN!!
YOU GOT THE BEST SCORE SO FAR, KEIICHI!
NOTHIN' TO IT.
SHUCKS...

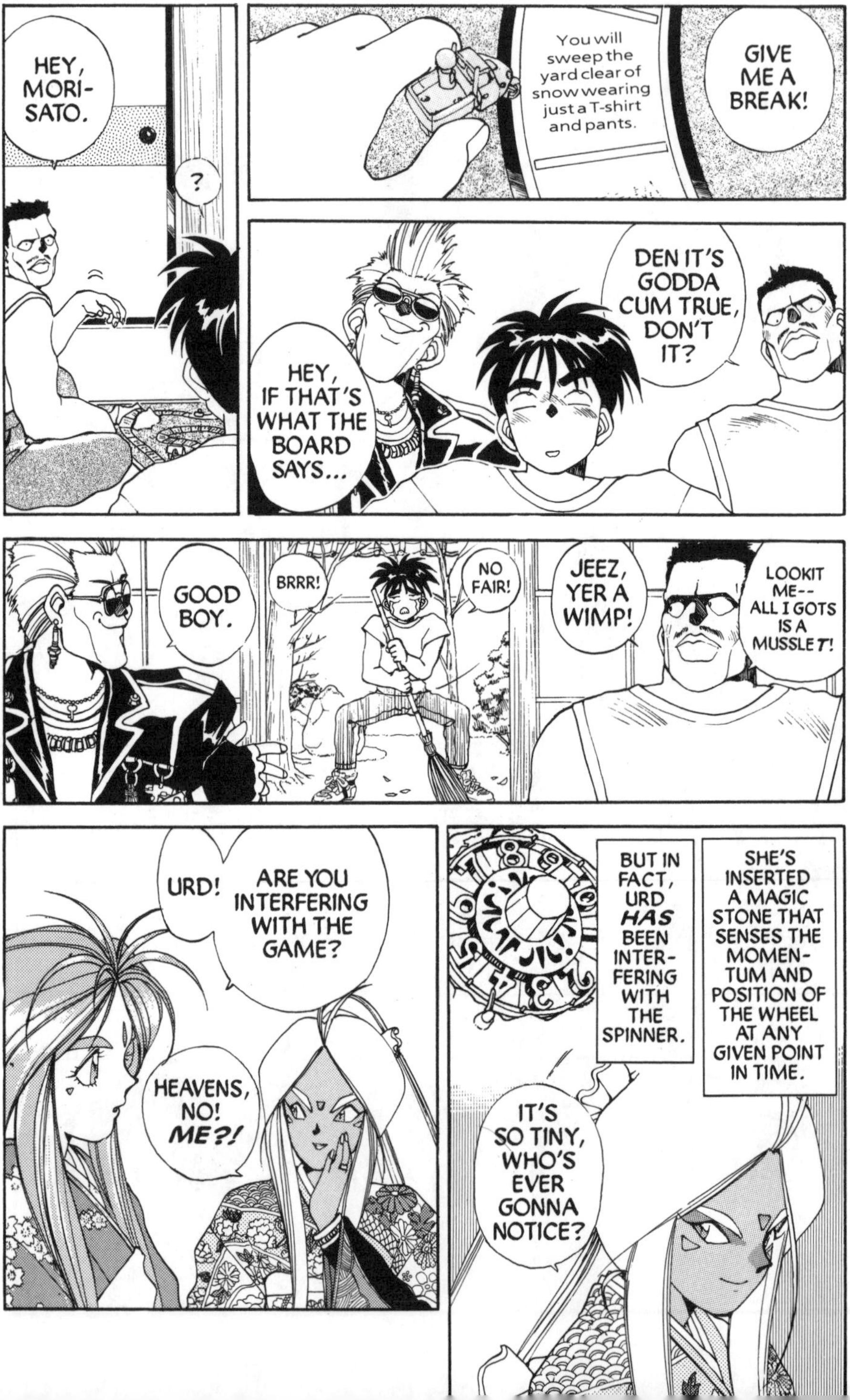
HEY, MORI-SATO.
?
You will sweep the yard clear of snow wearing just a T-shirt and pants.
GIVE ME A BREAK!
HEY, IF THAT'S WHAT THE BOARD SAYS...
DEN IT'S GODDA CUM TRUE, DON'T IT?
GOOD BOY.
BRRR!
NO FAIR!
JEEZ, YER A WIMP!
LOOKIT ME-- ALL I GOTS IS A MUSSLE *T*!
URD!
ARE YOU INTERFERING WITH THE GAME?
HEAVENS, NO! ***ME?!***
BUT IN FACT, URD ***HAS*** BEEN INTER-FERING WITH THE SPINNER.
SHE'S INSERTED A MAGIC STONE THAT SENSES THE MOMEN-TUM AND POSITION OF THE WHEEL AT ANY GIVEN POINT IN TIME.
IT'S SO TINY, WHO'S EVER GONNA NOTICE?

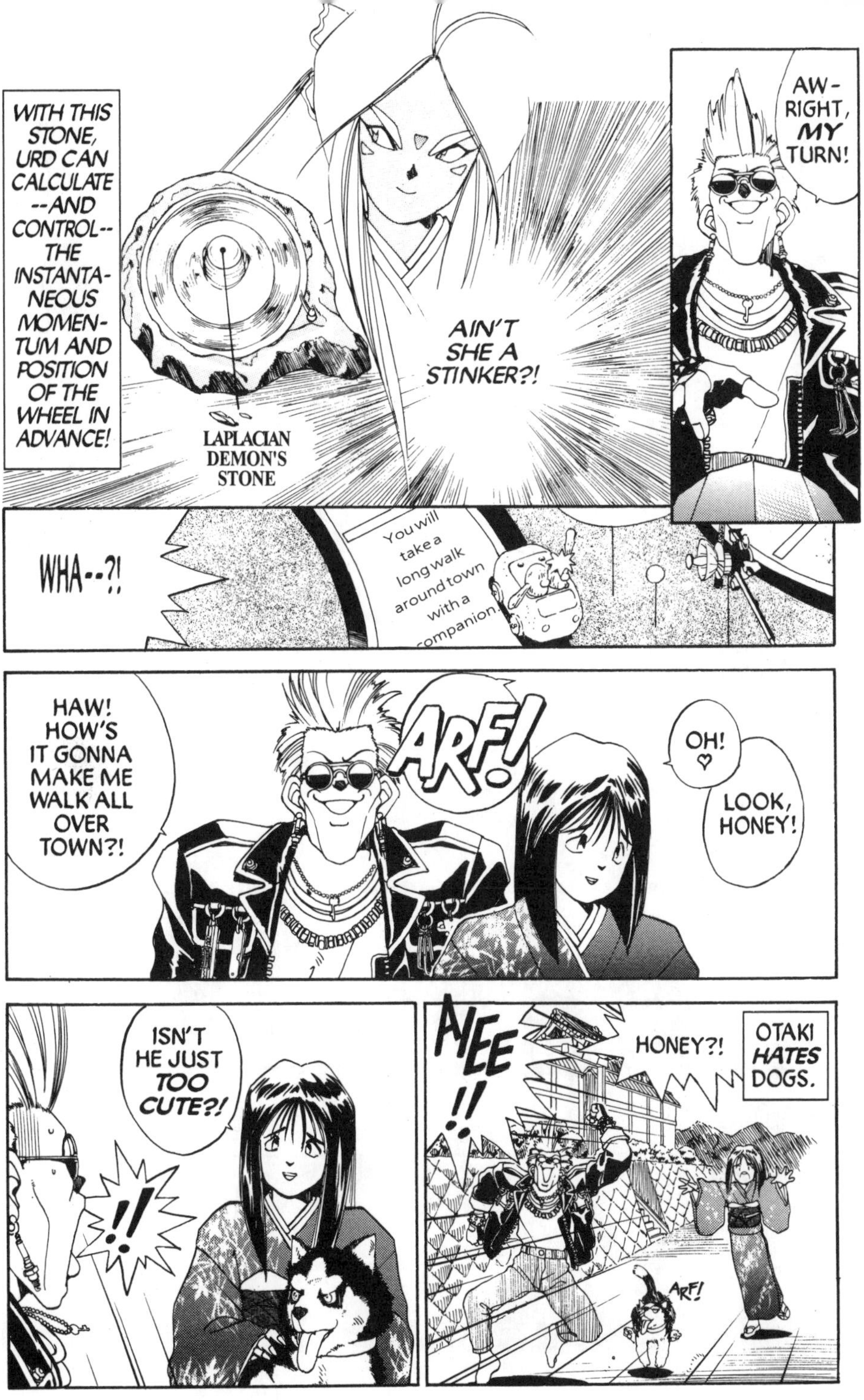
WITH THIS STONE, URD CAN CALCULATE --AND CONTROL-- THE INSTANTANEOUS MOMENTUM AND POSITION OF THE WHEEL IN ADVANCE!
LAPLACIAN DEMON'S STONE
AIN'T SHE A STINKER?!
AW-RIGHT, MY TURN!
WHA--?!
You will take a long walk around town with a companion.
HAW! HOW'S IT GONNA MAKE ME WALK ALL OVER TOWN?!
ARF!
OH! ♡
LOOK, HONEY!
ISN'T HE JUST TOO CUTE?!
!!
AIEE !!
HONEY?!
OTAKI HATES DOGS.
ARF!

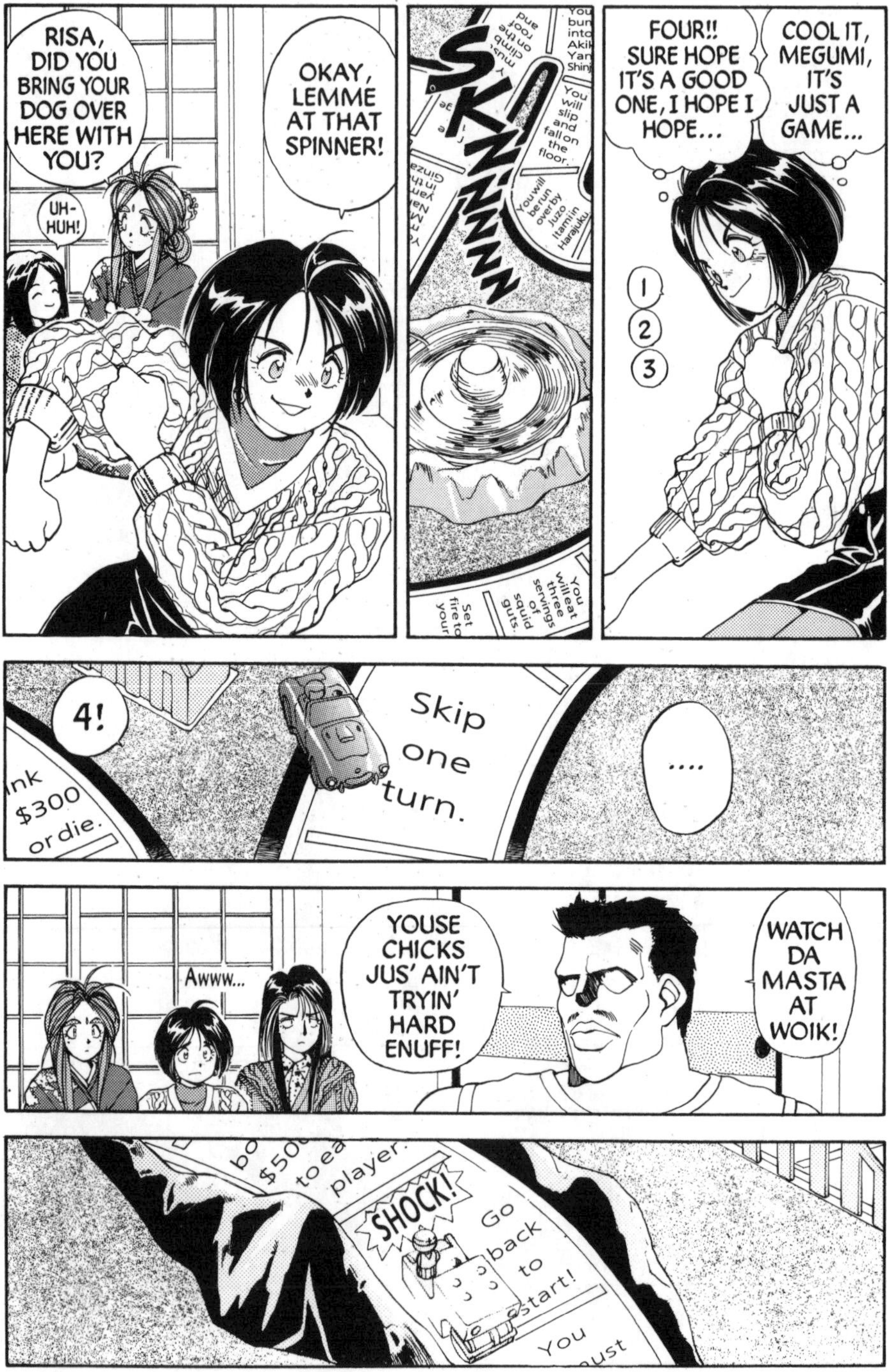
RISA, DID YOU BRING YOUR DOG OVER HERE WITH YOU?
UH-HUH!
OKAY, LEMME AT THAT SPINNER!
SKINNNNN
You will slip and fall on the floor.
You will be run over by Juzo Itami in Harajuku
You will eat three servings of squid guts.
FOUR!! SURE HOPE IT'S A GOOD ONE, I HOPE I HOPE...
COOL IT, MEGUMI, IT'S JUST A GAME...
1
2
3
4!
$300 or die.
Skip one turn.
....
AWWW...
YOUSE CHICKS JUS' AIN'T TRYIN' HARD ENUFF!
WATCH DA MASTA AT WOIK!
player.
SHOCK!
Go back to start!
You

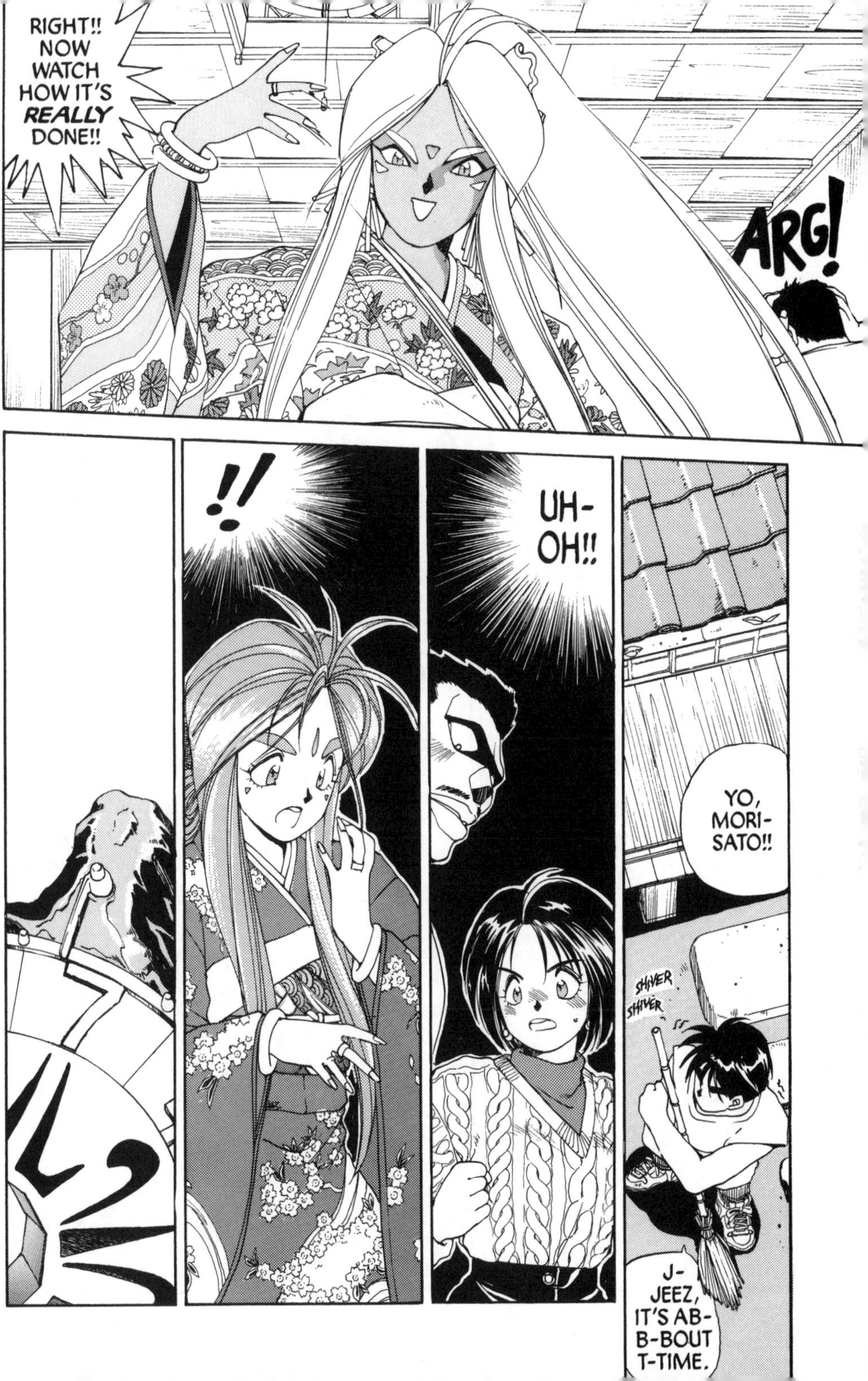
RIGHT!! NOW WATCH HOW IT'S *REALLY* DONE!!
ARG!
!!
UH-OH!!
YO, MORI-SATO!!
SHIVER SHIVER
J-JEEZ, IT'S AB-B-BOUT T-TIME.

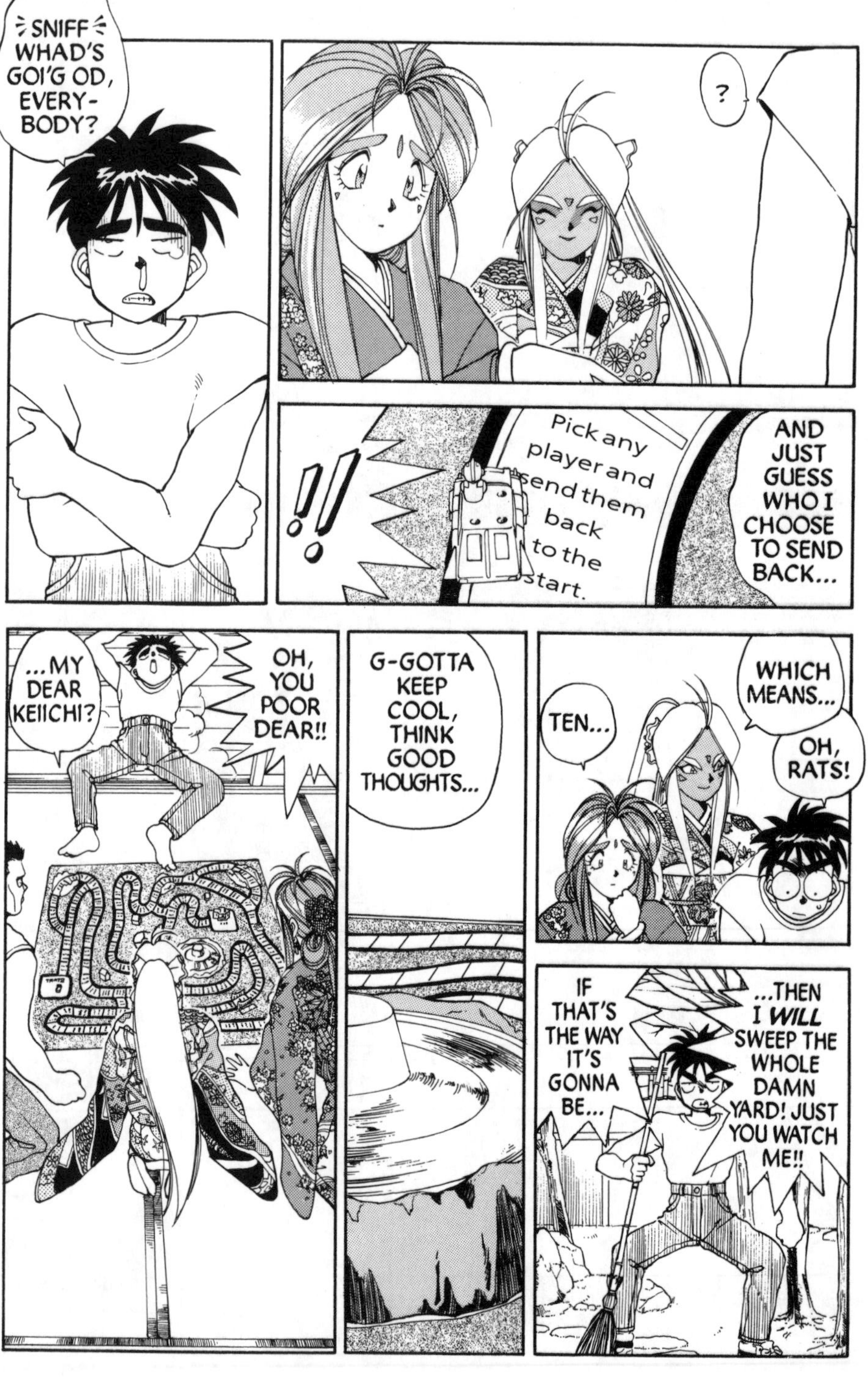
SNIFF WHAD'S GOI'G OD, EVERY-BODY?
?
!!
Pick any player and send them back to the start.
AND JUST GUESS WHO I CHOOSE TO SEND BACK...
...MY DEAR KEIICHI?
OH, YOU POOR DEAR!!
G-GOTTA KEEP COOL, THINK GOOD THOUGHTS...
TEN...
WHICH MEANS...
OH, RATS!
IF THAT'S THE WAY IT'S GONNA BE...
...THEN I *WILL* SWEEP THE WHOLE DAMN YARD! JUST YOU WATCH ME!!

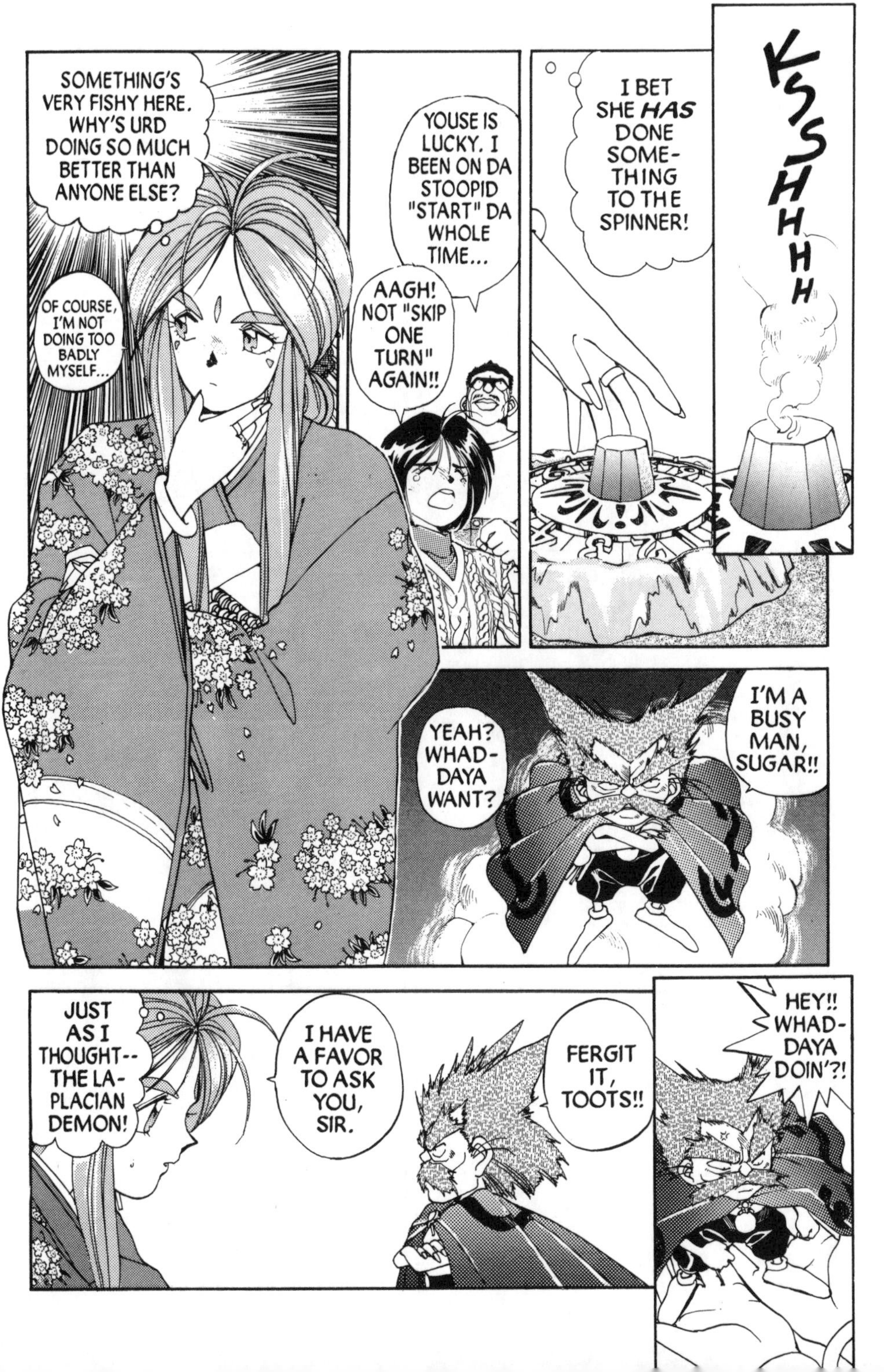
SOMETHING'S VERY FISHY HERE. WHY'S URD DOING SO MUCH BETTER THAN ANYONE ELSE?
OF COURSE, I'M NOT DOING TOO BADLY MYSELF...
YOUSE IS LUCKY. I BEEN ON DA STOOPID "START" DA WHOLE TIME...
AAGH! NOT "SKIP ONE TURN" AGAIN!!
I BET SHE *HAS* DONE SOME-THING TO THE SPINNER!
KSSHHHH
YEAH? WHAD-DAYA WANT?
I'M A BUSY MAN, SUGAR!!
JUST AS I THOUGHT-- THE LA-PLACIAN DEMON!
I HAVE A FAVOR TO ASK YOU, SIR.
FERGIT IT, TOOTS!!
HEY!! WHAD-DAYA DOIN'?!

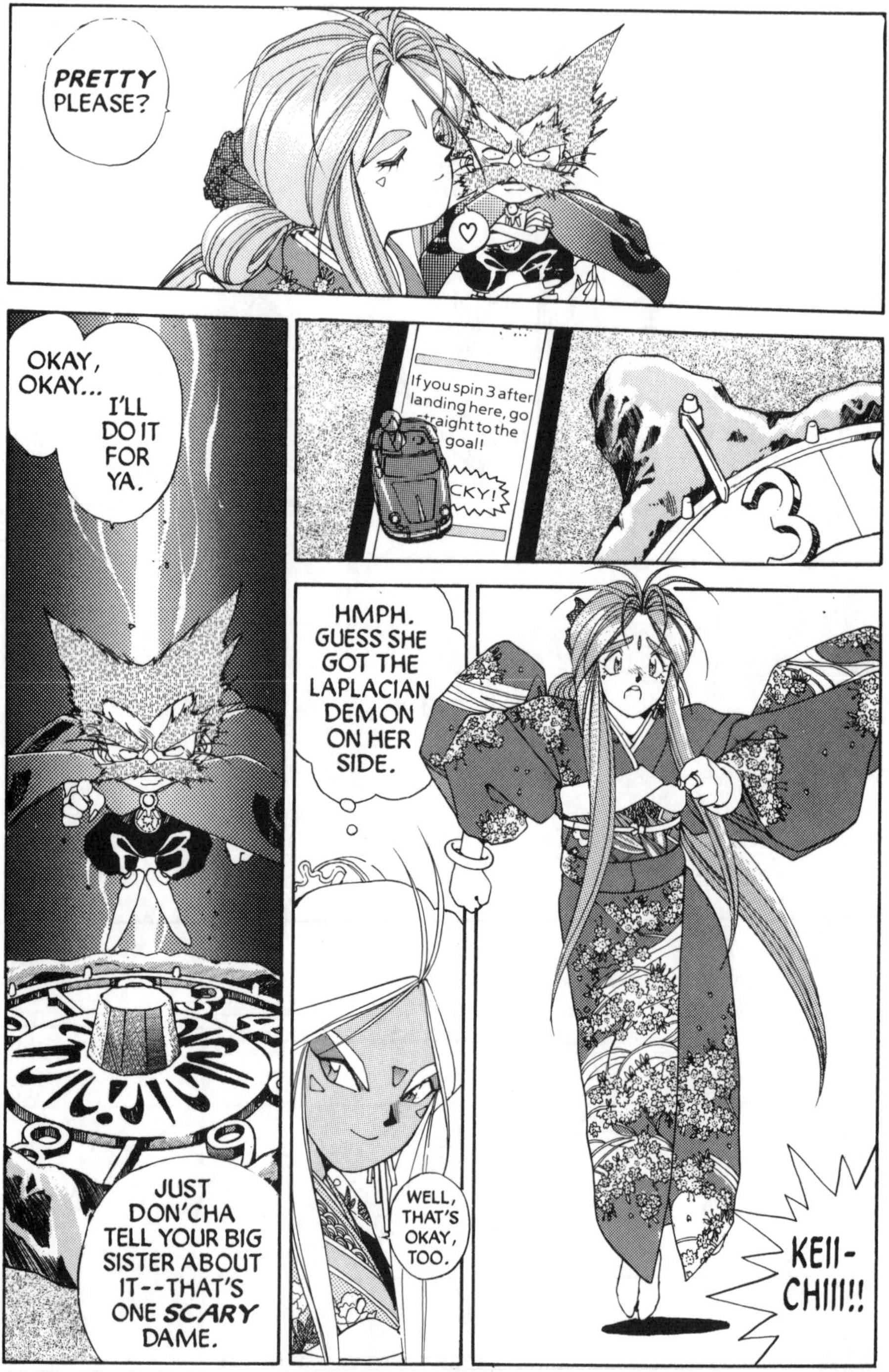
***PRETTY*** PLEASE?
OKAY, OKAY...
I'LL DO IT FOR YA.
JUST DON'CHA TELL YOUR BIG SISTER ABOUT IT--THAT'S ONE ***SCARY*** DAME.
If you spin 3 after landing here, go straight to the goal!
HMPH. GUESS SHE GOT THE LAPLACIAN DEMON ON HER SIDE.
WELL, THAT'S OKAY, TOO.
KEII-CHIII!!

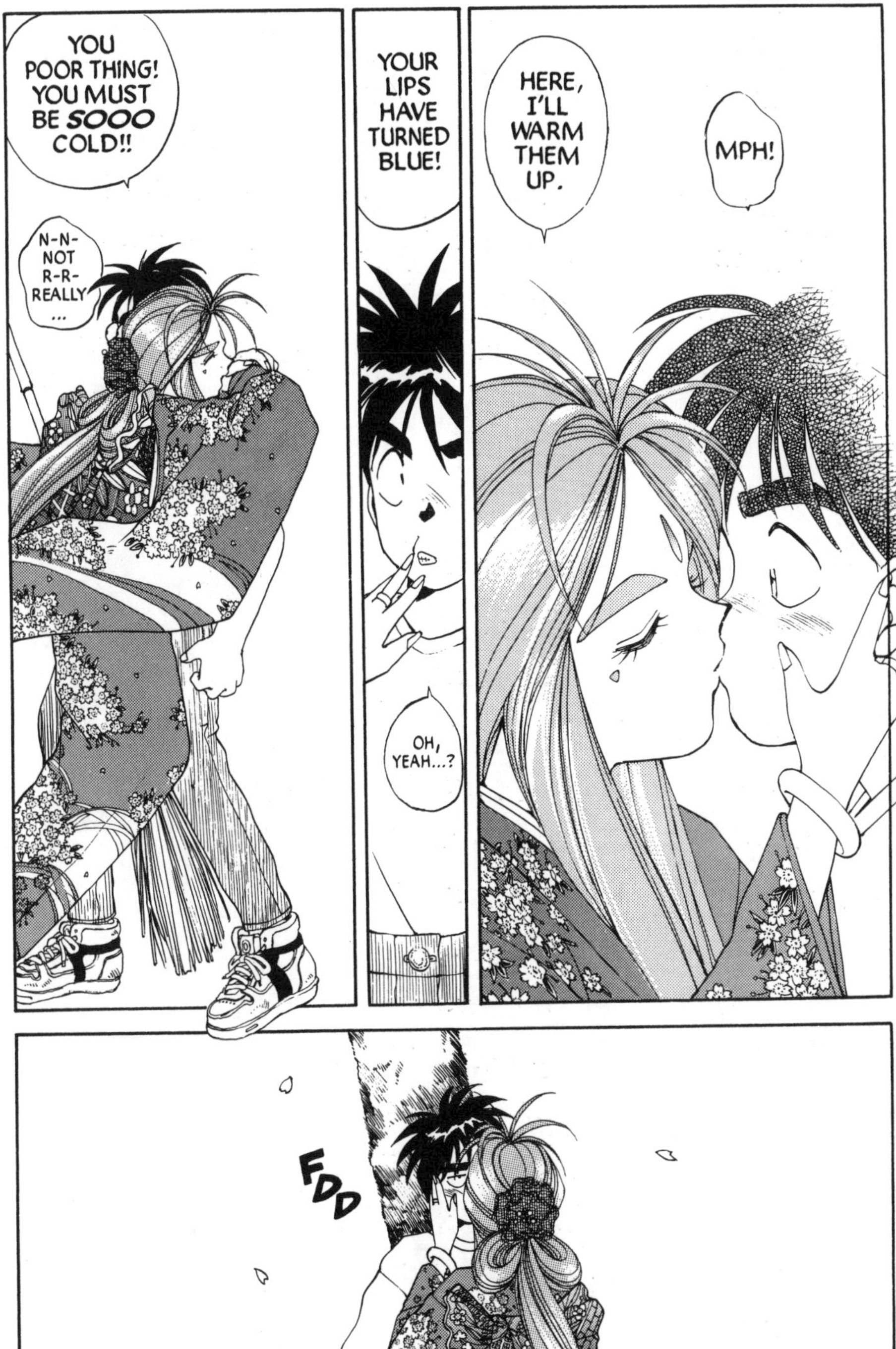

YOU POOR THING! YOU MUST BE SOOO COLD!!
N-N-NOT R-R-REALLY...
YOUR LIPS HAVE TURNED BLUE!
OH, YEAH...?
HERE, I'LL WARM THEM UP.
MPH!
FDD

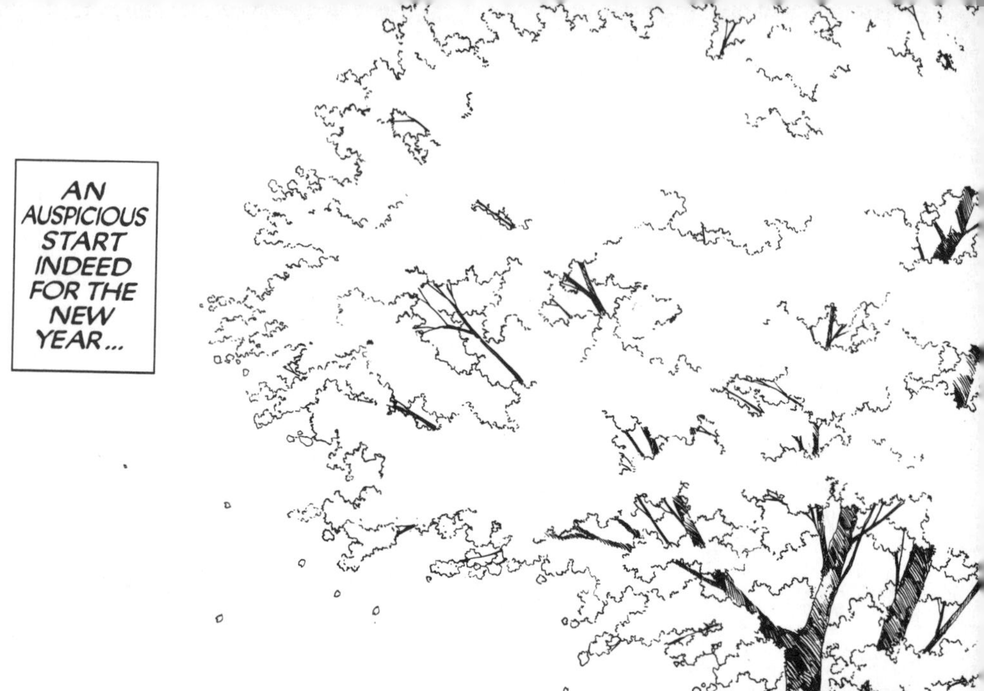
AN AUSPICIOUS START INDEED FOR THE NEW YEAR...

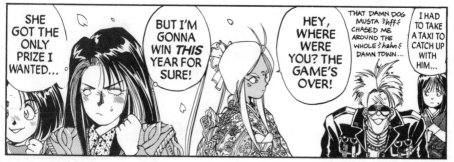

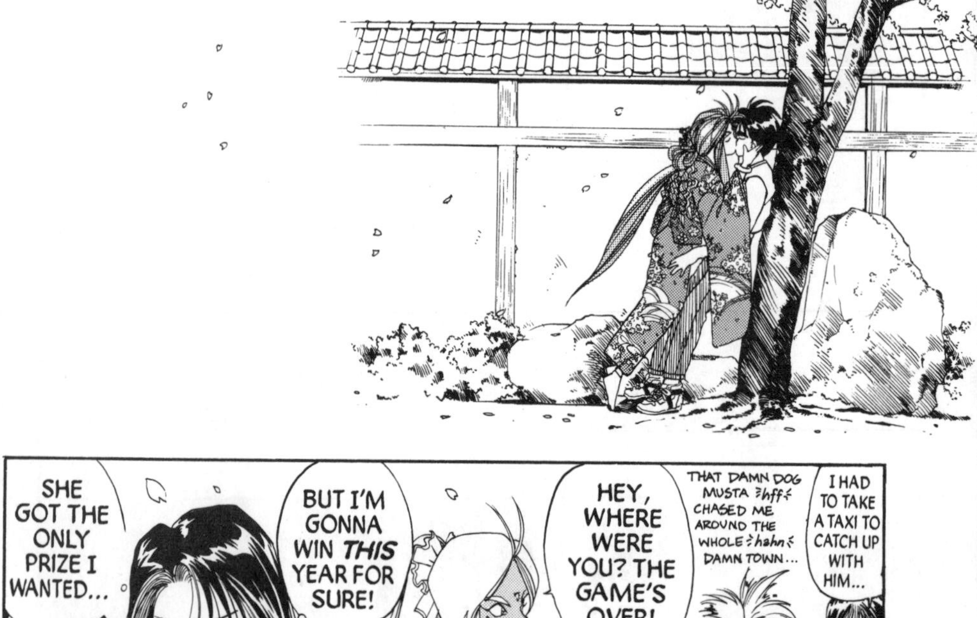
SHE GOT THE ONLY PRIZE I WANTED...
BUT I'M GONNA WIN *THIS* YEAR FOR SURE!
HEY, WHERE WERE YOU? THE GAME'S OVER!
THAT DAMN DOG MUSTA *hff* CHASED ME AROUND THE WHOLE *hahn* DAMN TOWN...
I HAD TO TAKE A TAXI TO CATCH UP WITH HIM...

# FINAL EXAM

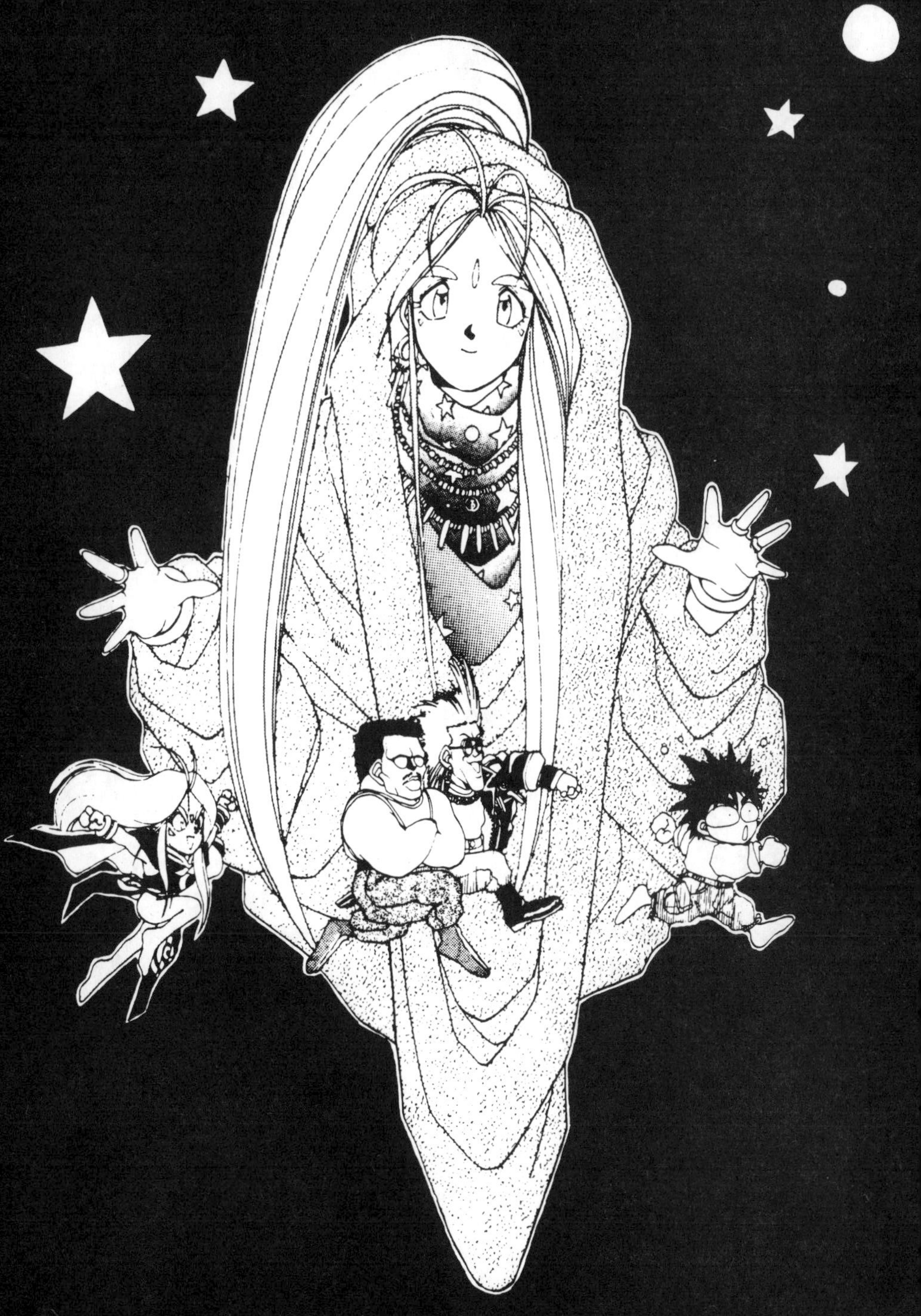

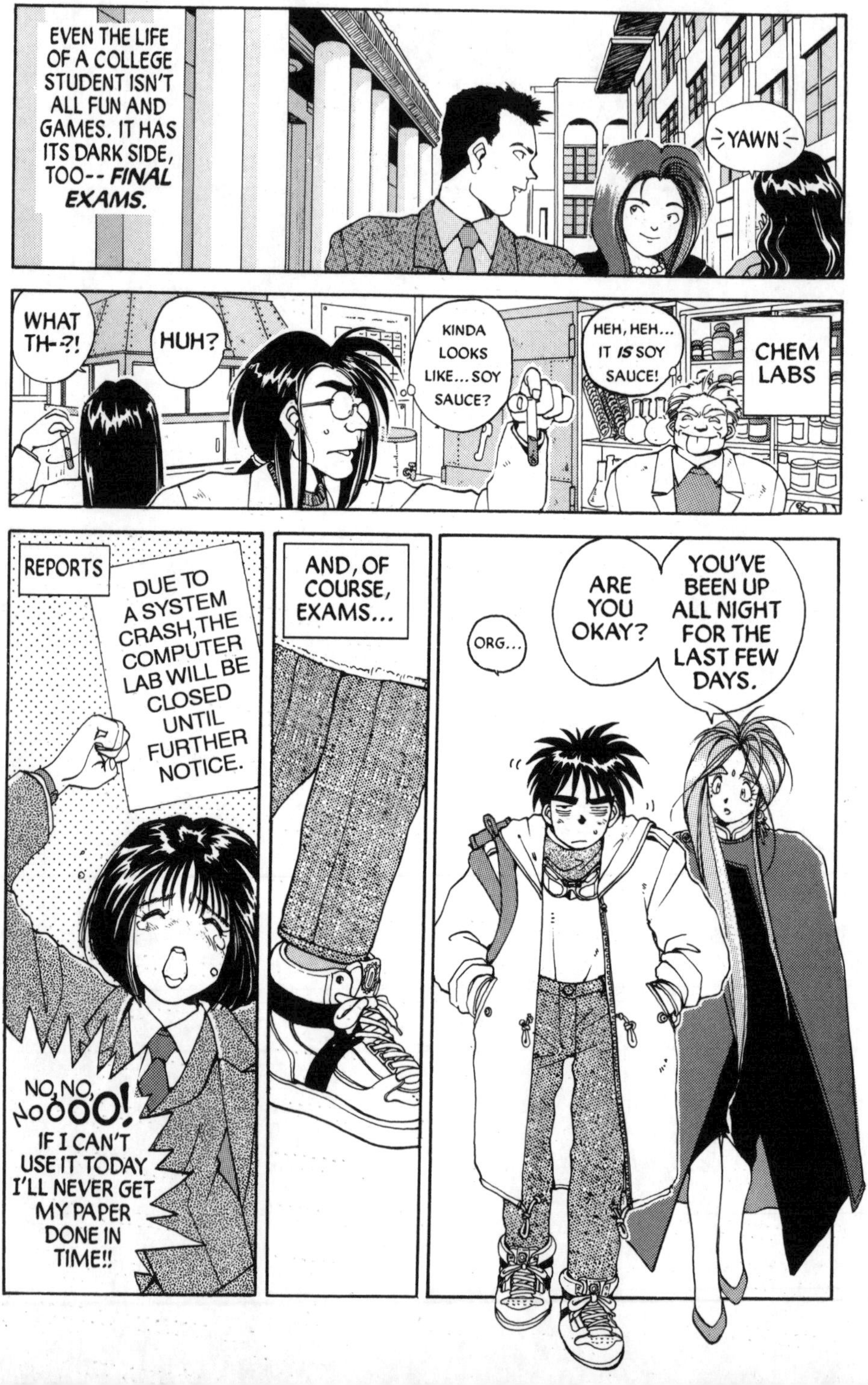
EVEN THE LIFE OF A COLLEGE STUDENT ISN'T ALL FUN AND GAMES. IT HAS ITS DARK SIDE, TOO-- *FINAL EXAMS.*
YAWN
WHAT TH-?!
HUH?
KINDA LOOKS LIKE... SOY SAUCE?
HEH, HEH... IT *IS* SOY SAUCE!
CHEM LABS
REPORTS
DUE TO A SYSTEM CRASH, THE COMPUTER LAB WILL BE CLOSED UNTIL FURTHER NOTICE.
NO, NO, NOOOO! IF I CAN'T USE IT TODAY I'LL NEVER GET MY PAPER DONE IN TIME!!
AND, OF COURSE, EXAMS...
ORG...
ARE YOU OKAY?
YOU'VE BEEN UP ALL NIGHT FOR THE LAST FEW DAYS.

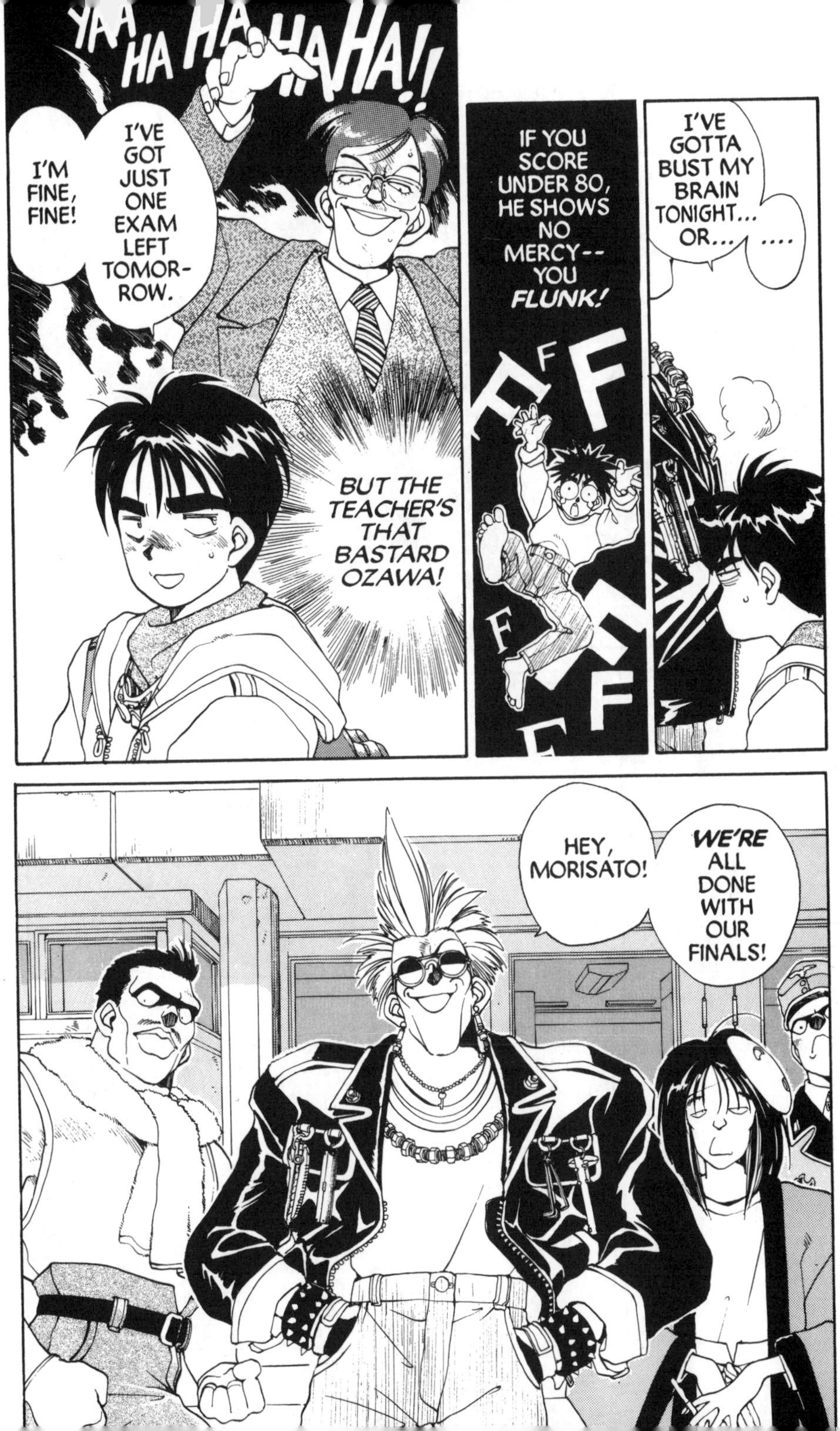
YAA HA HA HAHAHA!!
I'M FINE, FINE!
I'VE GOT JUST ONE EXAM LEFT TOMOR-ROW.
BUT THE TEACHER'S THAT BASTARD OZAWA!
IF YOU SCORE UNDER 80, HE SHOWS NO MERCY-- YOU *FLUNK!*
F F F F F F
I'VE GOTTA BUST MY BRAIN TONIGHT... OR... ....
HEY, MORISATO!
*WE'RE* ALL DONE WITH OUR FINALS!

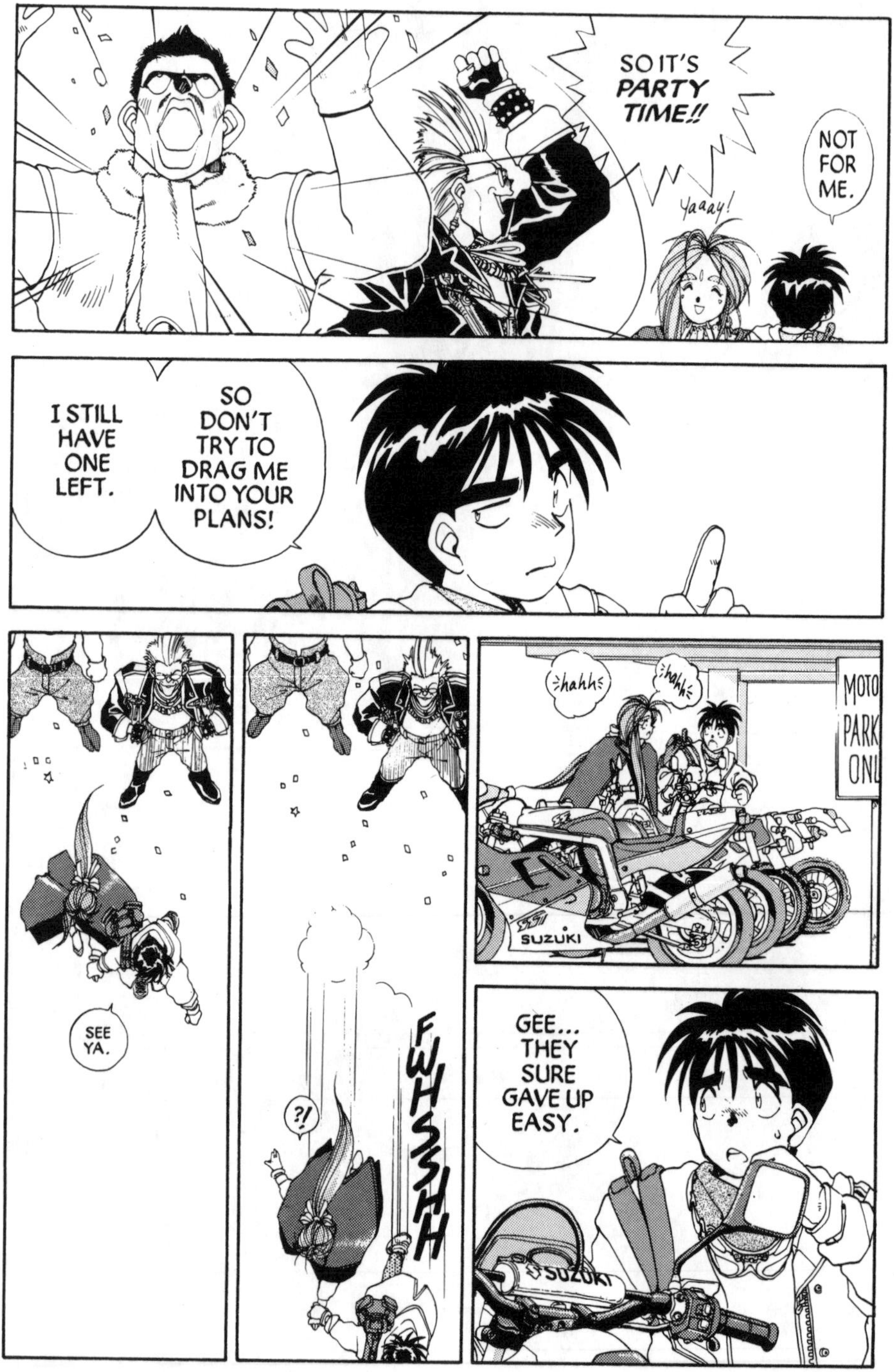
SO IT'S *PARTY TIME!!*
Yaaay!
NOT FOR ME.
I STILL HAVE ONE LEFT.
SO DON'T TRY TO DRAG ME INTO YOUR PLANS!
SEE YA.
?!
FWHSSHH
hahh
hahh
MOTO
PARK
ONL
SUZUKI
GEE... THEY SURE GAVE UP EASY.
SUZUKI

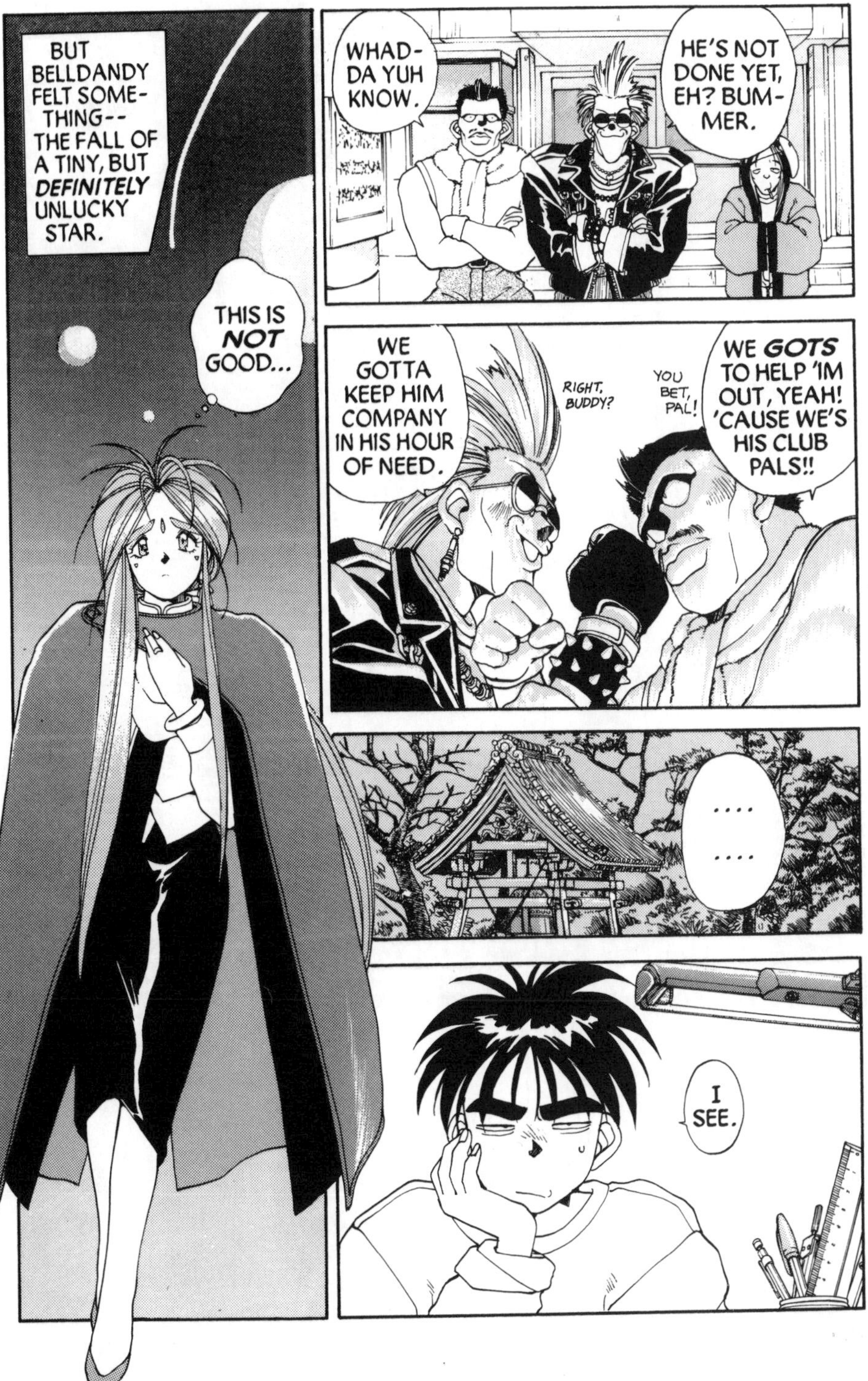
BUT BELLDANDY FELT SOME-THING-- THE FALL OF A TINY, BUT *DEFINITELY* UNLUCKY STAR.
THIS IS *NOT* GOOD...
WHAD-DA YUH KNOW.
HE'S NOT DONE YET, EH? BUM-MER.
WE GOTTA KEEP HIM COMPANY IN HIS HOUR OF NEED.
RIGHT, BUDDY?
YOU BET, PAL!
WE *GOTS* TO HELP 'IM OUT, YEAH! 'CAUSE WE'S HIS CLUB PALS!!
....
....
I SEE.

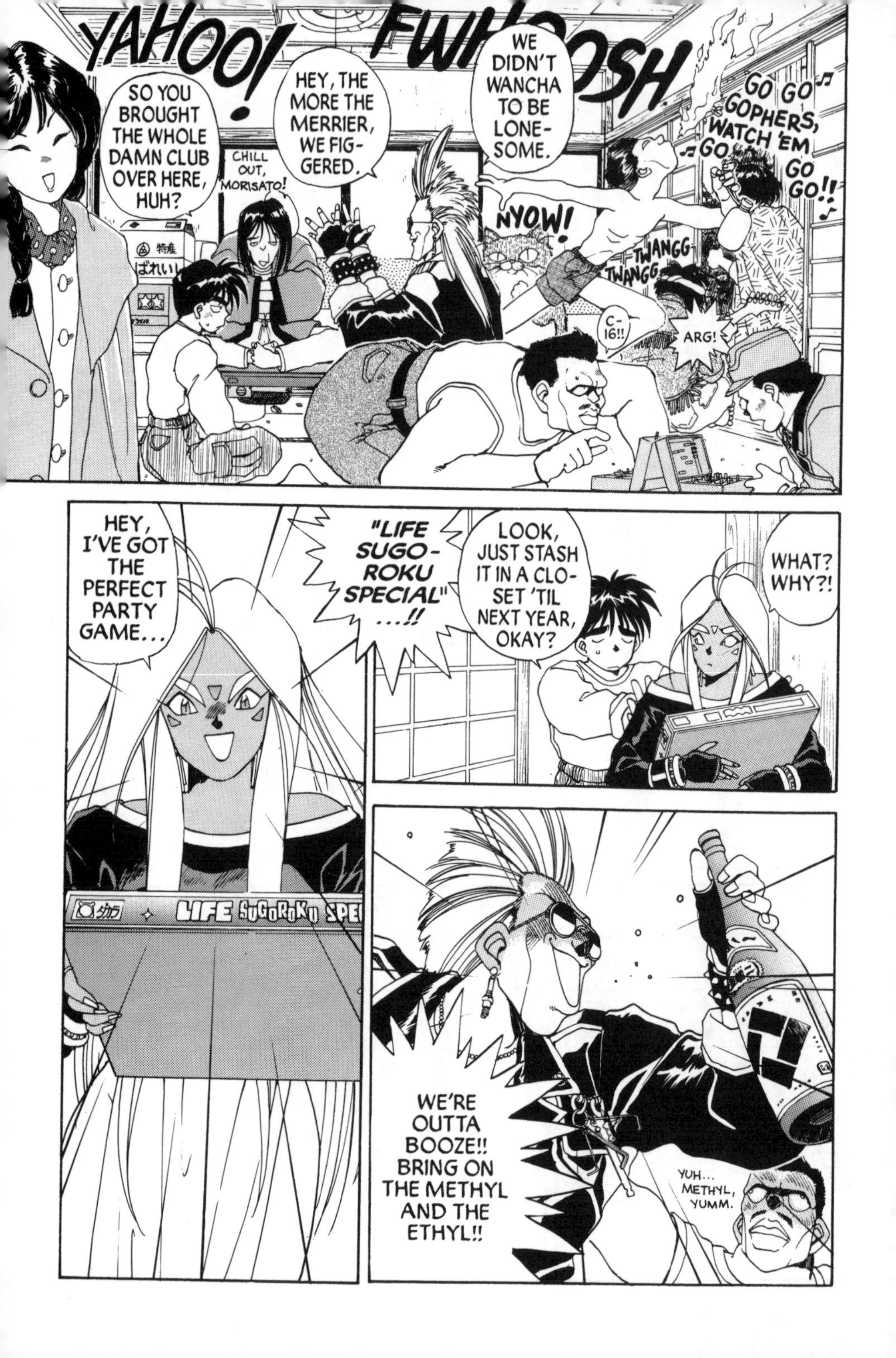
YAHOO!
FWHOOSH
SO YOU BROUGHT THE WHOLE DAMN CLUB OVER HERE, HUH?
CHILL OUT, MORISATO!
HEY, THE MORE THE MERRIER, WE FIGGERED.
WE DIDN'T WANCHA TO BE LONESOME.
NYOW!
GO GO GOPHERS, WATCH 'EM GO GO GO!!
TWANGG TWANGG
C-16!!
ARG!
特産
ばれいし
HEY, I'VE GOT THE PERFECT PARTY GAME...
"LIFE SUGOROKU SPECIAL" ...!!
LIFE SUGOROKU SPE
LOOK, JUST STASH IT IN A CLOSET 'TIL NEXT YEAR, OKAY?
WHAT? WHY?!
WE'RE OUTTA BOOZE!! BRING ON THE METHYL AND THE ETHYL!!
YUH... METHYL, YUMM.

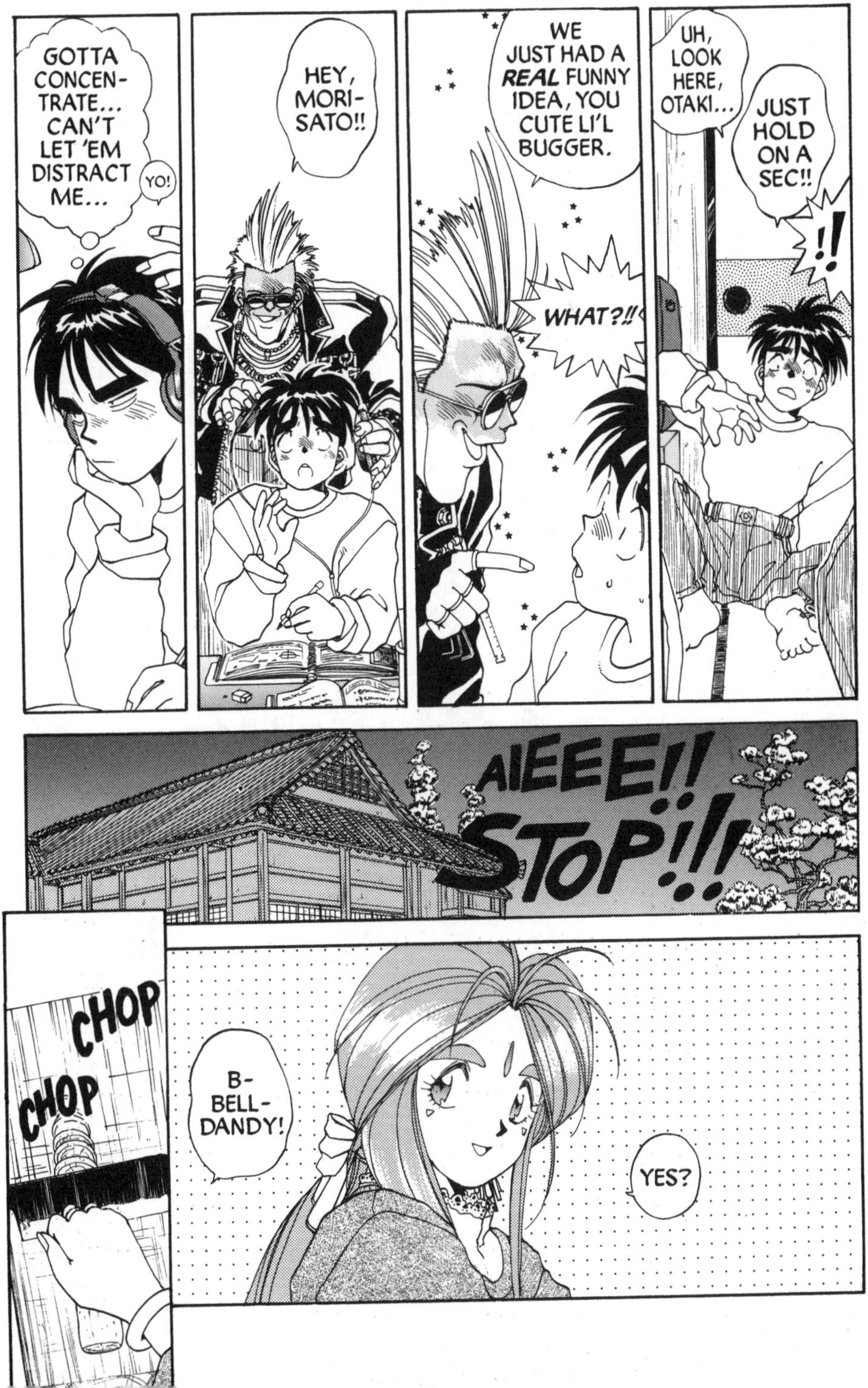
GOTTA CONCEN-TRATE... CAN'T LET 'EM DISTRACT ME...
YO!
HEY, MORI-SATO!!
WE JUST HAD A REAL FUNNY IDEA, YOU CUTE LI'L BUGGER.
WHAT?!!
UH, LOOK HERE, OTAKI...
JUST HOLD ON A SEC!!
!!
AIEEE!! STOP!!!
CHOP
CHOP
B-BELL-DANDY!
YES?

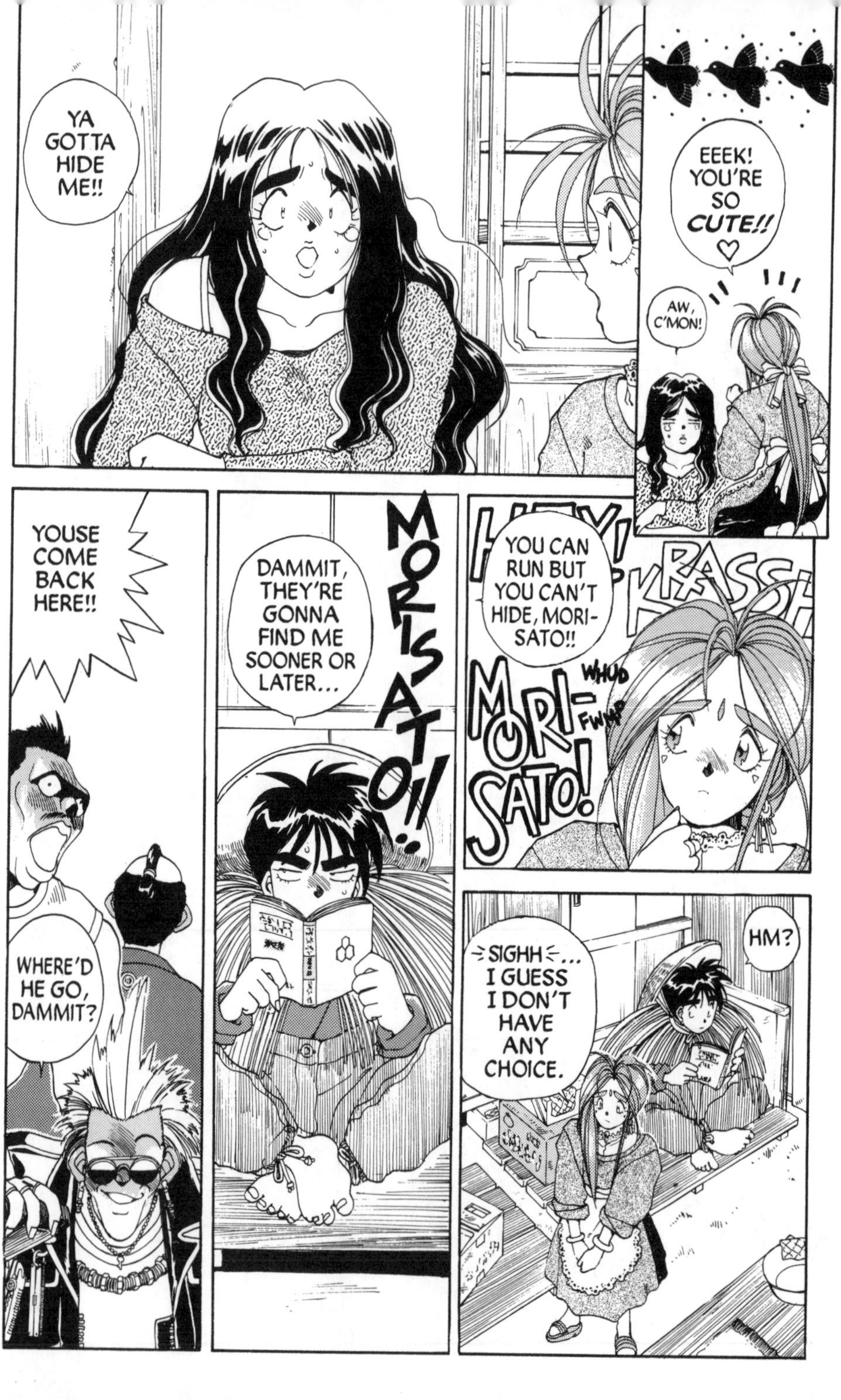
YA GOTTA HIDE ME!!
EEEK! YOU'RE SO *CUTE!!* ♡
AW, C'MON!
YOUSE COME BACK HERE!!
WHERE'D HE GO, DAMMIT?
DAMMIT, THEY'RE GONNA FIND ME SOONER OR LATER...
MORISATO!!
KRASSH
YOU CAN RUN BUT YOU CAN'T HIDE, MORI-SATO!!
MORI-SATO!
WHUD
FWAP
SIGHH... I GUESS I DON'T HAVE ANY CHOICE.
HM?

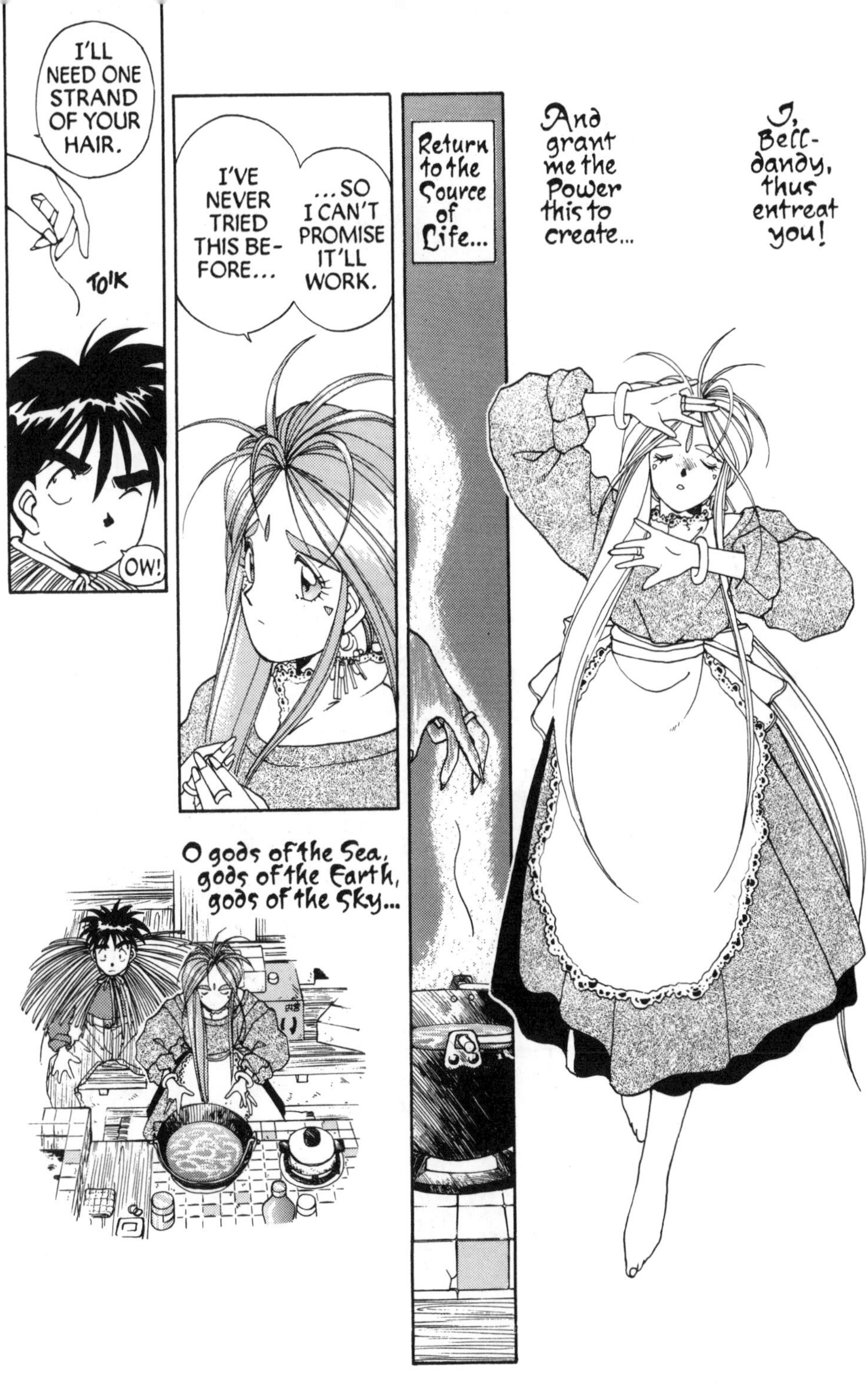
I'LL NEED ONE STRAND OF YOUR HAIR.
TOIK
OW!
I'VE NEVER TRIED THIS BEFORE...
...SO I CAN'T PROMISE IT'LL WORK.
O gods of the Sea, gods of the Earth, gods of the Sky...
Return to the Source of Life...
And grant me the Power this to create...
I, Belldandy, thus entreat you!

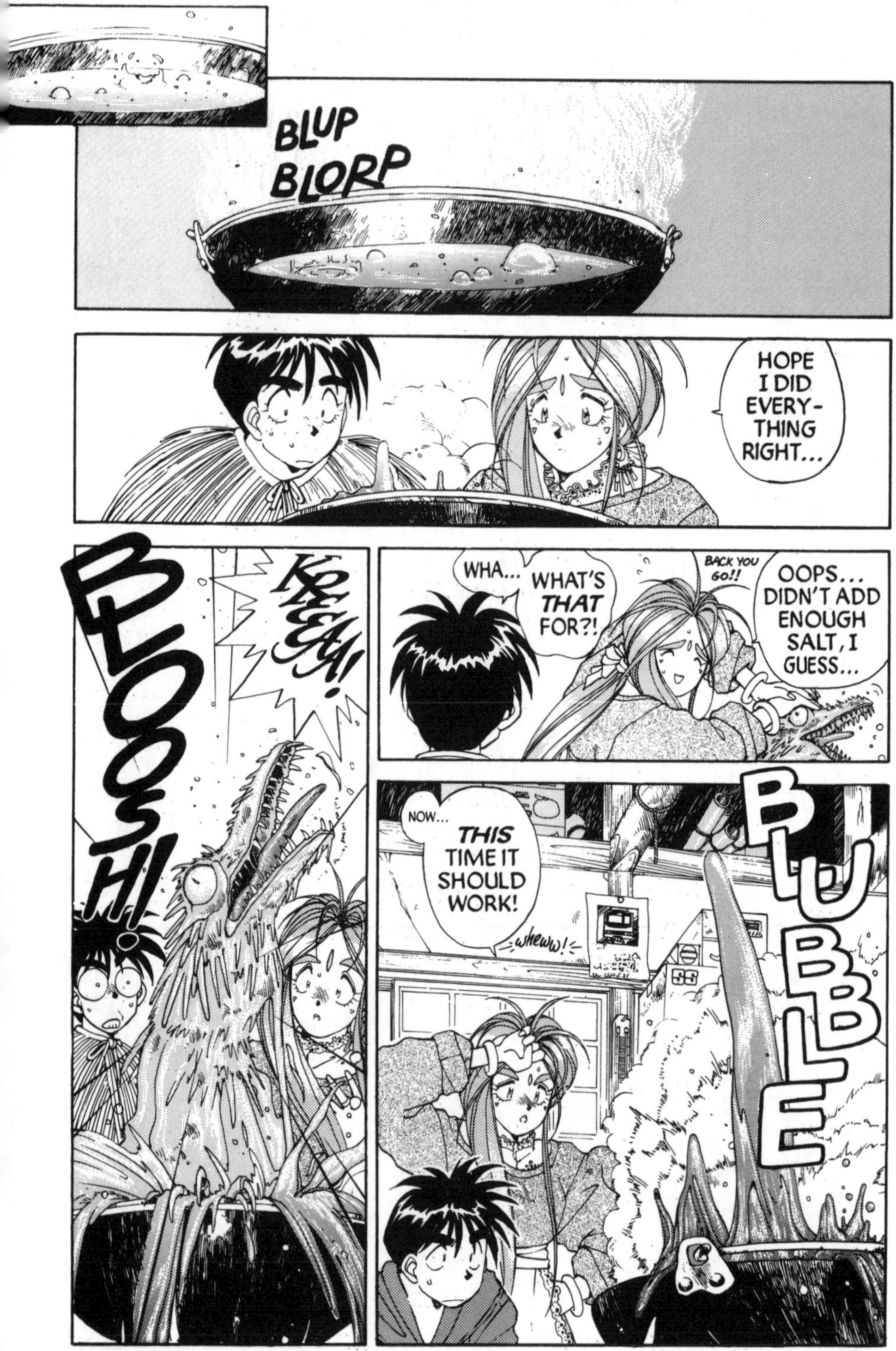
BLUP
BLORP
HOPE I DID EVERY-THING RIGHT...
BLOOSH!
KREEAAA!
WHA...
WHAT'S *THAT* FOR?!
BACK YOU GO!!
OOPS... DIDN'T ADD ENOUGH SALT, I GUESS...
NOW...
*THIS* TIME IT SHOULD WORK!
wheww!
BLUBBLE

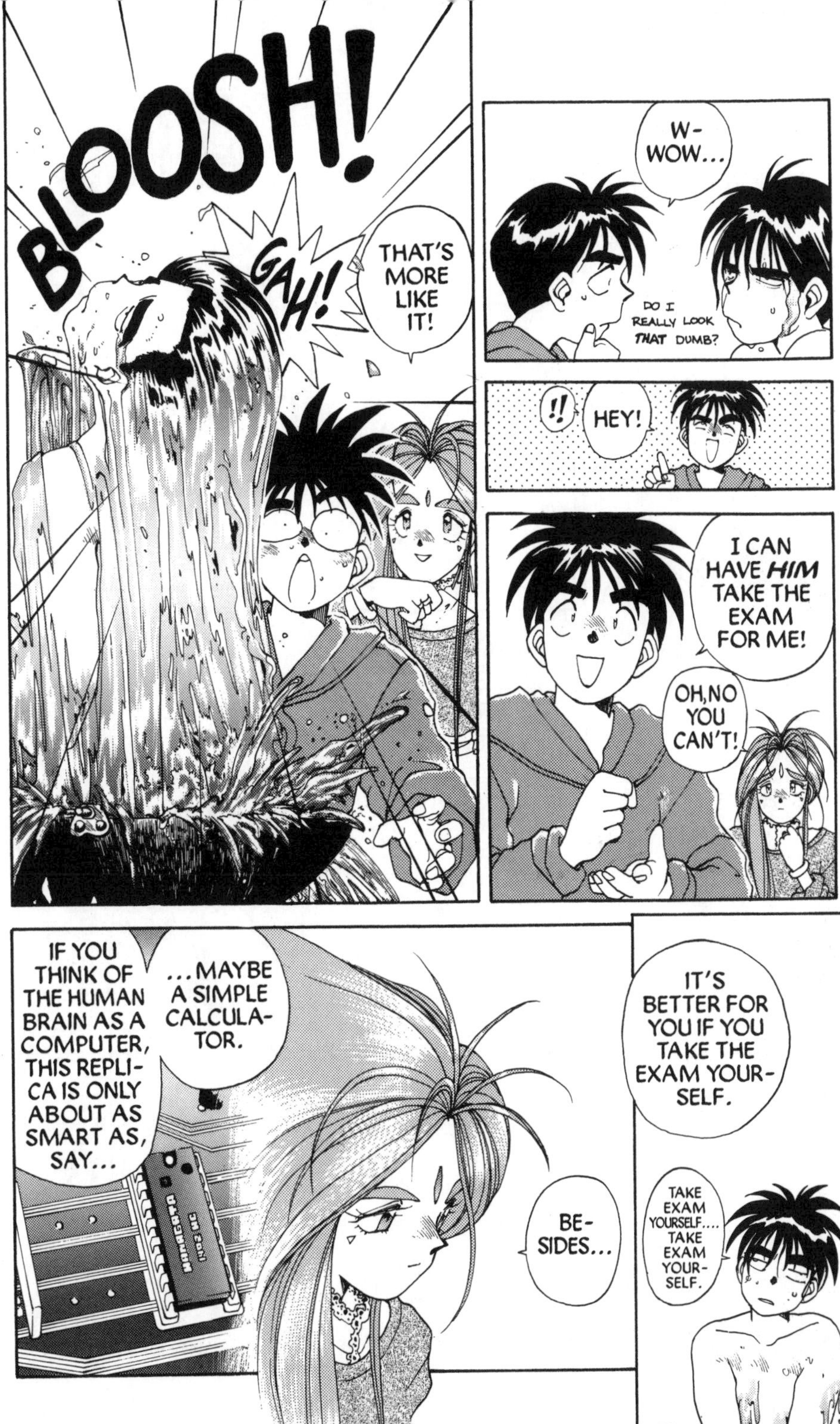
BLOOSH!
GAH!
THAT'S MORE LIKE IT!
W-WOW...
DO I REALLY LOOK THAT DUMB?
!!
HEY!
I CAN HAVE HIM TAKE THE EXAM FOR ME!
OH, NO YOU CAN'T!
IF YOU THINK OF THE HUMAN BRAIN AS A COMPUTER, THIS REPLICA IS ONLY ABOUT AS SMART AS, SAY...
...MAYBE A SIMPLE CALCULATOR.
BE-SIDES...
IT'S BETTER FOR YOU IF YOU TAKE THE EXAM YOURSELF.
TAKE EXAM YOURSELF.... TAKE EXAM YOURSELF.

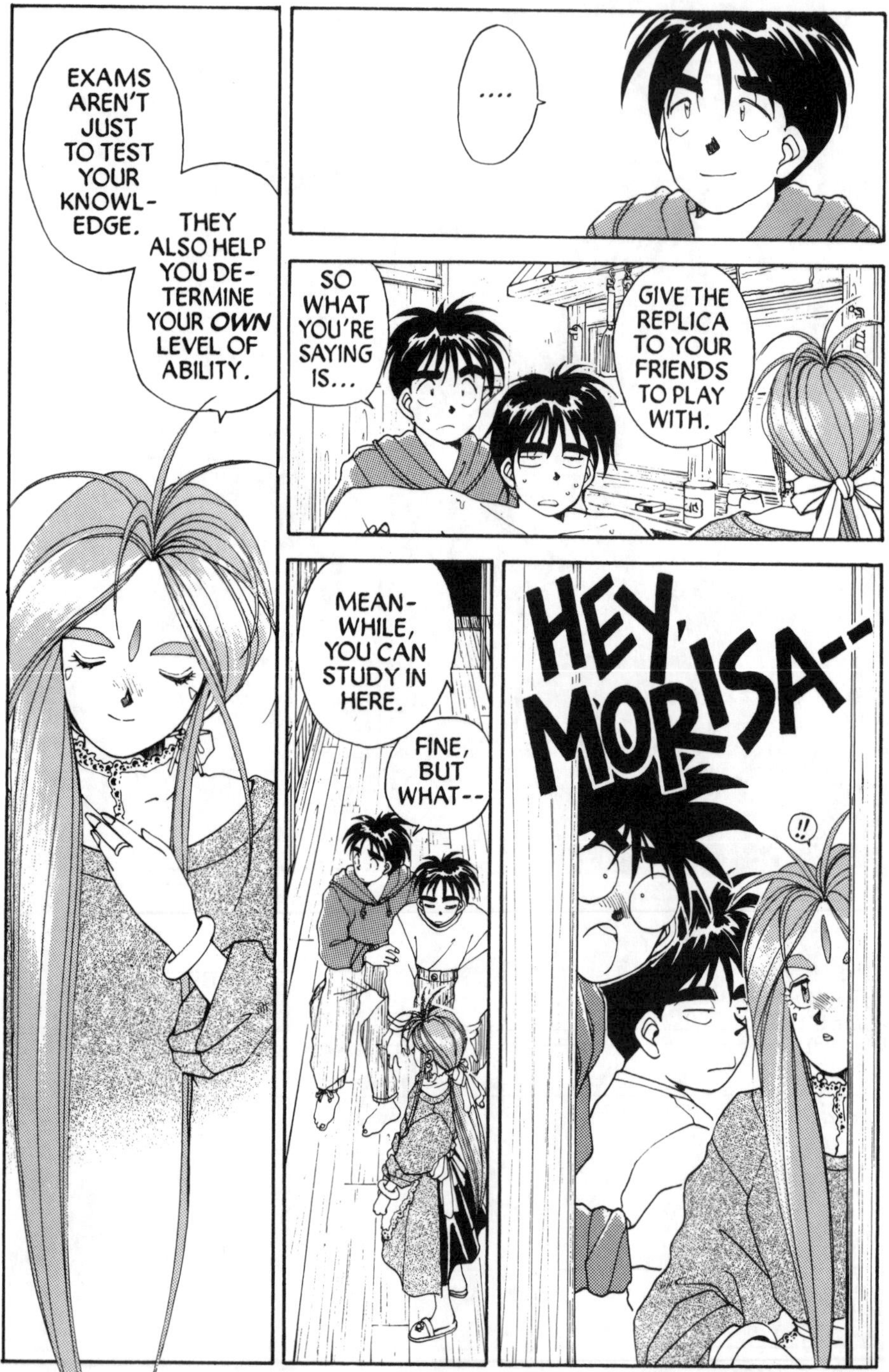
EXAMS AREN'T JUST TO TEST YOUR KNOWL-EDGE.
THEY ALSO HELP YOU DE-TERMINE YOUR *OWN* LEVEL OF ABILITY.
....
SO WHAT YOU'RE SAYING IS...
GIVE THE REPLICA TO YOUR FRIENDS TO PLAY WITH.
MEAN-WHILE, YOU CAN STUDY IN HERE.
FINE, BUT WHAT--
HEY, MORISA--
!!

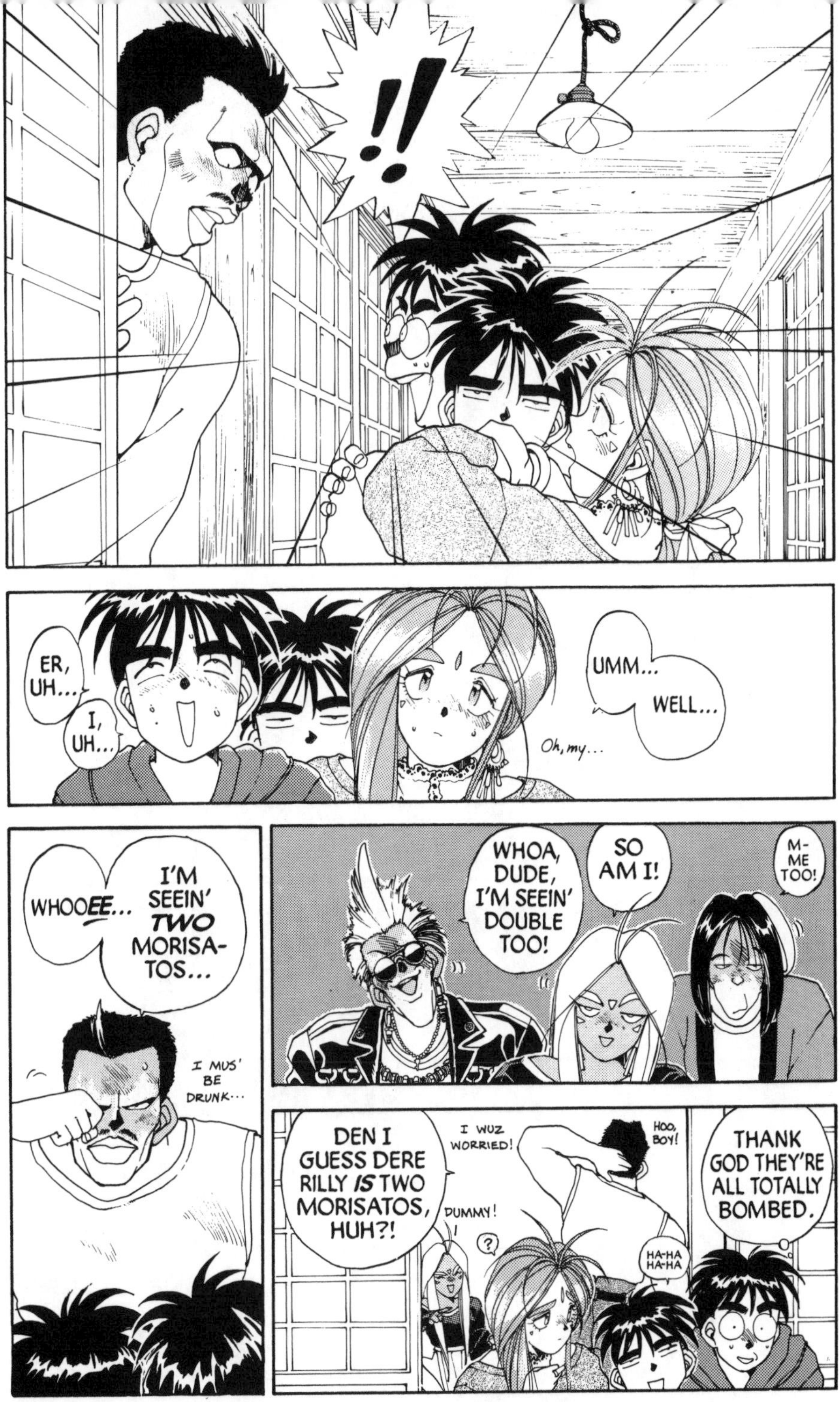
!!
ER, UH...
I, UH...
Oh, my...
UMM... WELL...
WHOOEE... I'M SEEIN' TWO MORISATOS...
I MUS' BE DRUNK...
WHOA, DUDE, I'M SEEIN' DOUBLE TOO!
SO AM I!
M-ME TOO!
DEN I GUESS DERE RILLY IS TWO MORISATOS, HUH?!
I WUZ WORRIED!
HOO, BOY!
DUMMY!!
?
HA-HA HA-HA
THANK GOD THEY'RE ALL TOTALLY BOMBED.

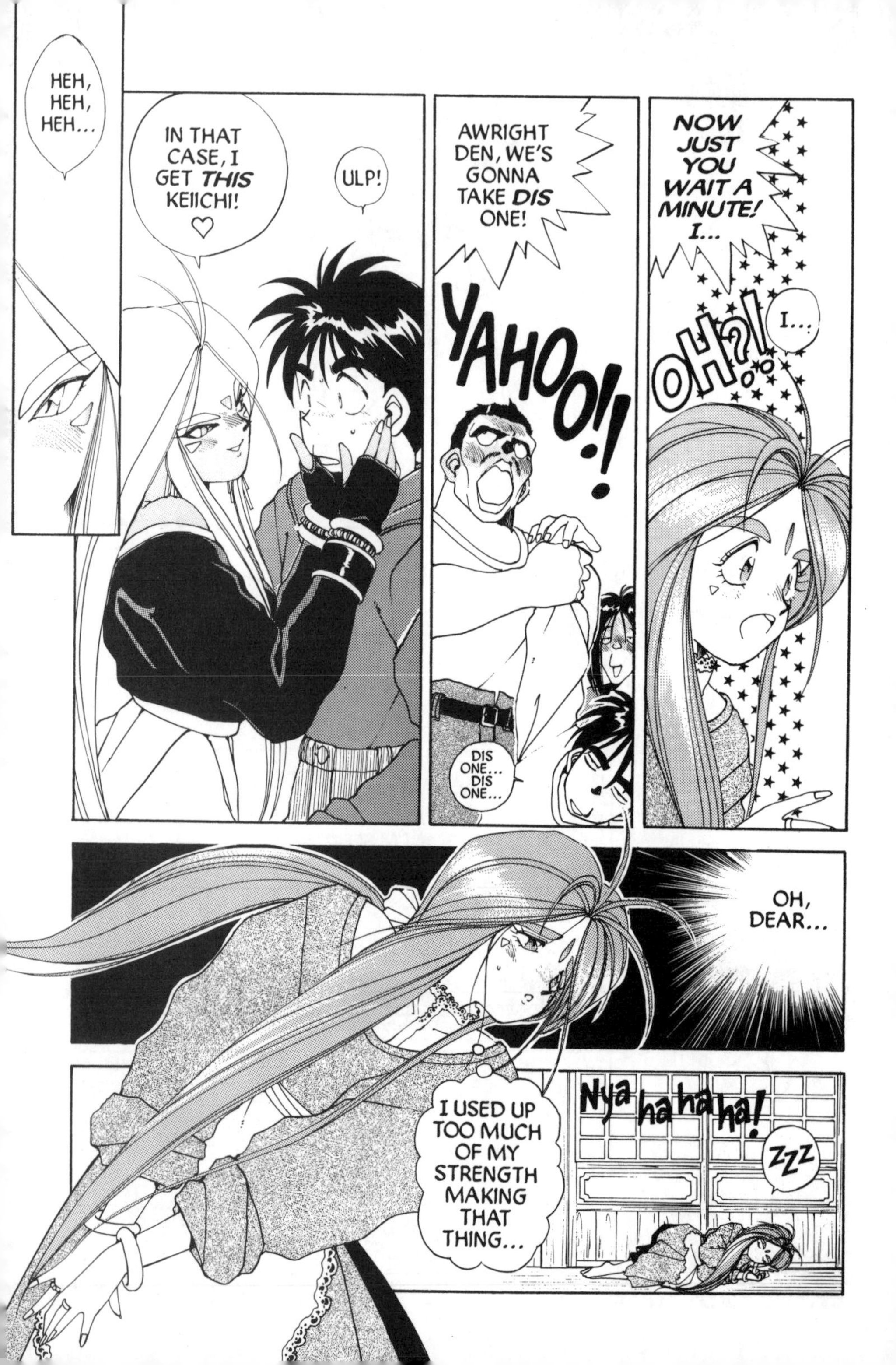

HEH, HEH, HEH...
IN THAT CASE, I GET THIS KEIICHI! ♡
ULP!
AWRIGHT DEN, WE'S GONNA TAKE DIS ONE!
YAHOO!!
DIS ONE... DIS ONE...
NOW JUST YOU WAIT A MINUTE! I...
OH?!
I...
OH, DEAR...
I USED UP TOO MUCH OF MY STRENGTH MAKING THAT THING...
Nya ha ha ha ha!
ZZZ

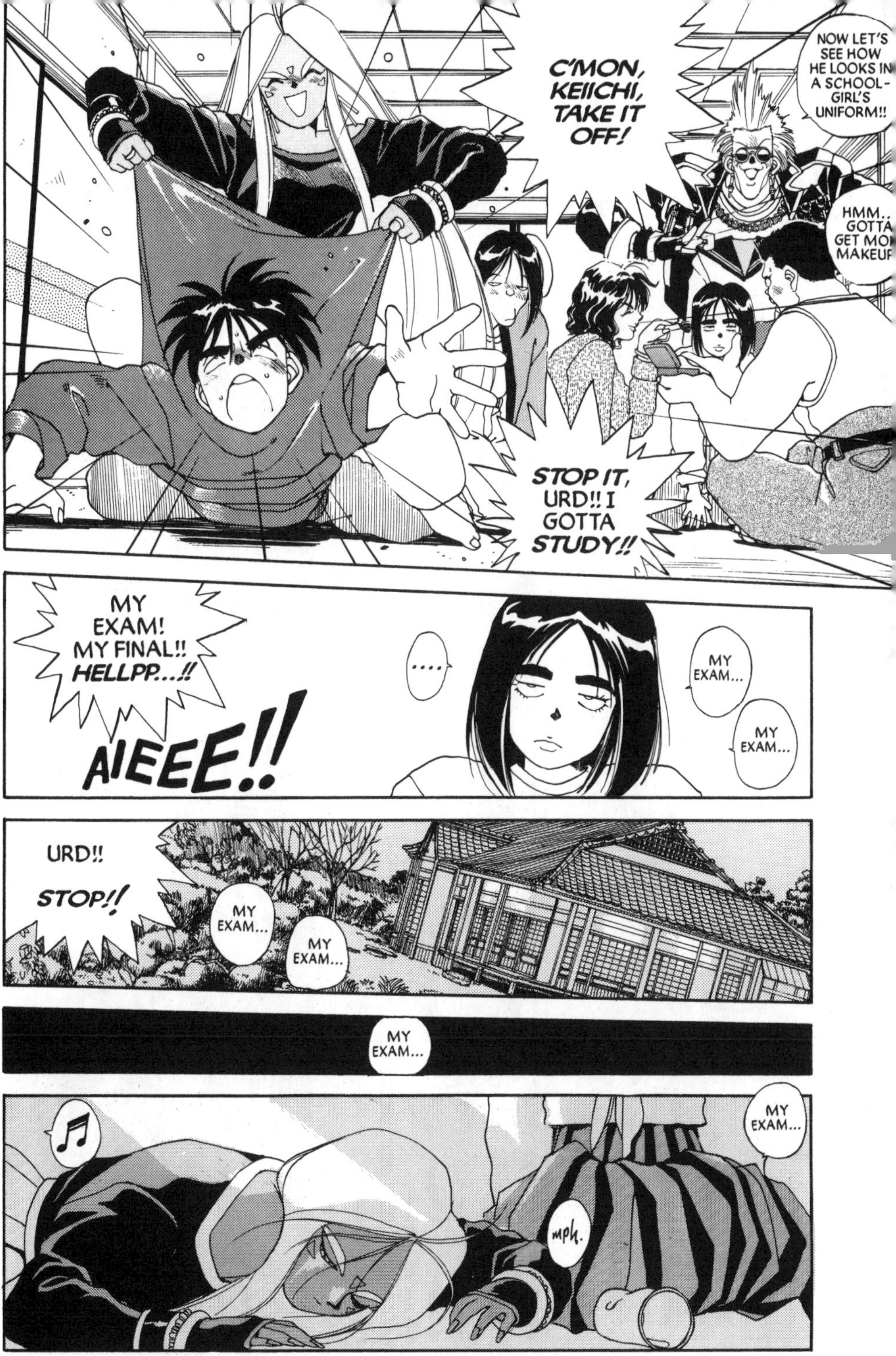
C'MON, KEIICHI, TAKE IT OFF!
NOW LET'S SEE HOW HE LOOKS IN A SCHOOL-GIRL'S UNIFORM!!
HMM.. GOTTA GET MO MAKEU
STOP IT, URD!! I GOTTA STUDY!!
MY EXAM! MY FINAL!! HELLPP...!!
AIEEE!!
....
MY EXAM...
MY EXAM...
URD!!
STOP!!
MY EXAM...
MY EXAM...
MY EXAM...
♫
MY EXAM...
mph.

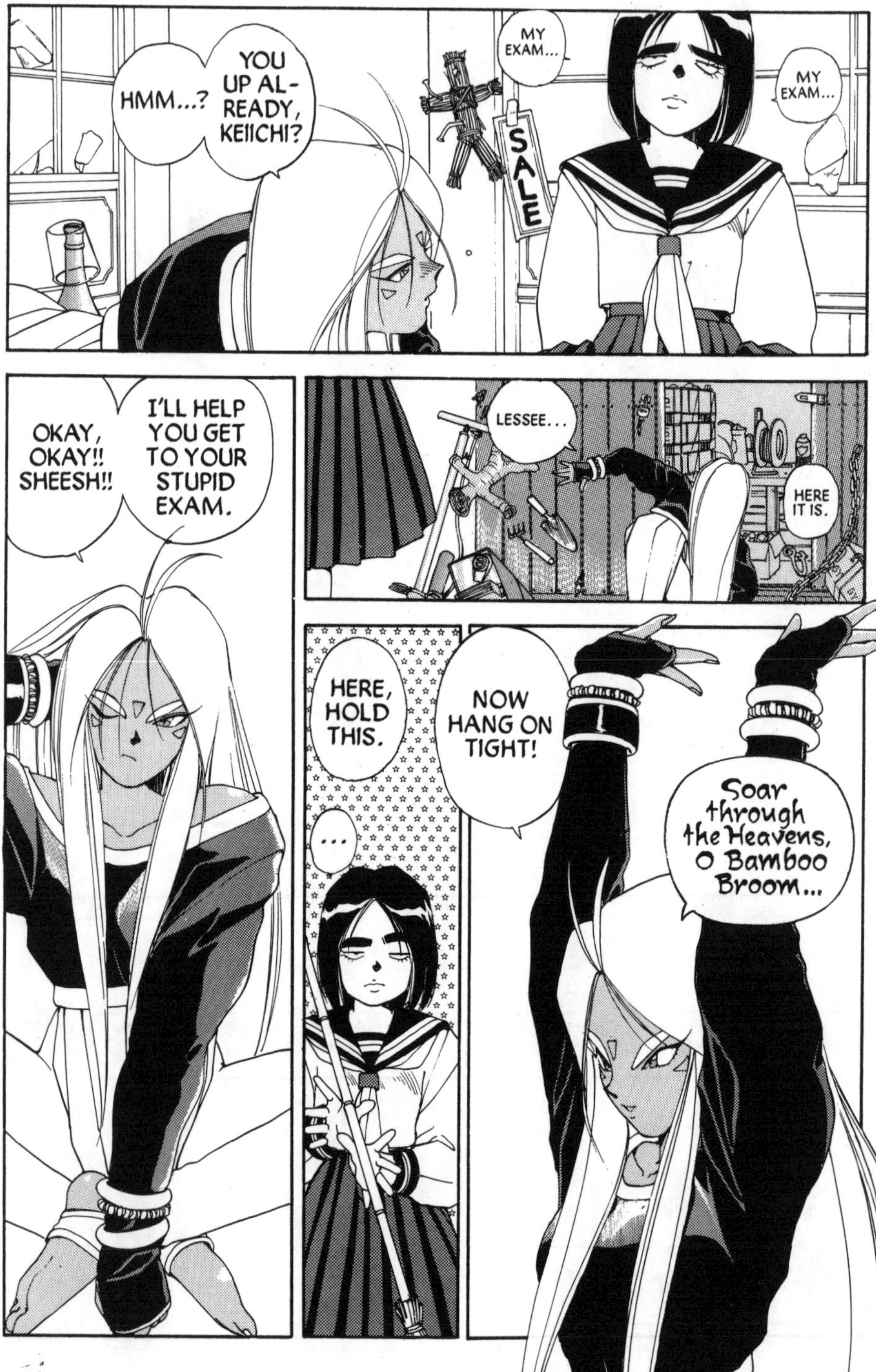
HMM...?
YOU UP AL- READY, KEIICHI?
MY EXAM...
SALE
MY EXAM...
OKAY, OKAY!! SHEESH!!
I'LL HELP YOU GET TO YOUR STUPID EXAM.
LESSEE...
HERE IT IS.
HERE, HOLD THIS.
...
NOW HANG ON TIGHT!
Soar through the Heavens, O Bamboo Broom...

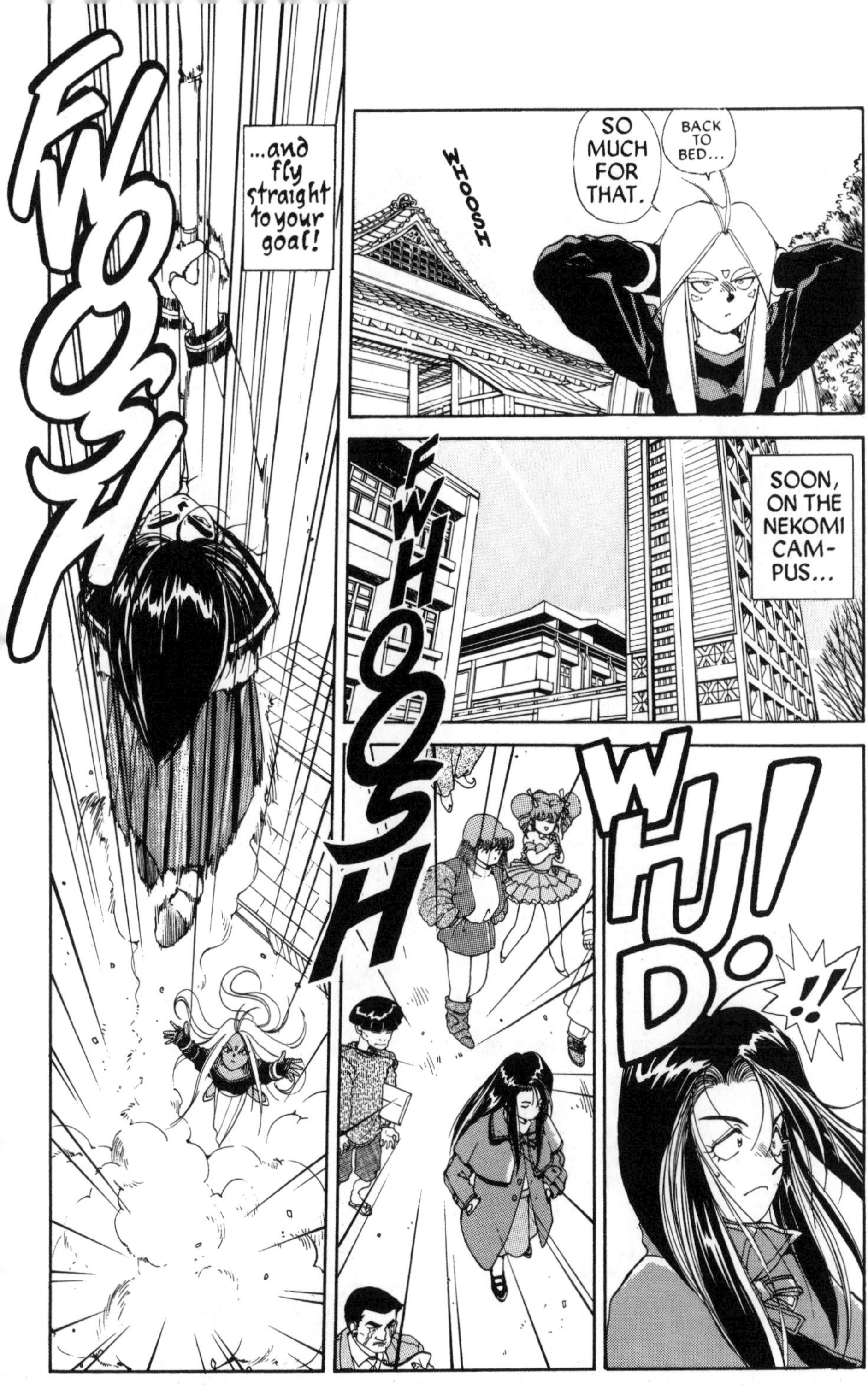
FWOOSH
...and fly straight to your goal!
WHOOSH
SO MUCH FOR THAT.
BACK TO BED...
SOON, ON THE NEKOMI CAMPUS...
FWHOOSH
WHUD!
!!

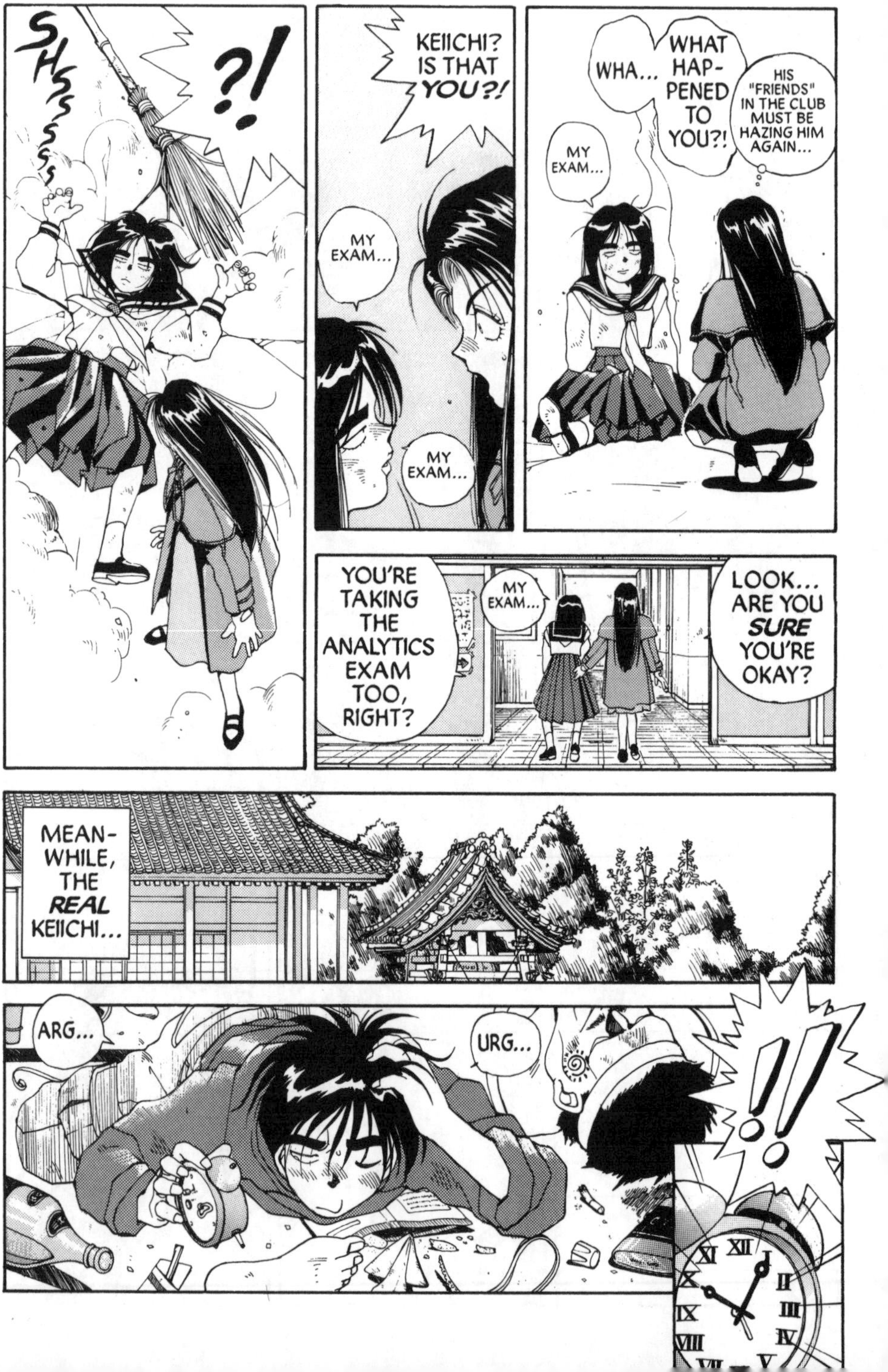
SHSSSSSS
?!
KEIICHI? IS THAT YOU?!
MY EXAM...
MY EXAM...
WHA...
WHAT HAP-PENED TO YOU?!
MY EXAM...
HIS "FRIENDS" IN THE CLUB MUST BE HAZING HIM AGAIN...
YOU'RE TAKING THE ANALYTICS EXAM TOO, RIGHT?
MY EXAM...
LOOK... ARE YOU SURE YOU'RE OKAY?
MEAN-WHILE, THE REAL KEIICHI...
ARG...
URG...
!!

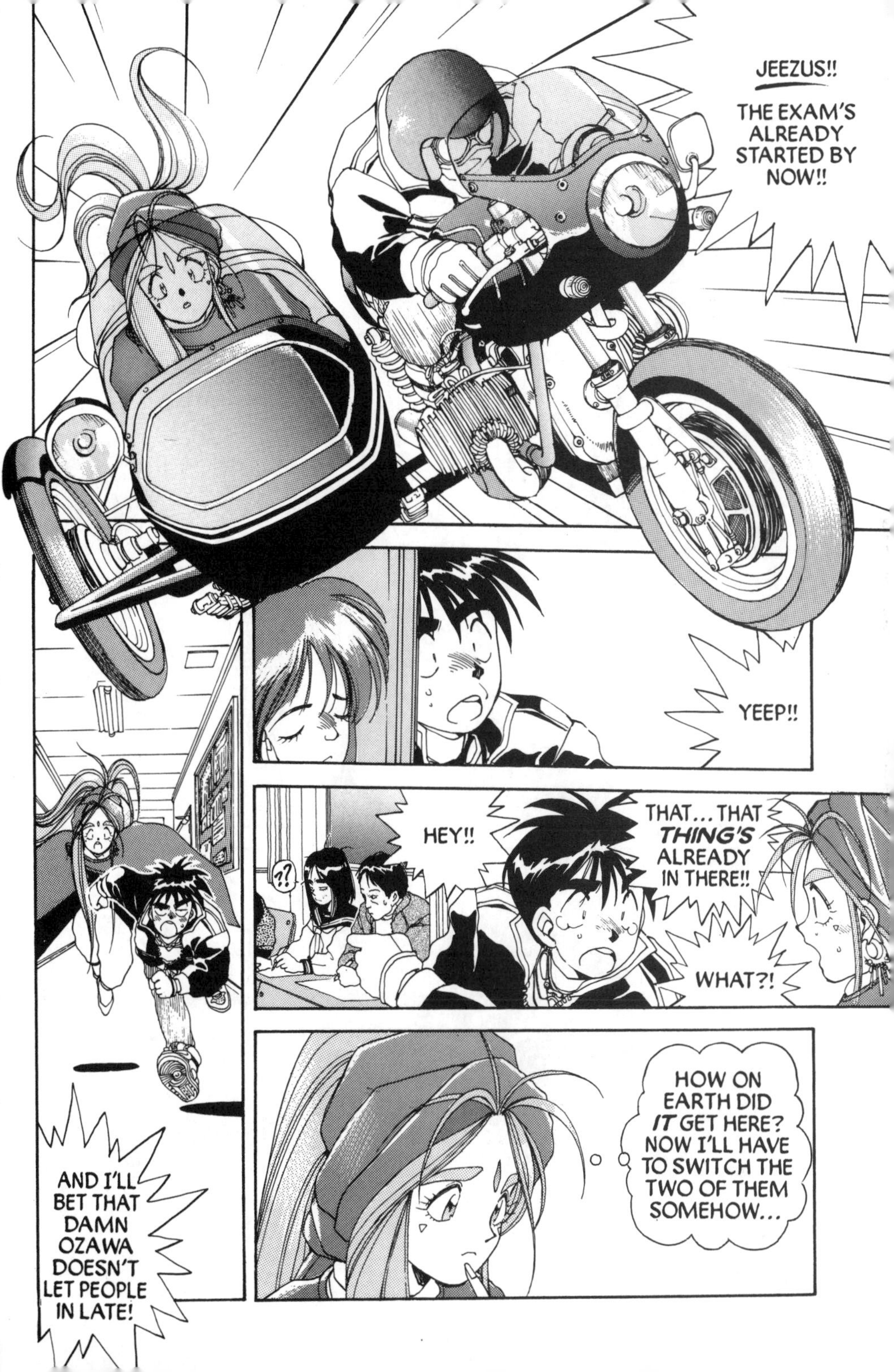
JEEZUS!!
THE EXAM'S ALREADY STARTED BY NOW!!
AND I'LL BET THAT DAMN OZAWA DOESN'T LET PEOPLE IN LATE!
YEEP!!
HEY!!
THAT... THAT *THING'S* ALREADY IN THERE!!
WHAT?!
HOW ON EARTH DID *IT* GET HERE? NOW I'LL HAVE TO SWITCH THE TWO OF THEM SOMEHOW...

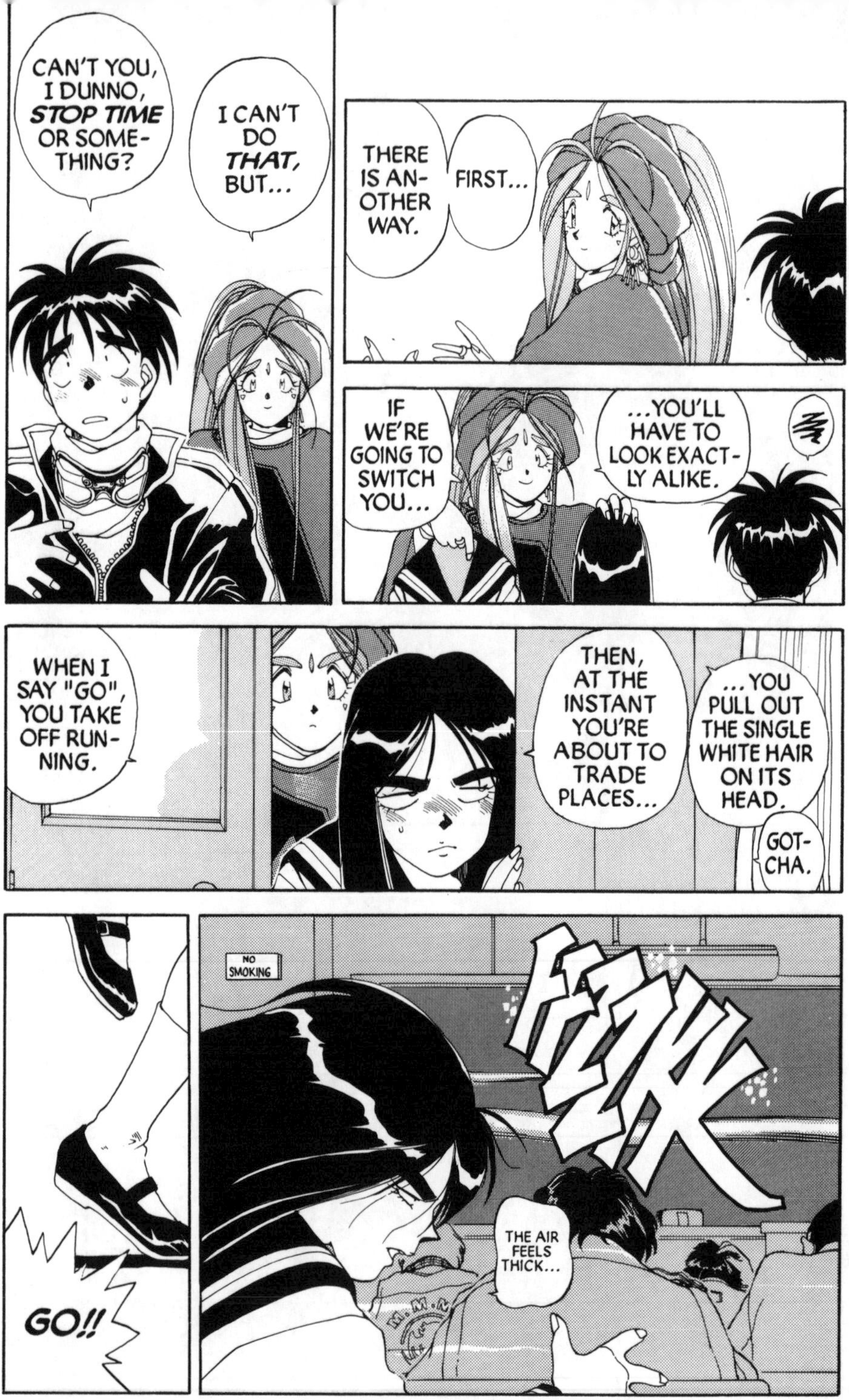
CAN'T YOU, I DUNNO, *STOP TIME* OR SOMETHING?
I CAN'T DO *THAT,* BUT...
THERE IS ANOTHER WAY.
FIRST...
IF WE'RE GOING TO SWITCH YOU...
...YOU'LL HAVE TO LOOK EXACTLY ALIKE.
WHEN I SAY "GO", YOU TAKE OFF RUNNING.
THEN, AT THE INSTANT YOU'RE ABOUT TO TRADE PLACES...
...YOU PULL OUT THE SINGLE WHITE HAIR ON ITS HEAD.
GOTCHA.
GO!!
NO SMOKING
THE AIR FEELS THICK...

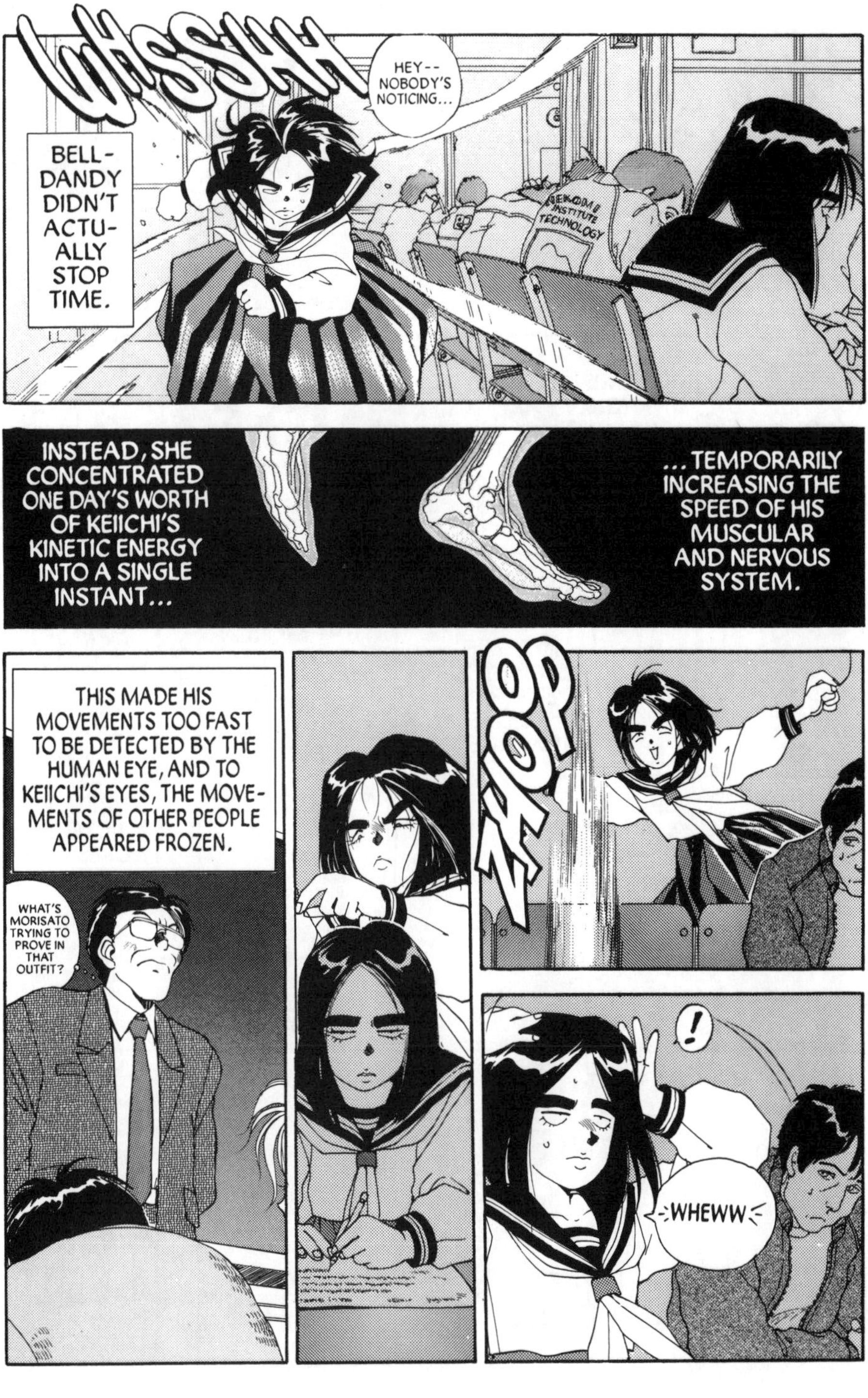
WHSSH
HEY-- NOBODY'S NOTICING...
BELL-DANDY DIDN'T ACTU-ALLY STOP TIME.
NEKOMI INSTITUTE TECHNOLOGY
INSTEAD, SHE CONCENTRATED ONE DAY'S WORTH OF KEIICHI'S KINETIC ENERGY INTO A SINGLE INSTANT...
...TEMPORARILY INCREASING THE SPEED OF HIS MUSCULAR AND NERVOUS SYSTEM.
THIS MADE HIS MOVEMENTS TOO FAST TO BE DETECTED BY THE HUMAN EYE, AND TO KEIICHI'S EYES, THE MOVE-MENTS OF OTHER PEOPLE APPEARED FROZEN.
WHAT'S MORISATO TRYING TO PROVE IN THAT OUTFIT?
ZHOOP
!
WHEWW

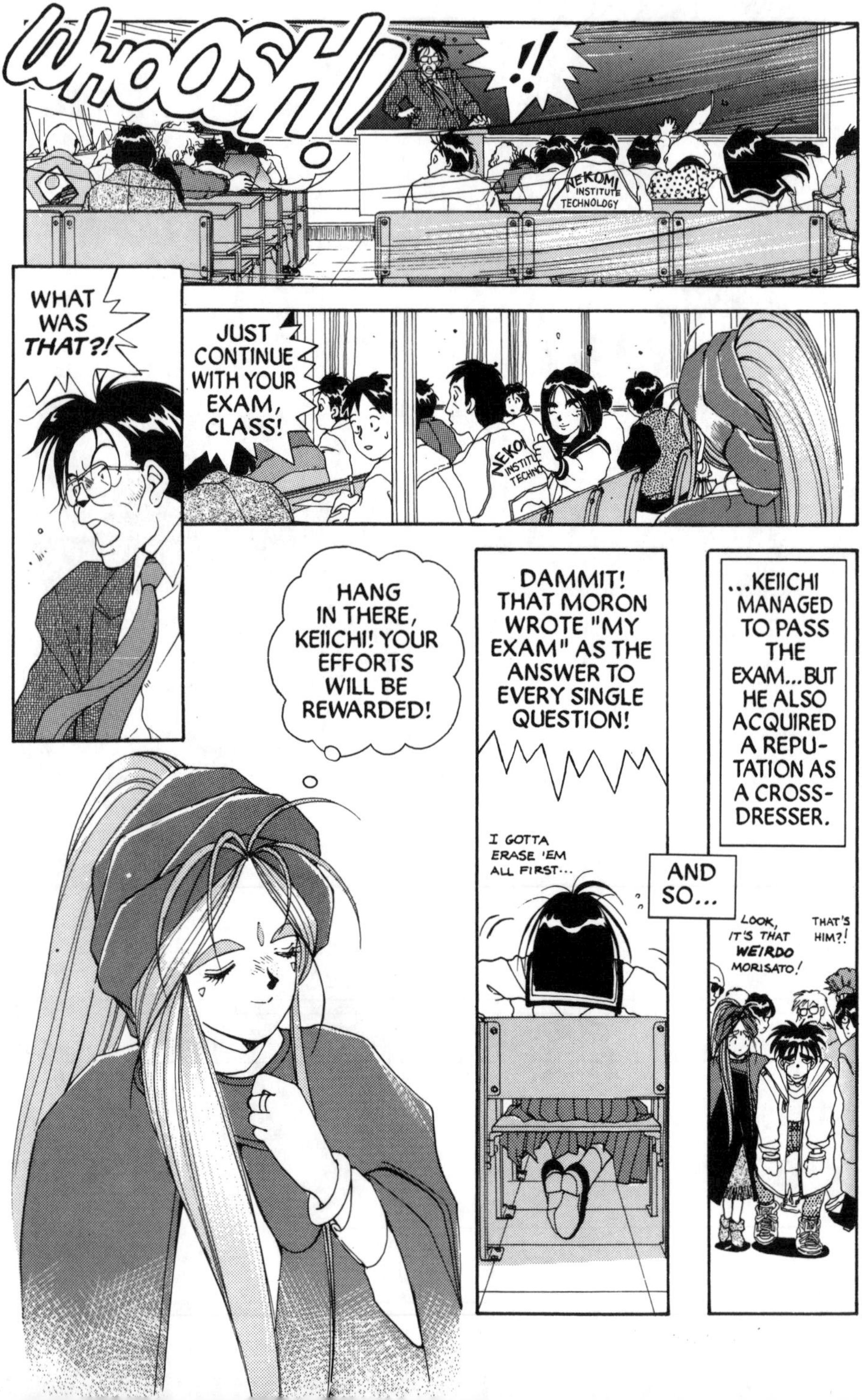
WHOOSH!
!!
WHAT WAS THAT?!
JUST CONTINUE WITH YOUR EXAM, CLASS!
NEKOMI INSTITUTE TECHNOLOGY
HANG IN THERE, KEIICHI! YOUR EFFORTS WILL BE REWARDED!
DAMMIT! THAT MORON WROTE "MY EXAM" AS THE ANSWER TO EVERY SINGLE QUESTION!
I GOTTA ERASE 'EM ALL FIRST...
AND SO...
...KEIICHI MANAGED TO PASS THE EXAM...BUT HE ALSO ACQUIRED A REPUTATION AS A CROSS-DRESSER.
LOOK, IT'S THAT WEIRDO MORISATO!
THAT'S HIM?!

# BELLDANDY'S NARROW ESCAPE

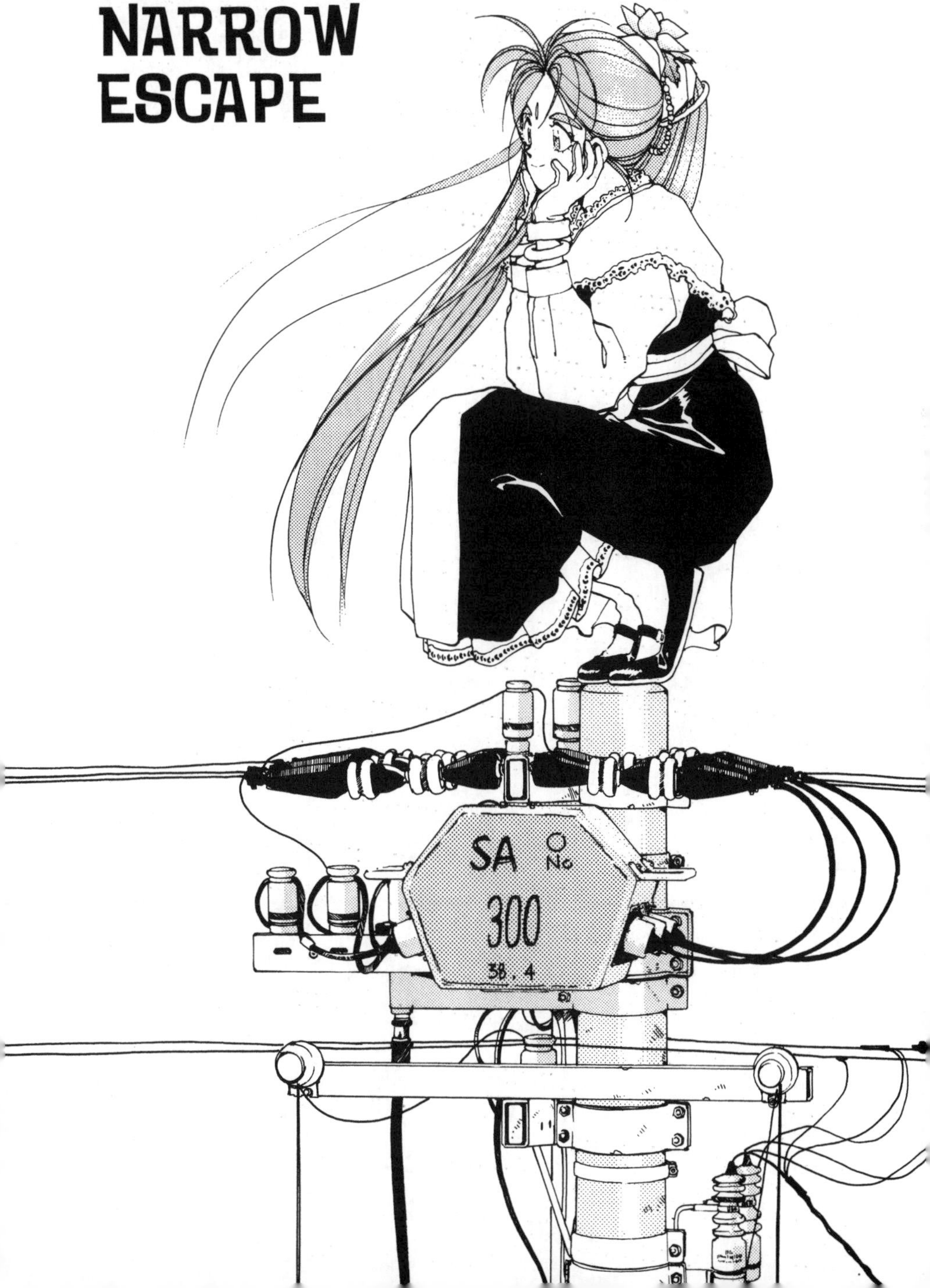
SA No
300
3B. 4

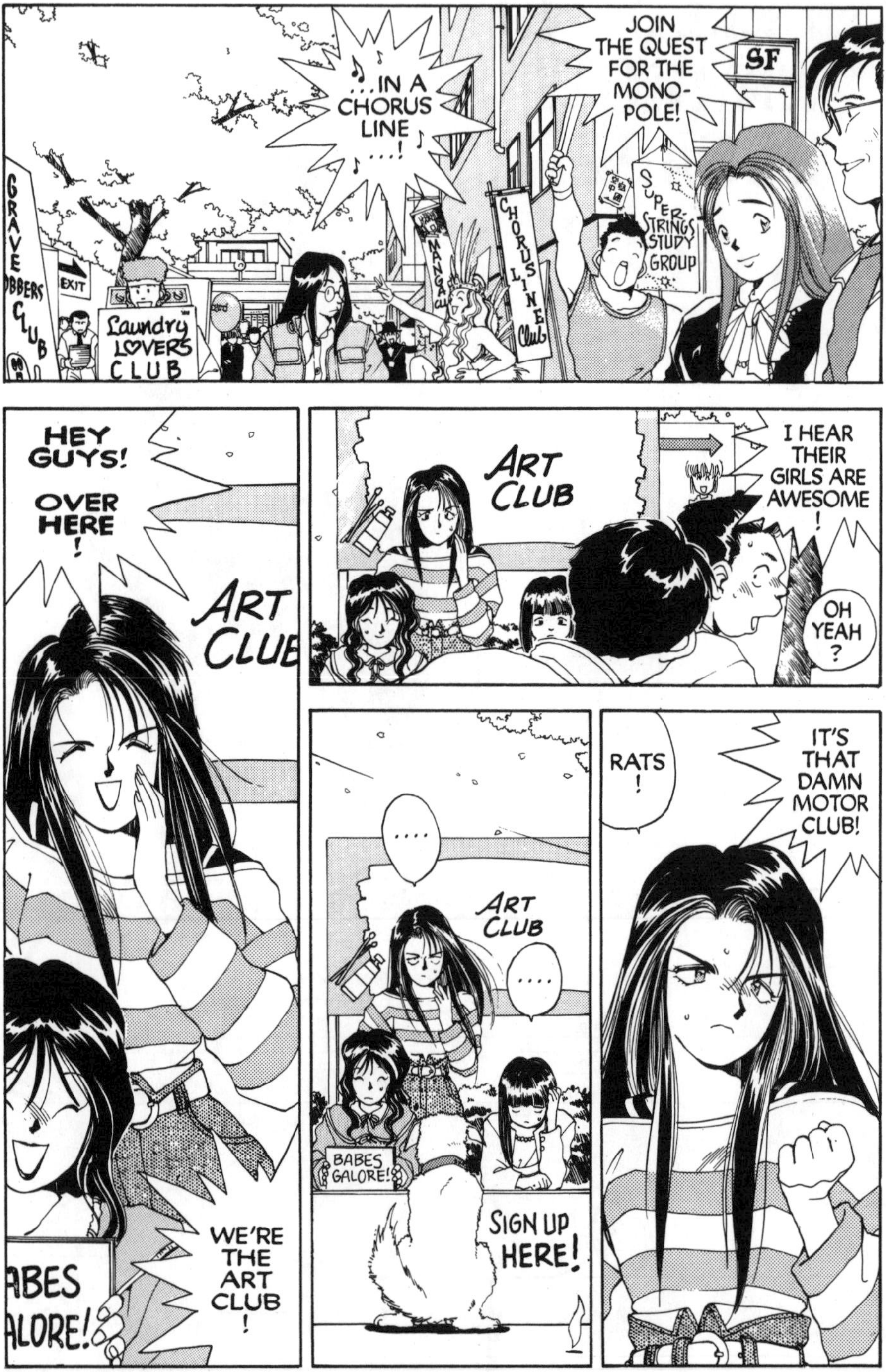

GRAVE
OBBERS
CLUB
EXIT
Laundry LOVERS CLUB
...IN A CHORUS LINE ...!
CHORUS LINE Club
JOIN THE QUEST FOR THE MONO-POLE!
SUPER-STRINGS STUDY GROUP
SF
HEY GUYS!
OVER HERE!
ART CLUB
WE'RE THE ART CLUB!
ABES
ALORE!
ART CLUB
I HEAR THEIR GIRLS ARE AWESOME!
OH YEAH?
....
ART CLUB
....
BABES GALORE!
SIGN UP HERE!
RATS!
IT'S THAT DAMN MOTOR CLUB!

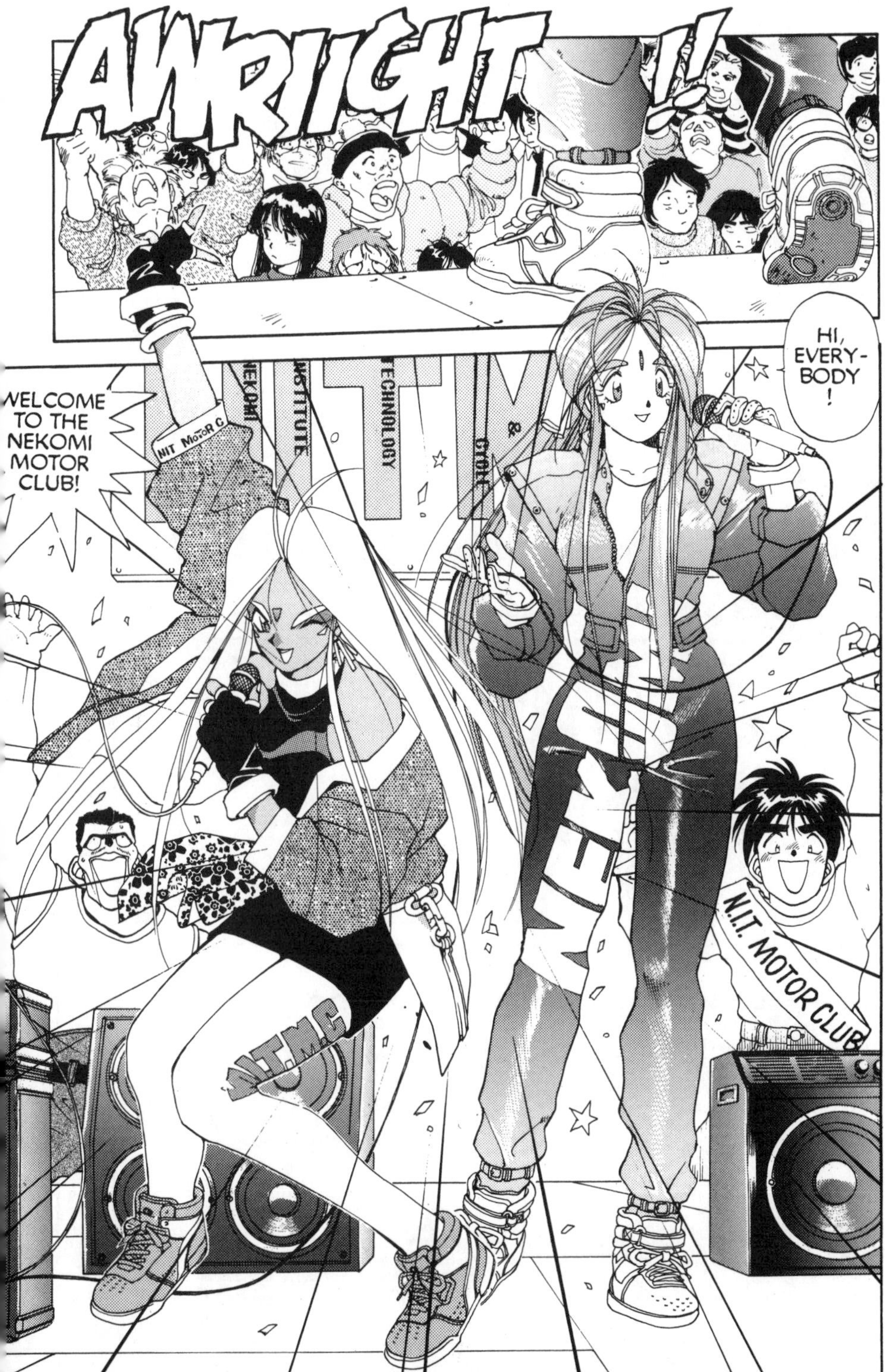
AWRIIGHT !!
WELCOME TO THE NEKOMI MOTOR CLUB!
HI, EVERY-BODY !
NIT MOTOR C
NEKOMI
INSTITUTE
TECHNOLOGY
N.I.T. MOTOR CLUB
N.I.T.M.C

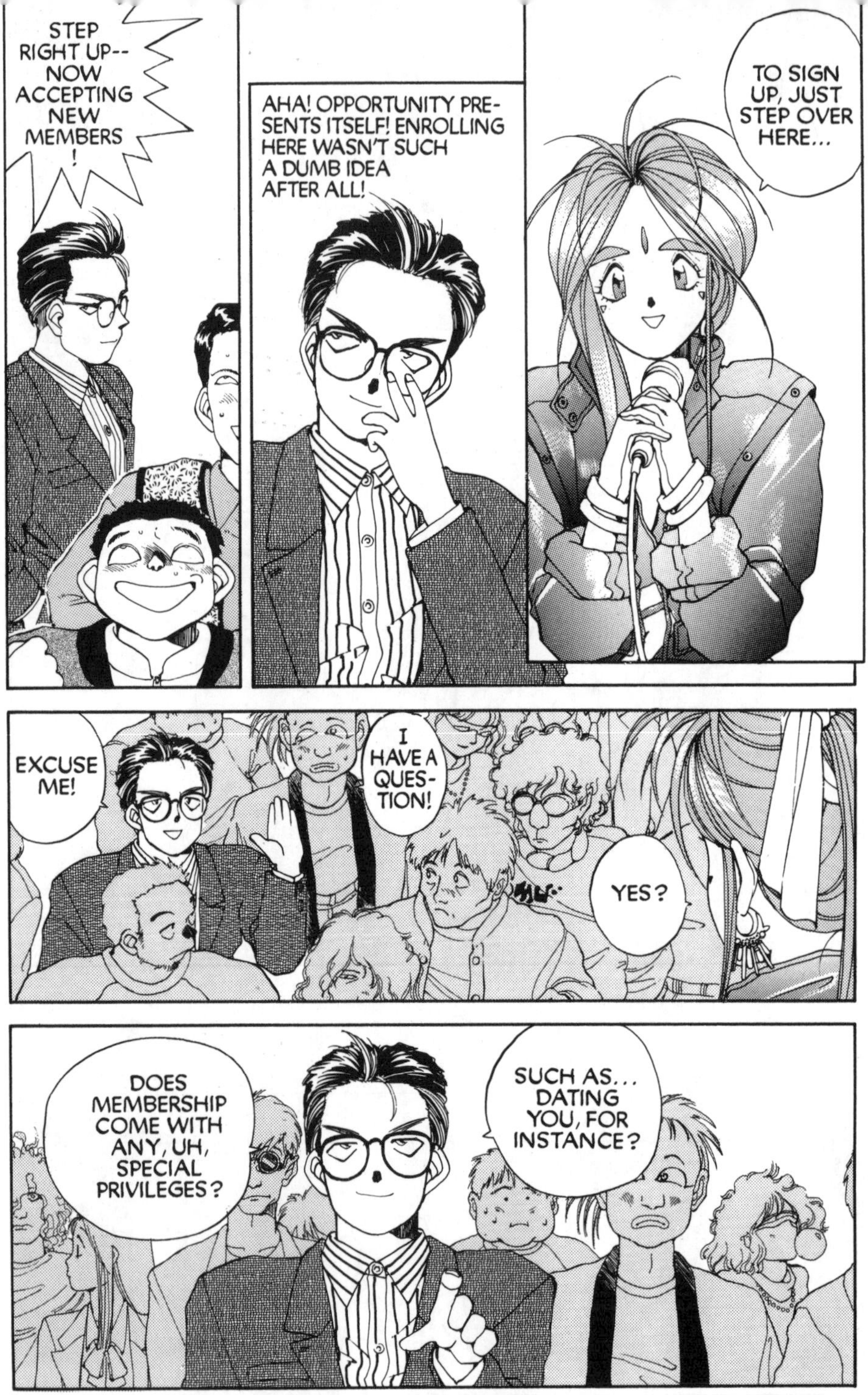
STEP RIGHT UP-- NOW ACCEPTING NEW MEMBERS!
AHA! OPPORTUNITY PRESENTS ITSELF! ENROLLING HERE WASN'T SUCH A DUMB IDEA AFTER ALL!
TO SIGN UP, JUST STEP OVER HERE...
EXCUSE ME!
I HAVE A QUESTION!
YES?
DOES MEMBERSHIP COME WITH ANY, UH, SPECIAL PRIVILEGES?
SUCH AS... DATING YOU, FOR INSTANCE?

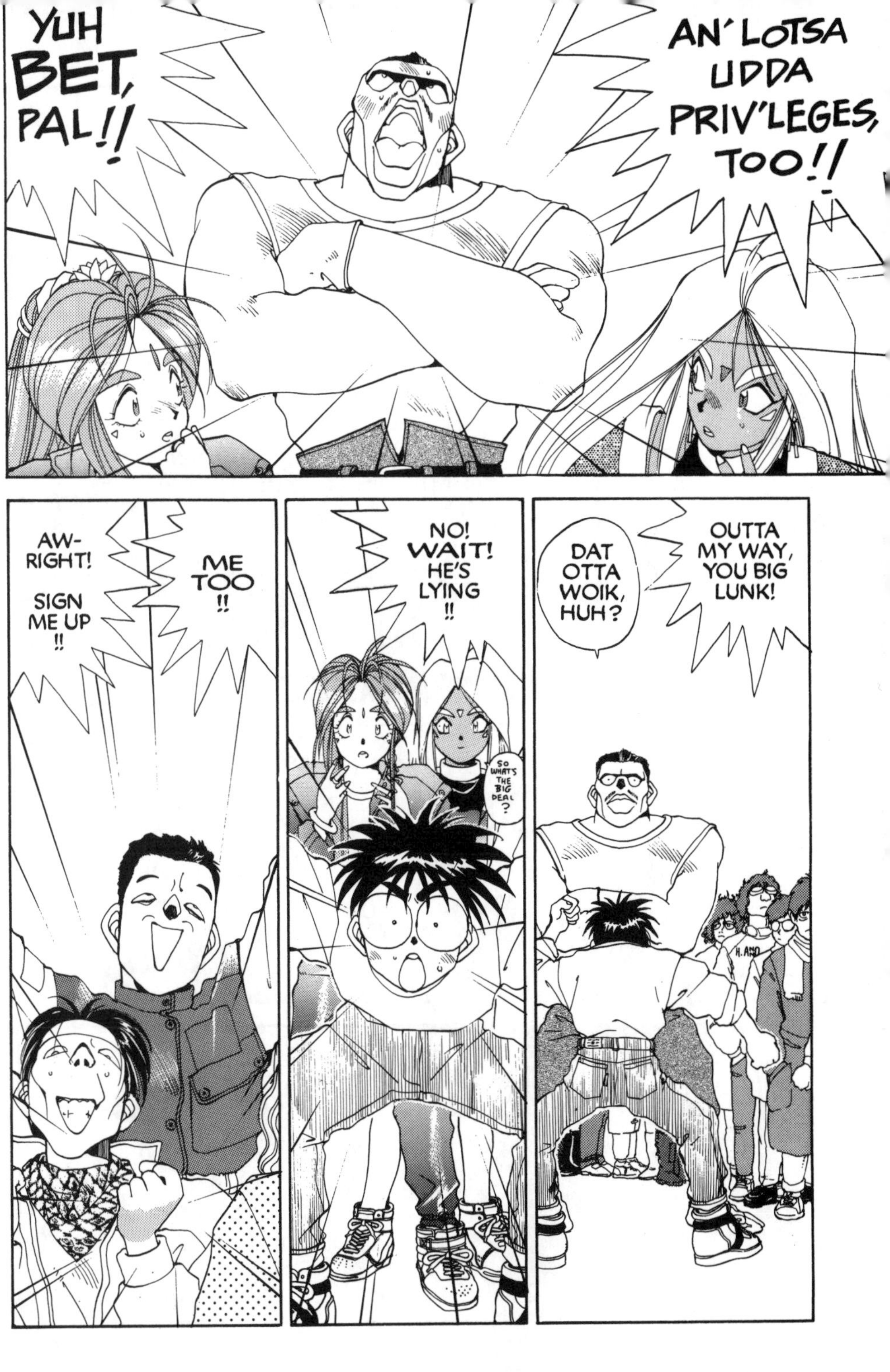
YUH BET, PAL!!
AN' LOTSA UDDA PRIV'LEGES, TOO!!
AW-RIGHT!
SIGN ME UP!!
ME TOO!!
NO! WAIT! HE'S LYING!!
SO WHAT'S THE BIG DEAL?
DAT OTTA WOIK, HUH?
OUTTA MY WAY, YOU BIG LUNK!

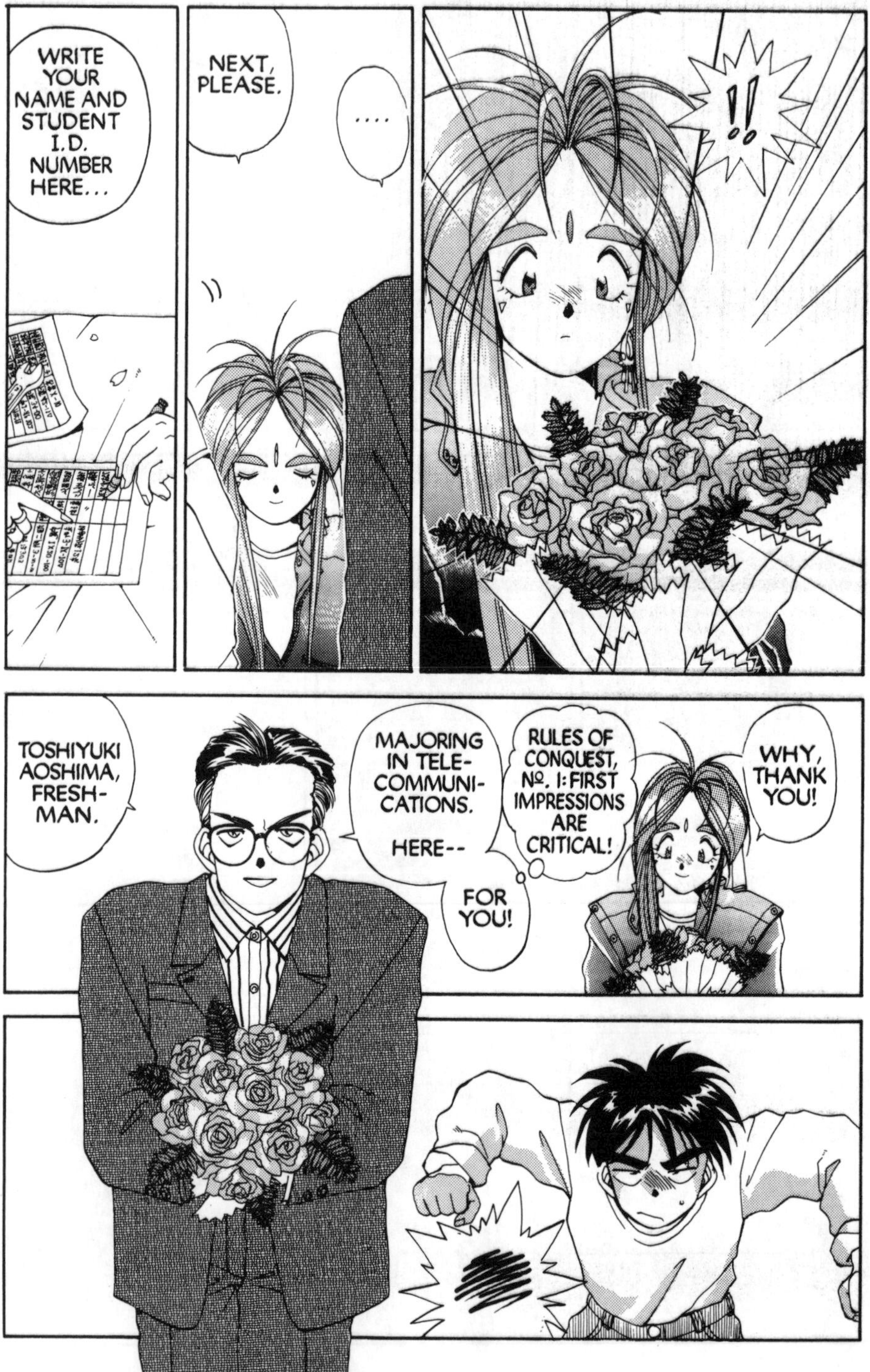
WRITE YOUR NAME AND STUDENT I.D. NUMBER HERE...
NEXT, PLEASE.
....
!!
TOSHIYUKI AOSHIMA, FRESH-MAN.
MAJORING IN TELE-COMMUNI-CATIONS.
HERE--
FOR YOU!
RULES OF CONQUEST, №. 1: FIRST IMPRESSIONS ARE CRITICAL!
WHY, THANK YOU!

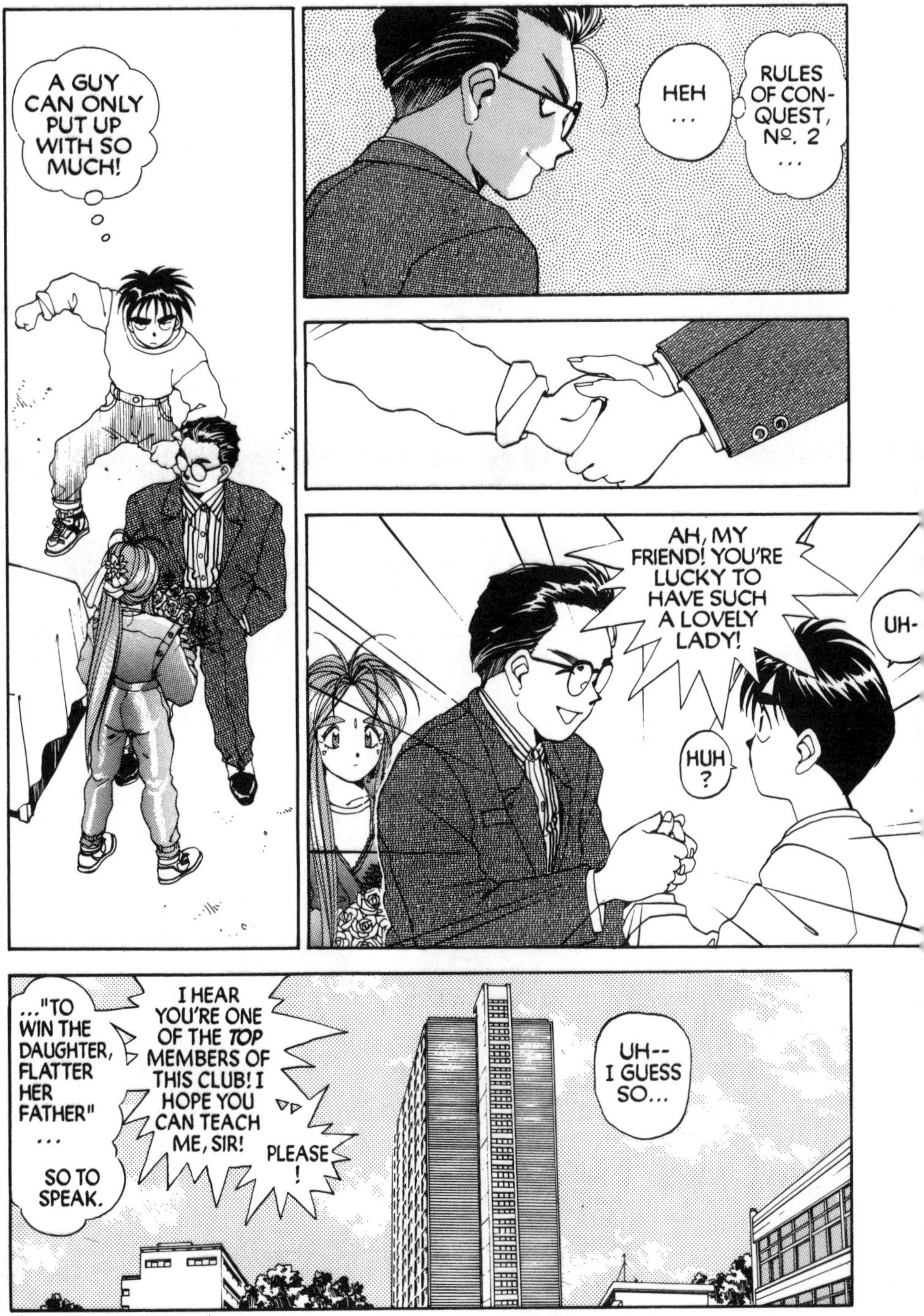

A GUY CAN ONLY PUT UP WITH SO MUCH!
HEH ...
RULES OF CONQUEST, №. 2 ...
AH, MY FRIEND! YOU'RE LUCKY TO HAVE SUCH A LOVELY LADY!
UH-
HUH ?
..."TO WIN THE DAUGHTER, FLATTER HER FATHER" ...
SO TO SPEAK.
I HEAR YOU'RE ONE OF THE *TOP* MEMBERS OF THIS CLUB! I HOPE YOU CAN TEACH ME, SIR!
PLEASE !
UH-- I GUESS SO...

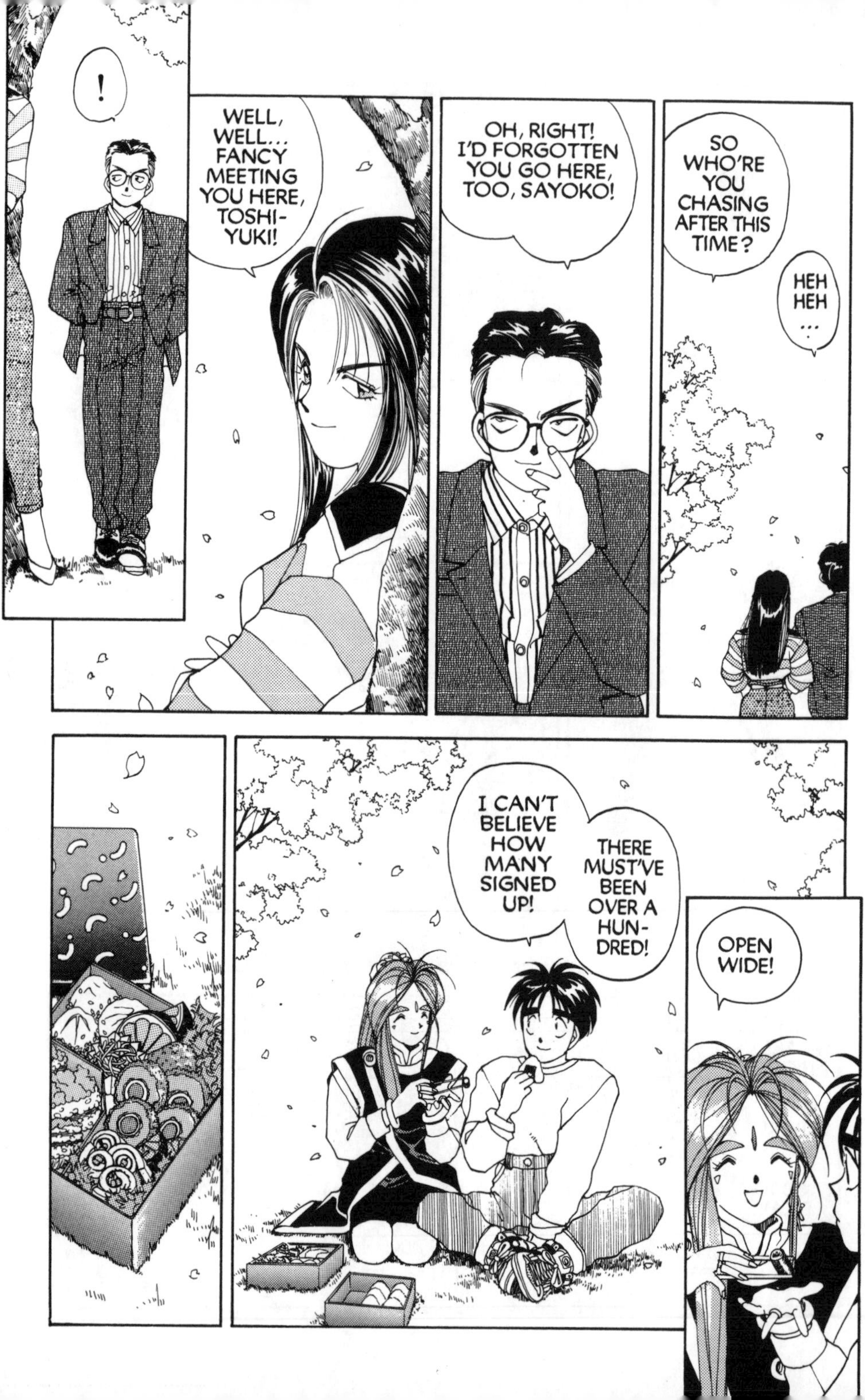
!
WELL, WELL... FANCY MEETING YOU HERE, TOSHI-YUKI!
OH, RIGHT! I'D FORGOTTEN YOU GO HERE, TOO, SAYOKO!
SO WHO'RE YOU CHASING AFTER THIS TIME?
HEH HEH ...
I CAN'T BELIEVE HOW MANY SIGNED UP!
THERE MUST'VE BEEN OVER A HUN-DRED!
OPEN WIDE!

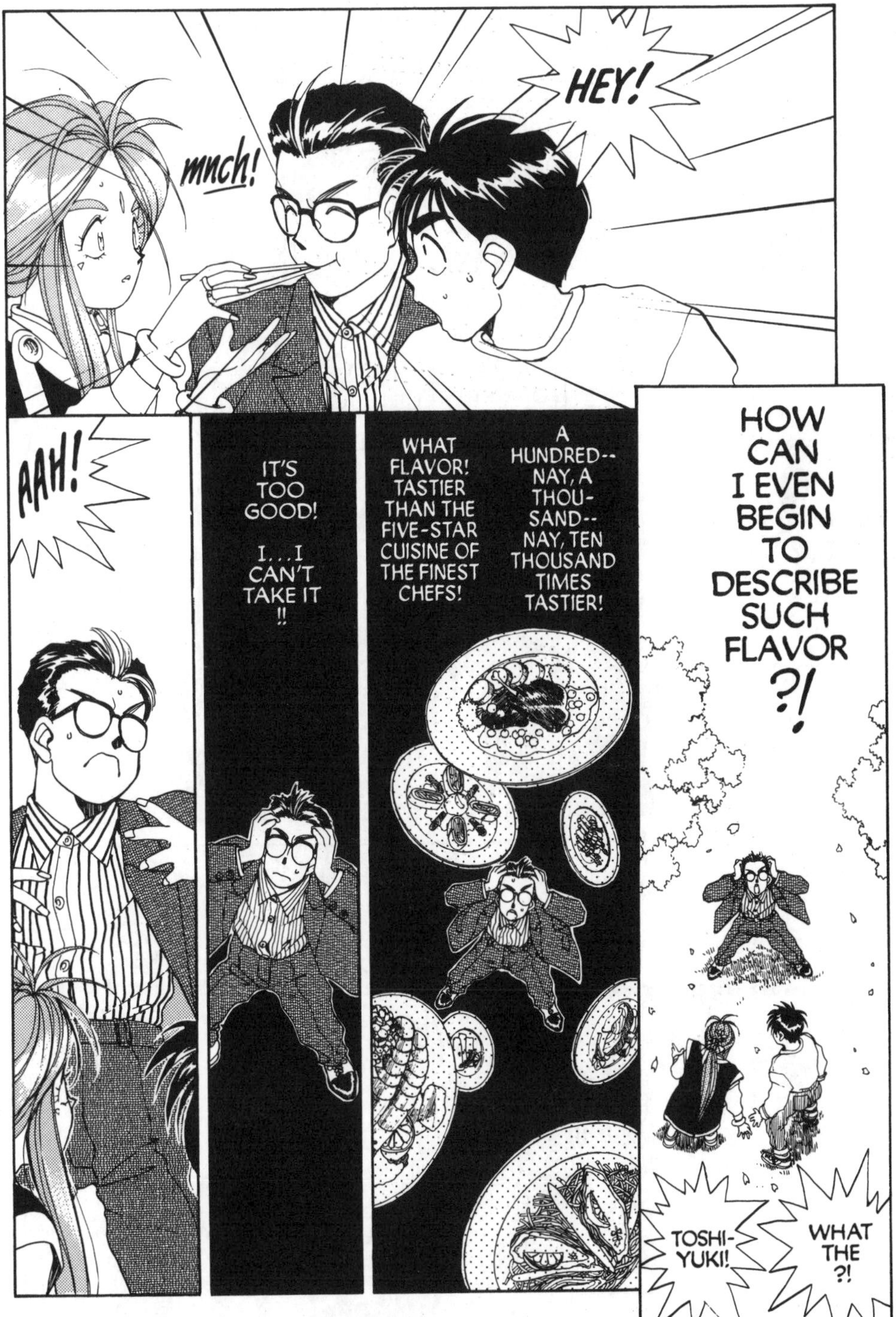
mnch!
HEY!
AAH!
IT'S TOO GOOD!
I...I CAN'T TAKE IT !!
WHAT FLAVOR! TASTIER THAN THE FIVE-STAR CUISINE OF THE FINEST CHEFS!
A HUNDRED-- NAY, A THOUSAND-- NAY, TEN THOUSAND TIMES TASTIER!
HOW CAN I EVEN BEGIN TO DESCRIBE SUCH FLAVOR ?!
TOSHI-YUKI!
WHAT THE ?!

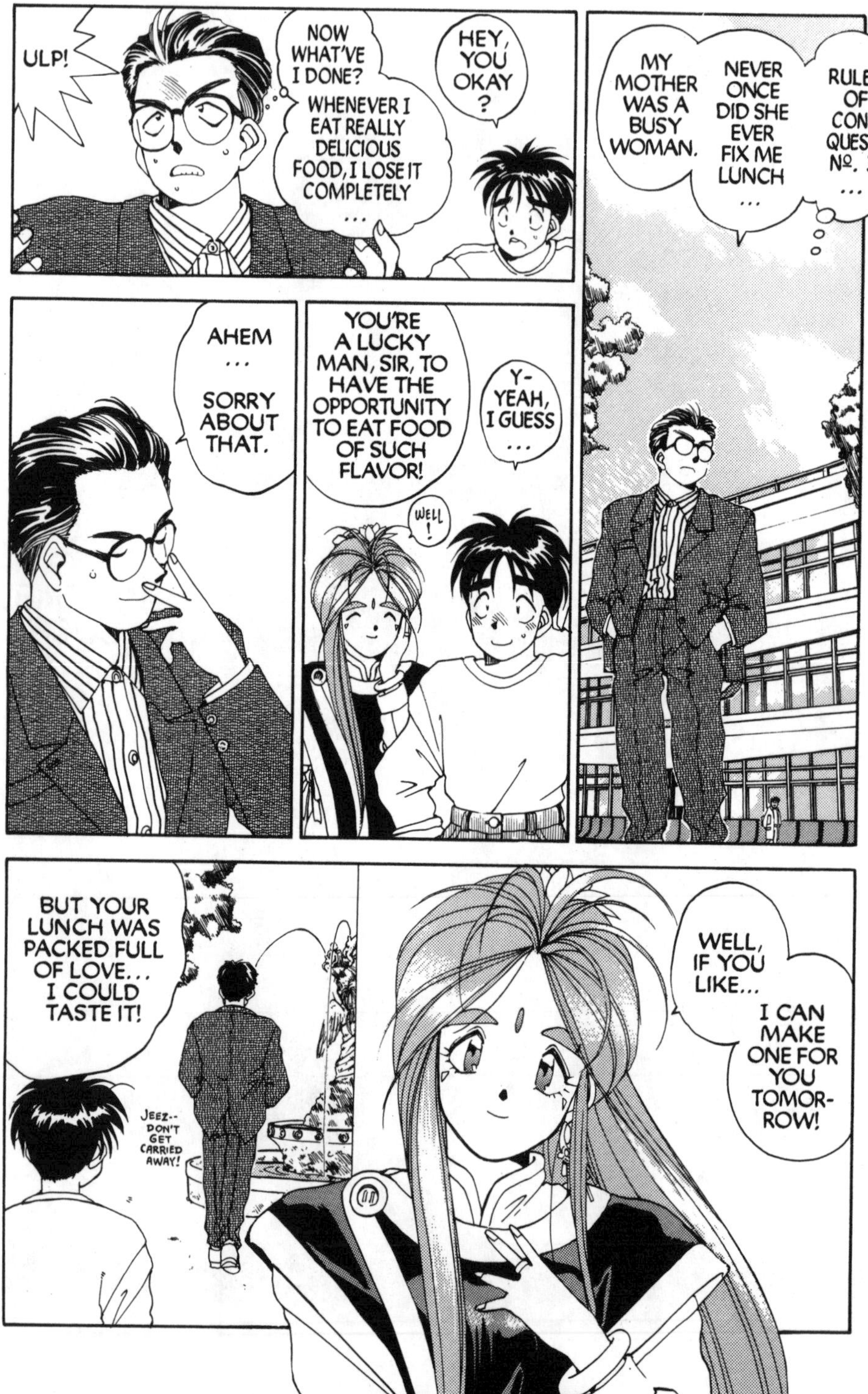
ULP!
NOW WHAT'VE I DONE?
WHENEVER I EAT REALLY DELICIOUS FOOD, I LOSE IT COMPLETELY ...
HEY, YOU OKAY ?
MY MOTHER WAS A BUSY WOMAN.
NEVER ONCE DID SHE EVER FIX ME LUNCH ...
RULES OF CON-QUEST, №. 3 ...
AHEM ...
SORRY ABOUT THAT.
YOU'RE A LUCKY MAN, SIR, TO HAVE THE OPPORTUNITY TO EAT FOOD OF SUCH FLAVOR!
Y-YEAH, I GUESS ...
WELL !
BUT YOUR LUNCH WAS PACKED FULL OF LOVE... I COULD TASTE IT!
JEEZ-- DON'T GET CARRIED AWAY!
WELL, IF YOU LIKE...
I CAN MAKE ONE FOR YOU TOMOR-ROW!

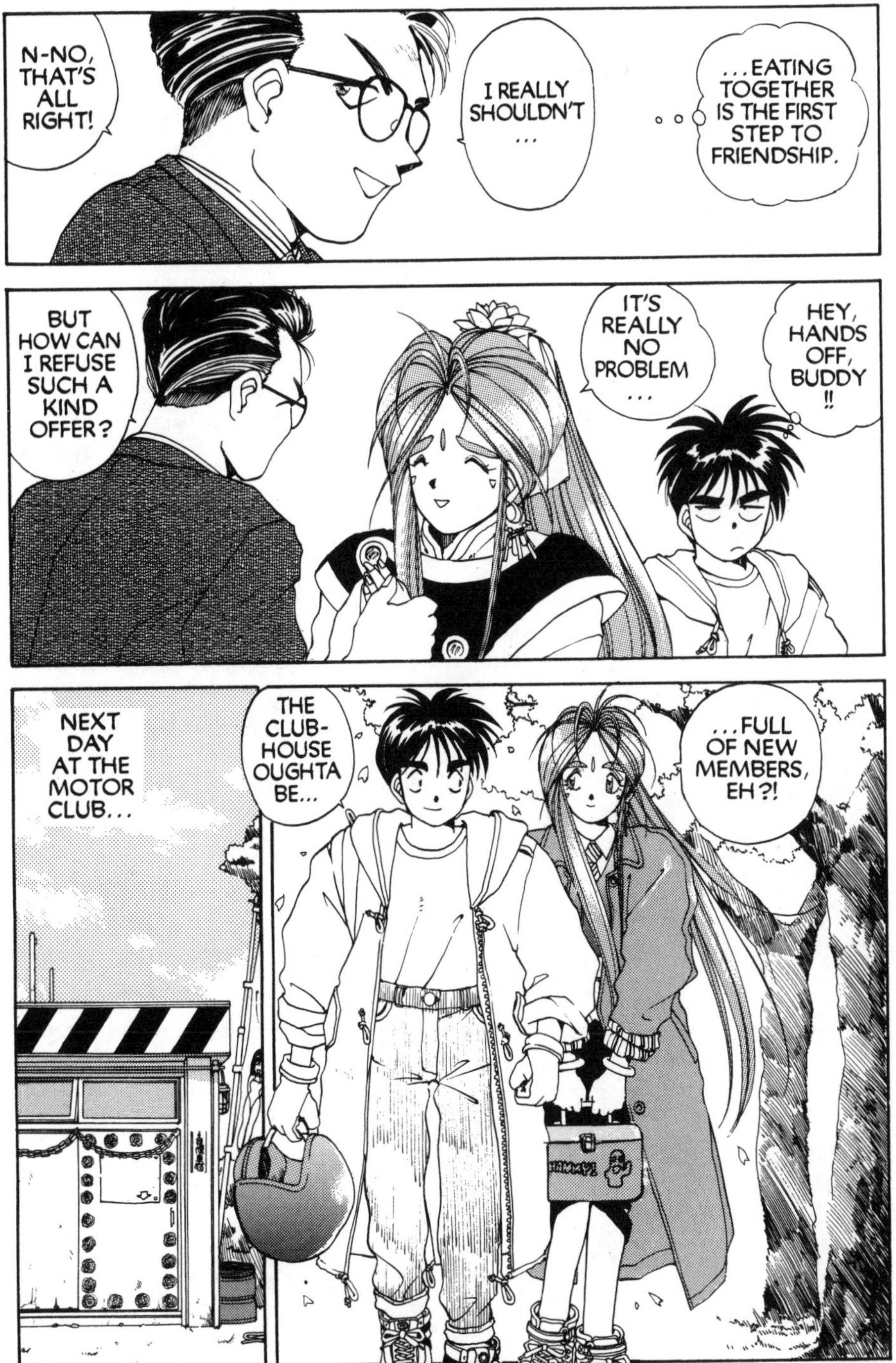
N-NO, THAT'S ALL RIGHT!
I REALLY SHOULDN'T ...
...EATING TOGETHER IS THE FIRST STEP TO FRIENDSHIP.
BUT HOW CAN I REFUSE SUCH A KIND OFFER?
IT'S REALLY NO PROBLEM ...
HEY, HANDS OFF, BUDDY!!
NEXT DAY AT THE MOTOR CLUB...
THE CLUB-HOUSE OUGHTA BE...
...FULL OF NEW MEMBERS, EH?!

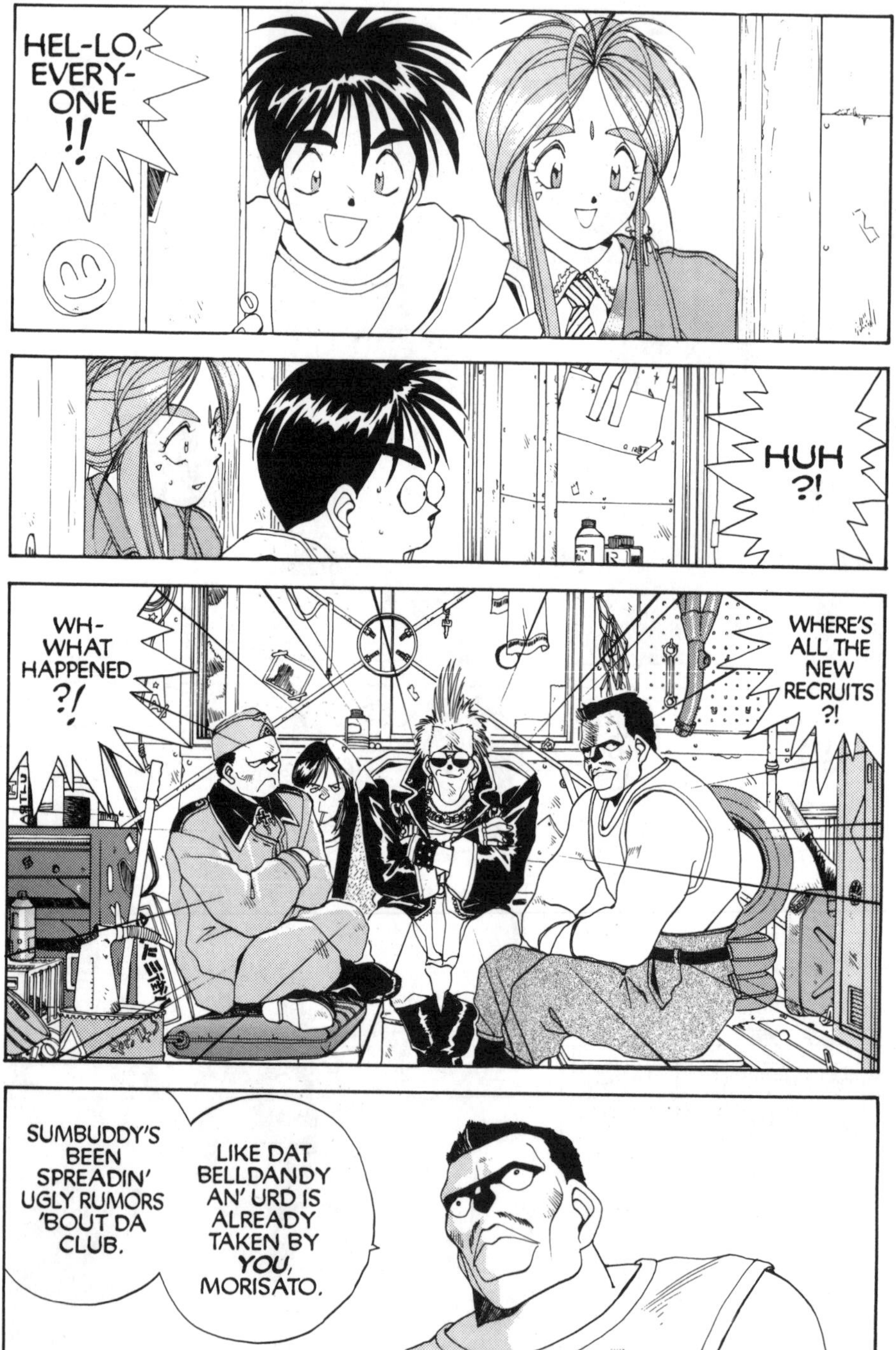
HEL-LO, EVERY-ONE!!
HUH?!
WH-WHAT HAPPENED?!
WHERE'S ALL THE NEW RECRUITS?!
SUMBUDDY'S BEEN SPREADIN' UGLY RUMORS 'BOUT DA CLUB.
LIKE DAT BELLDANDY AN' URD IS ALREADY TAKEN BY *YOU*, MORISATO.

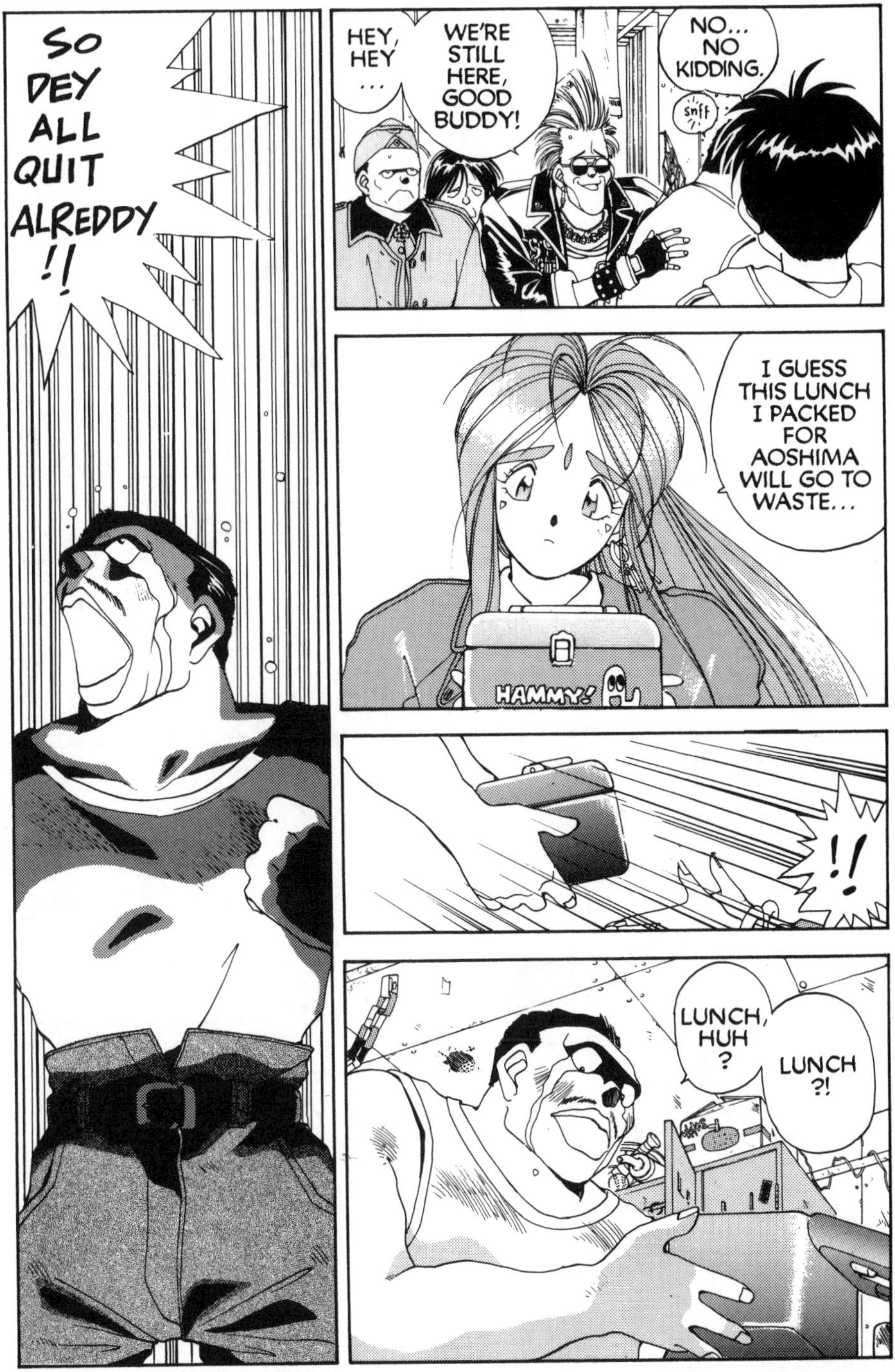
SO DEY ALL QUIT ALREDDY !!
HEY, HEY ...
WE'RE STILL HERE, GOOD BUDDY!
NO... NO KIDDING.
snff
I GUESS THIS LUNCH I PACKED FOR AOSHIMA WILL GO TO WASTE...
HAMMY!
!!
LUNCH, HUH ?
LUNCH ?!

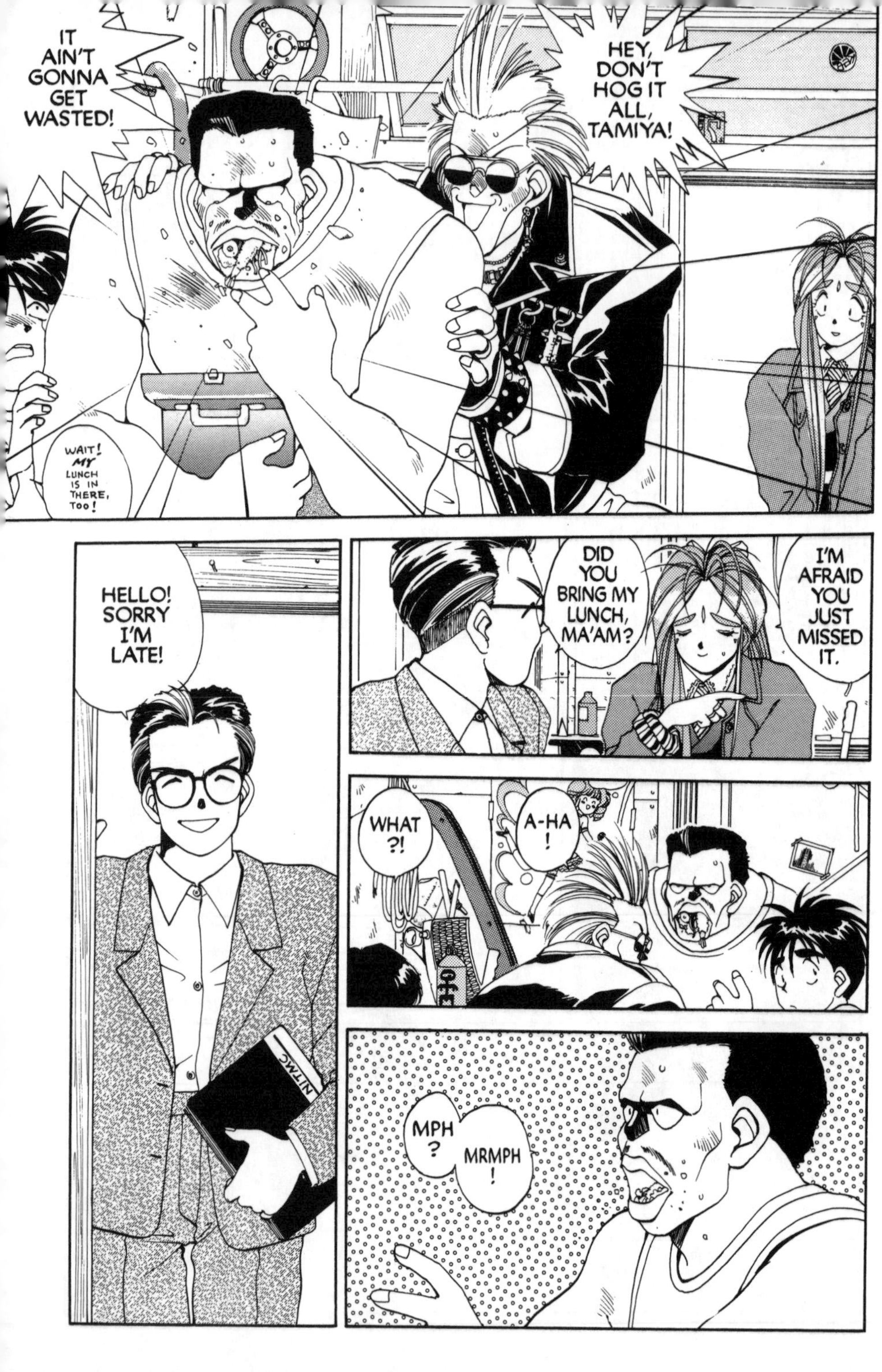
IT AIN'T GONNA GET WASTED!
HEY, DON'T HOG IT ALL, TAMIYA!
WAIT! MY LUNCH IS IN THERE, TOO!
HELLO! SORRY I'M LATE!
NITMC
DID YOU BRING MY LUNCH, MA'AM?
I'M AFRAID YOU JUST MISSED IT.
WHAT ?!
A-HA !
MPH ?
MRMPH !

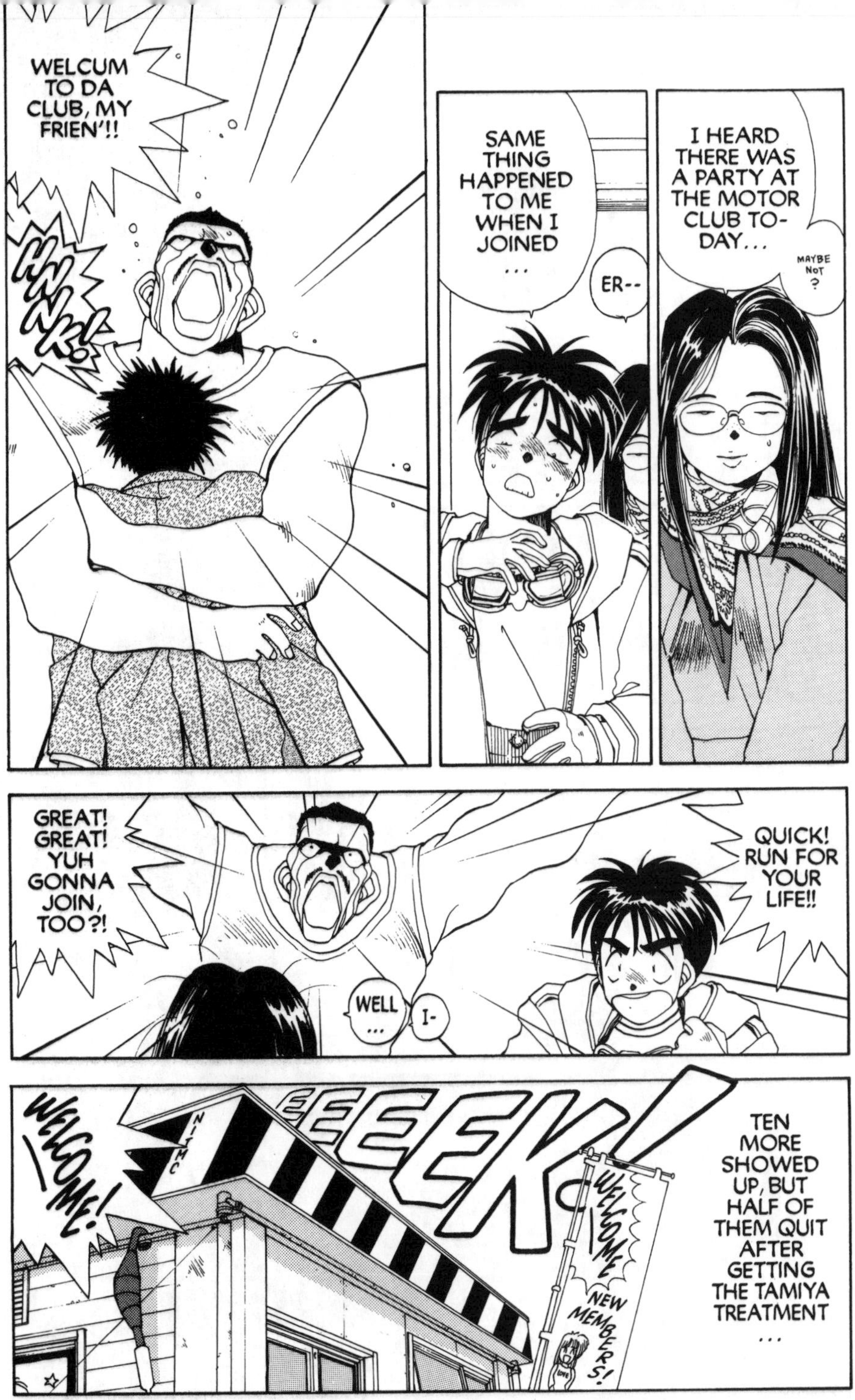
WELCUM TO DA CLUB, MY FRIEN'!!
HNNK!
SAME THING HAPPENED TO ME WHEN I JOINED...
ER--
I HEARD THERE WAS A PARTY AT THE MOTOR CLUB TO-DAY...
MAYBE NOT?
GREAT! GREAT! YUH GONNA JOIN, TOO?!
WELL...
I-
QUICK! RUN FOR YOUR LIFE!!
WELCOME!
NITMC
EEEEK!
WELCOME NEW MEMBERS!
TEN MORE SHOWED UP, BUT HALF OF THEM QUIT AFTER GETTING THE TAMIYA TREATMENT...

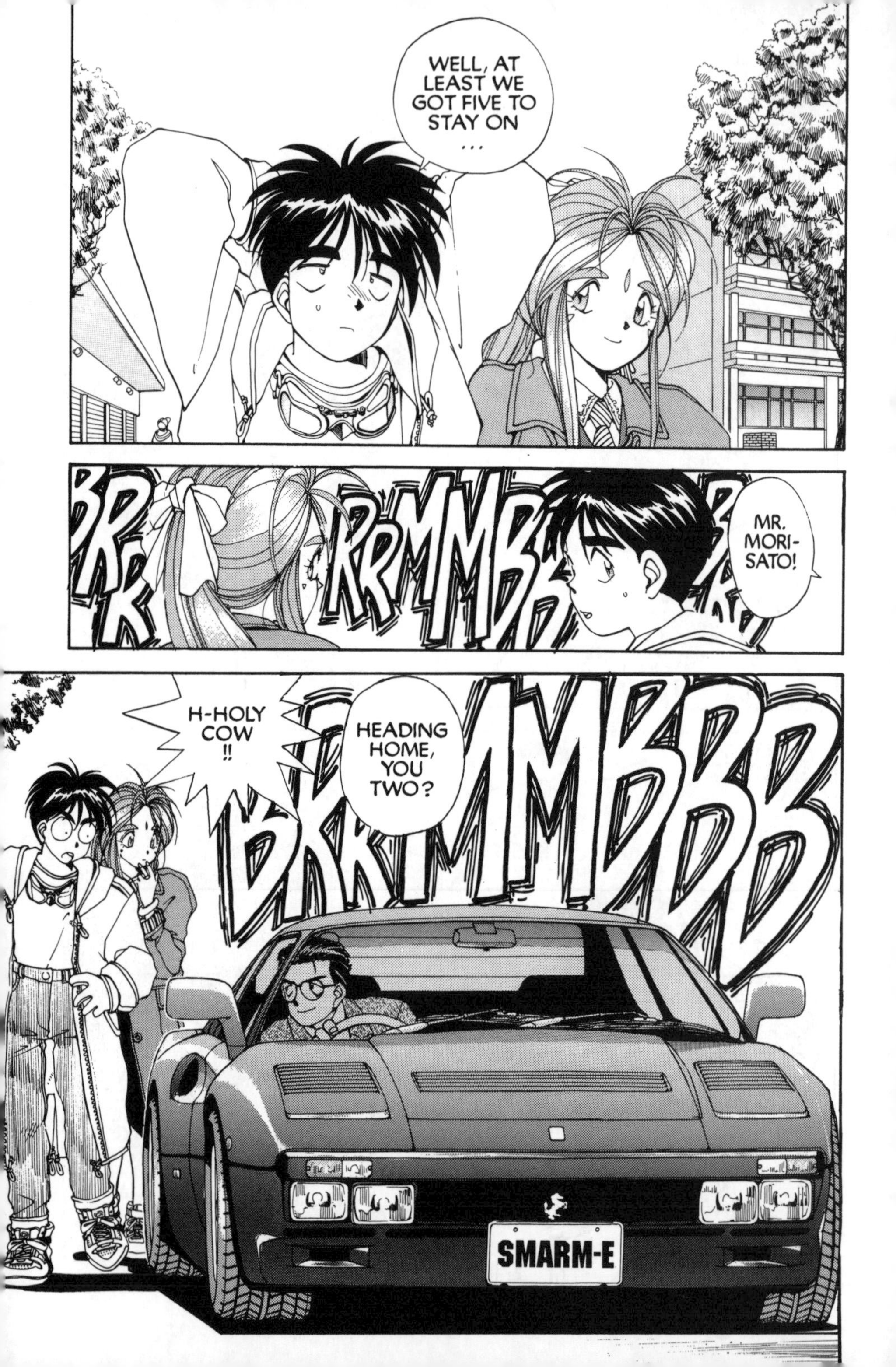
WELL, AT LEAST WE GOT FIVE TO STAY ON ...
BRRMMBRR
MR. MORI-SATO!
H-HOLY COW !!
HEADING HOME, YOU TWO?
BRRMMBBB
SMARM-E

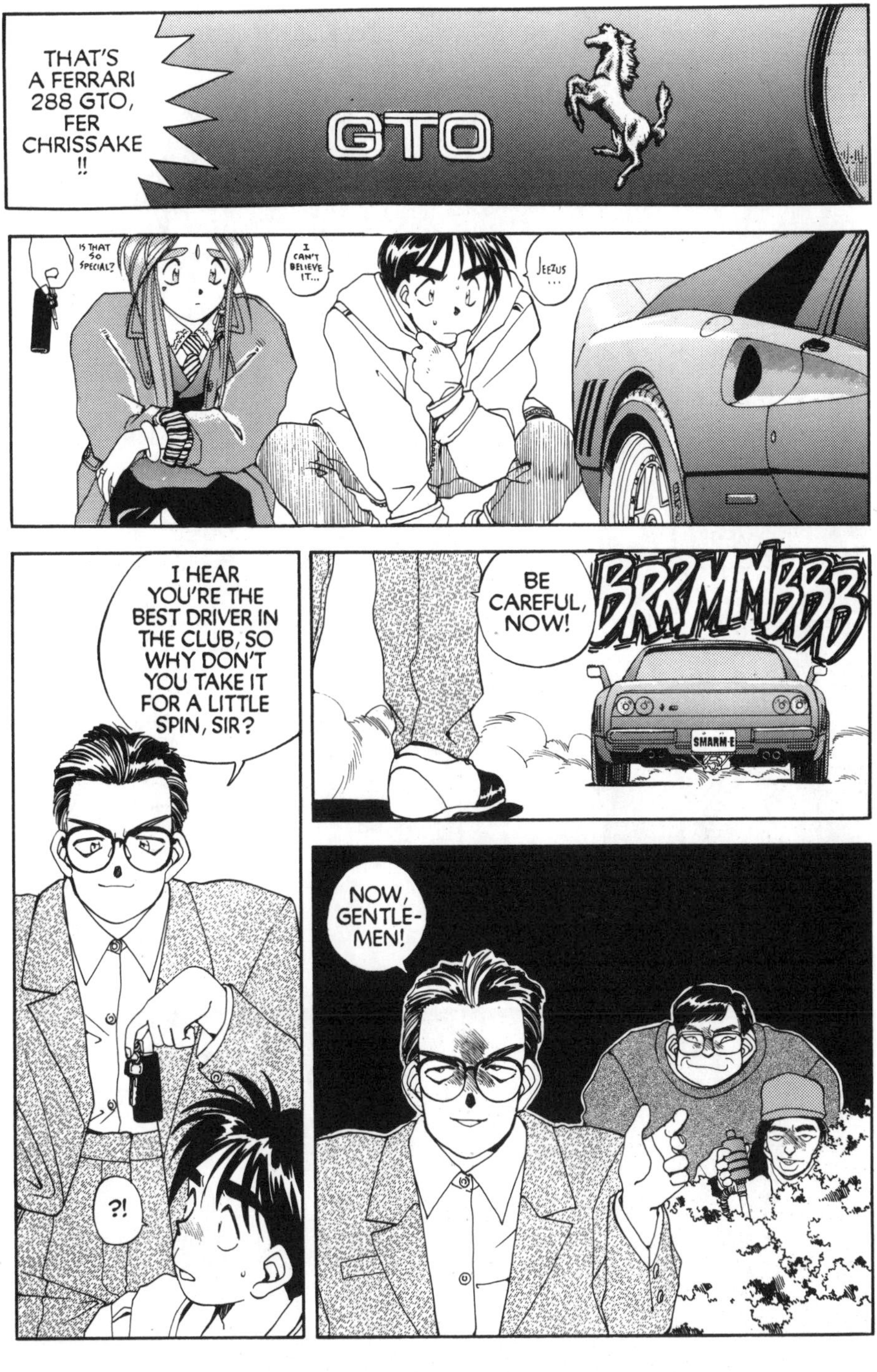
THAT'S A FERRARI 288 GTO, FER CHRISSAKE !!
GTO
IS THAT SO SPECIAL?
I CAN'T BELIEVE IT...
JEEZUS ...
I HEAR YOU'RE THE BEST DRIVER IN THE CLUB, SO WHY DON'T YOU TAKE IT FOR A LITTLE SPIN, SIR?
?!
BE CAREFUL, NOW!
BRRMMBBB
SMARM-E
NOW, GENTLE-MEN!

YOW! FEEL THAT ACCELERATION!

FERRARIS ARE THE GREATEST!

UM ... VERY NICE ...

BRRAAB VREEEE

THAT AOSHIMA... THERE'S A DARK SHADOW AROUND HIM THAT COMES AND GOES ...

WHAT IS IT, I WONDER?

HEY, THANKS A LOT!

THAT WAS INCREDIBLE!

FOR YOU, SIR, ANYTHING I CAN DO...!

EH?

VRMM

MY BIKE WON'T START.

ANYTHING WRONG?

WELL... IF IT'S ANY HELP, I'D BE GLAD TO DRIVE THE LADY HOME!

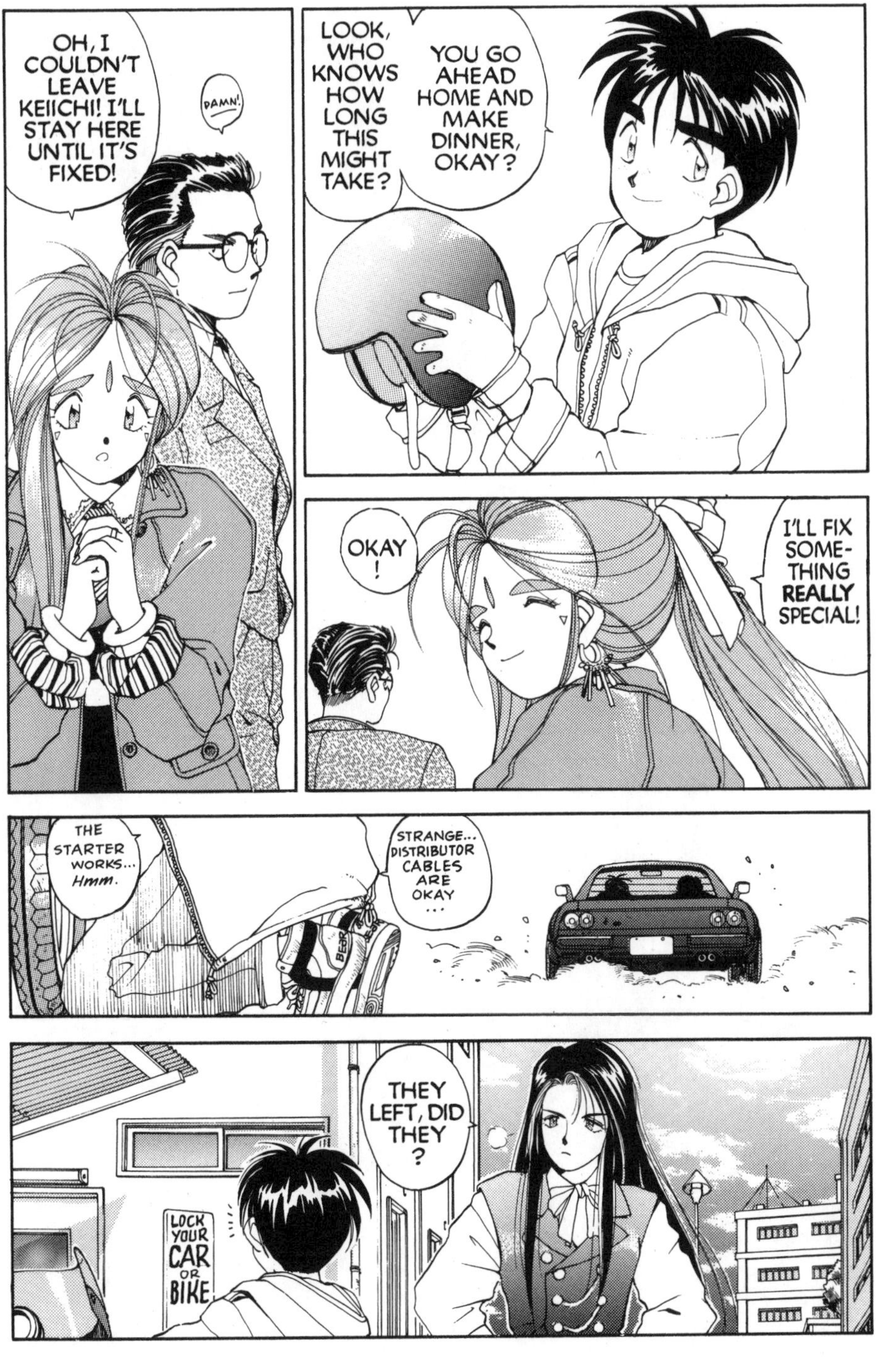
OH, I COULDN'T LEAVE KEIICHI! I'LL STAY HERE UNTIL IT'S FIXED!
DAMN!
LOOK, WHO KNOWS HOW LONG THIS MIGHT TAKE?
YOU GO AHEAD HOME AND MAKE DINNER, OKAY?
OKAY!
I'LL FIX SOMETHING **REALLY** SPECIAL!
THE STARTER WORKS... *Hmm.*
STRANGE... DISTRIBUTOR CABLES ARE OKAY...
LOCK YOUR CAR OR BIKE
THEY LEFT, DID THEY?

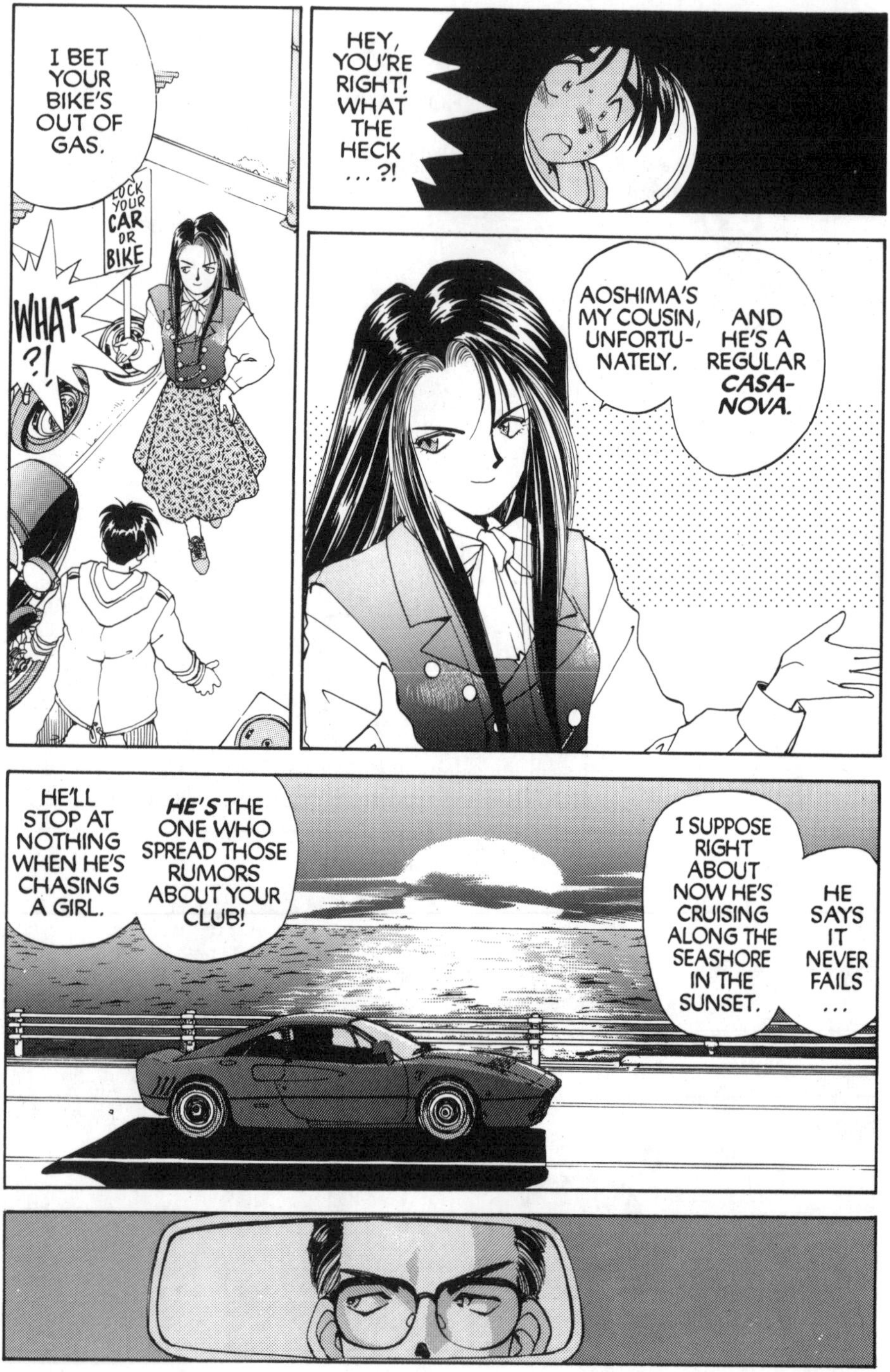
I BET YOUR BIKE'S OUT OF GAS.
LOCK YOUR CAR OR BIKE
WHAT ?!
HEY, YOU'RE RIGHT! WHAT THE HECK ...?!
AOSHIMA'S MY COUSIN, UNFORTU-NATELY.
AND HE'S A REGULAR *CASA-NOVA.*
HE'LL STOP AT NOTHING WHEN HE'S CHASING A GIRL.
*HE'S* THE ONE WHO SPREAD THOSE RUMORS ABOUT YOUR CLUB!
I SUPPOSE RIGHT ABOUT NOW HE'S CRUISING ALONG THE SEASHORE IN THE SUNSET.
HE SAYS IT NEVER FAILS ...

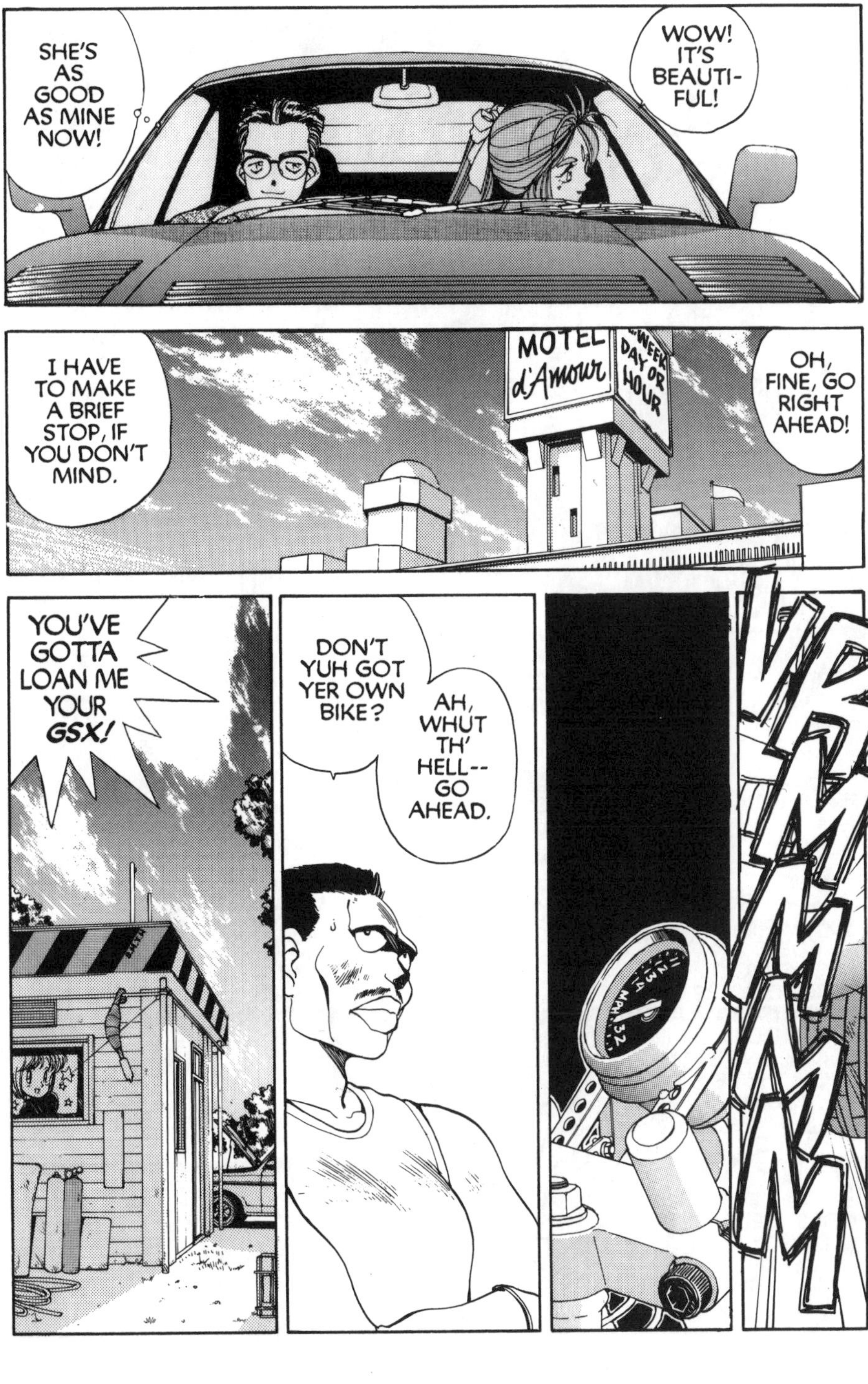
SHE'S AS GOOD AS MINE NOW!
WOW! IT'S BEAUTI-FUL!
I HAVE TO MAKE A BRIEF STOP, IF YOU DON'T MIND.
MOTEL d'Amour
WEEK DAY OR HOUR
OH, FINE, GO RIGHT AHEAD!
YOU'VE GOTTA LOAN ME YOUR *GSX!*
DON'T YUH GOT YER OWN BIKE?
AH, WHUT TH' HELL-- GO AHEAD.
VRMMMMM

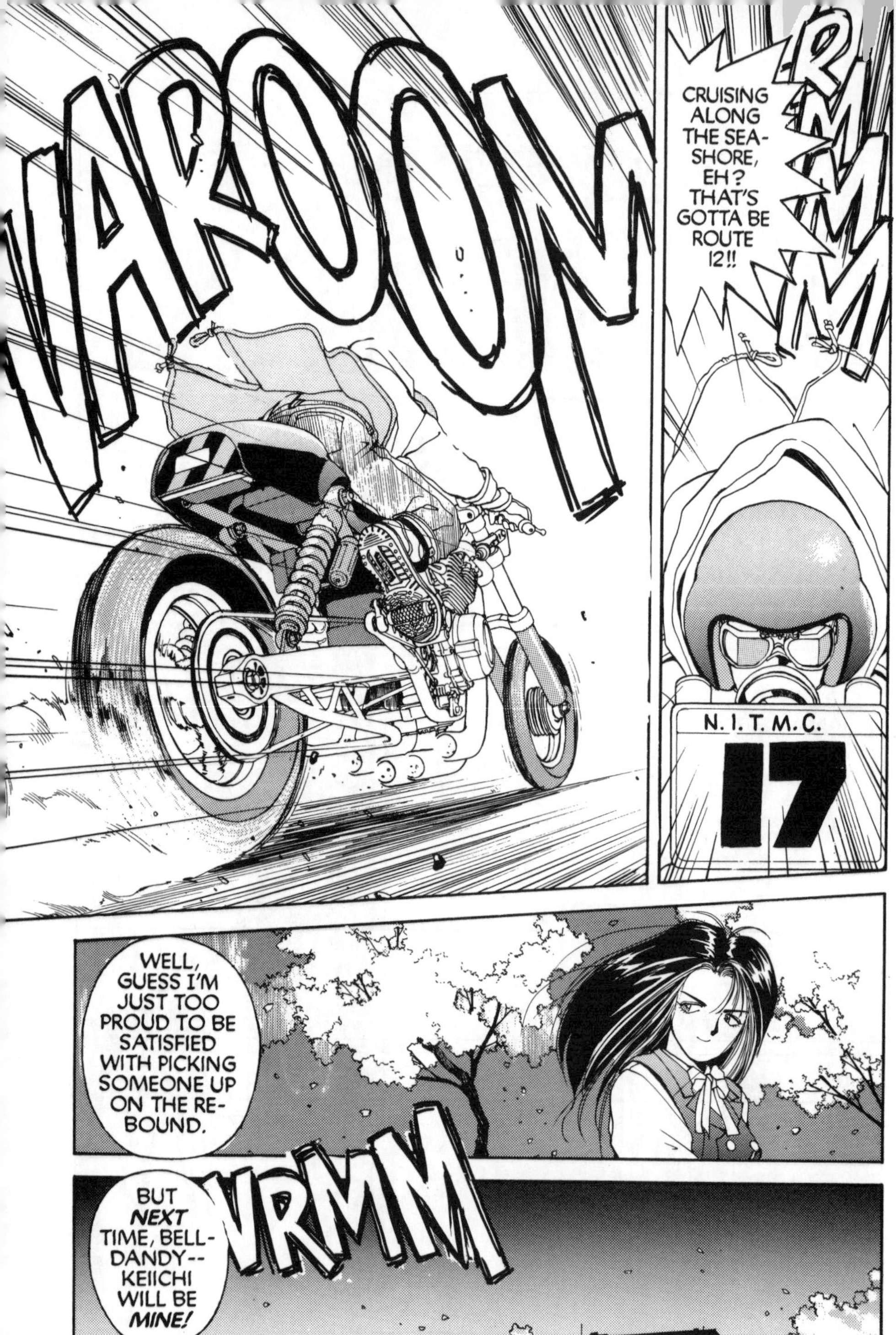
VAROOOM
RMMM
CRUISING ALONG THE SEA-SHORE, EH? THAT'S GOTTA BE ROUTE 12!!
N. I. T. M. C.
17
WELL, GUESS I'M JUST TOO PROUD TO BE SATISFIED WITH PICKING SOMEONE UP ON THE RE-BOUND.
BUT *NEXT* TIME, BELL-DANDY-- KEIICHI WILL BE *MINE!*
VRMM

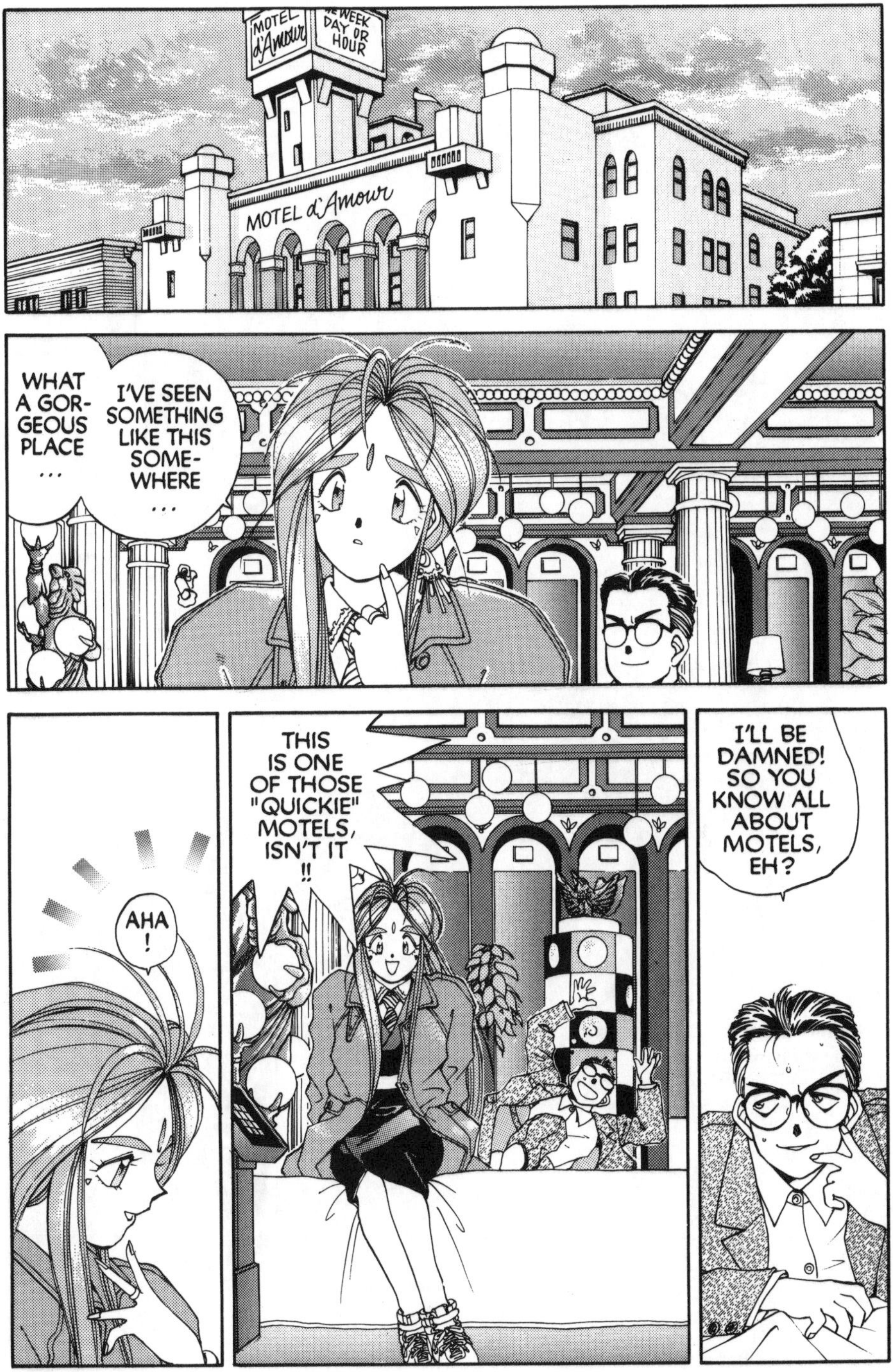

MOTEL d'Amour
WEEK DAY OR HOUR
MOTEL d'Amour
WHAT A GOR-GEOUS PLACE ...
I'VE SEEN SOMETHING LIKE THIS SOME-WHERE ...
AHA !
THIS IS ONE OF THOSE "QUICKIE" MOTELS, ISN'T IT !!
I'LL BE DAMNED! SO YOU KNOW ALL ABOUT MOTELS, EH?

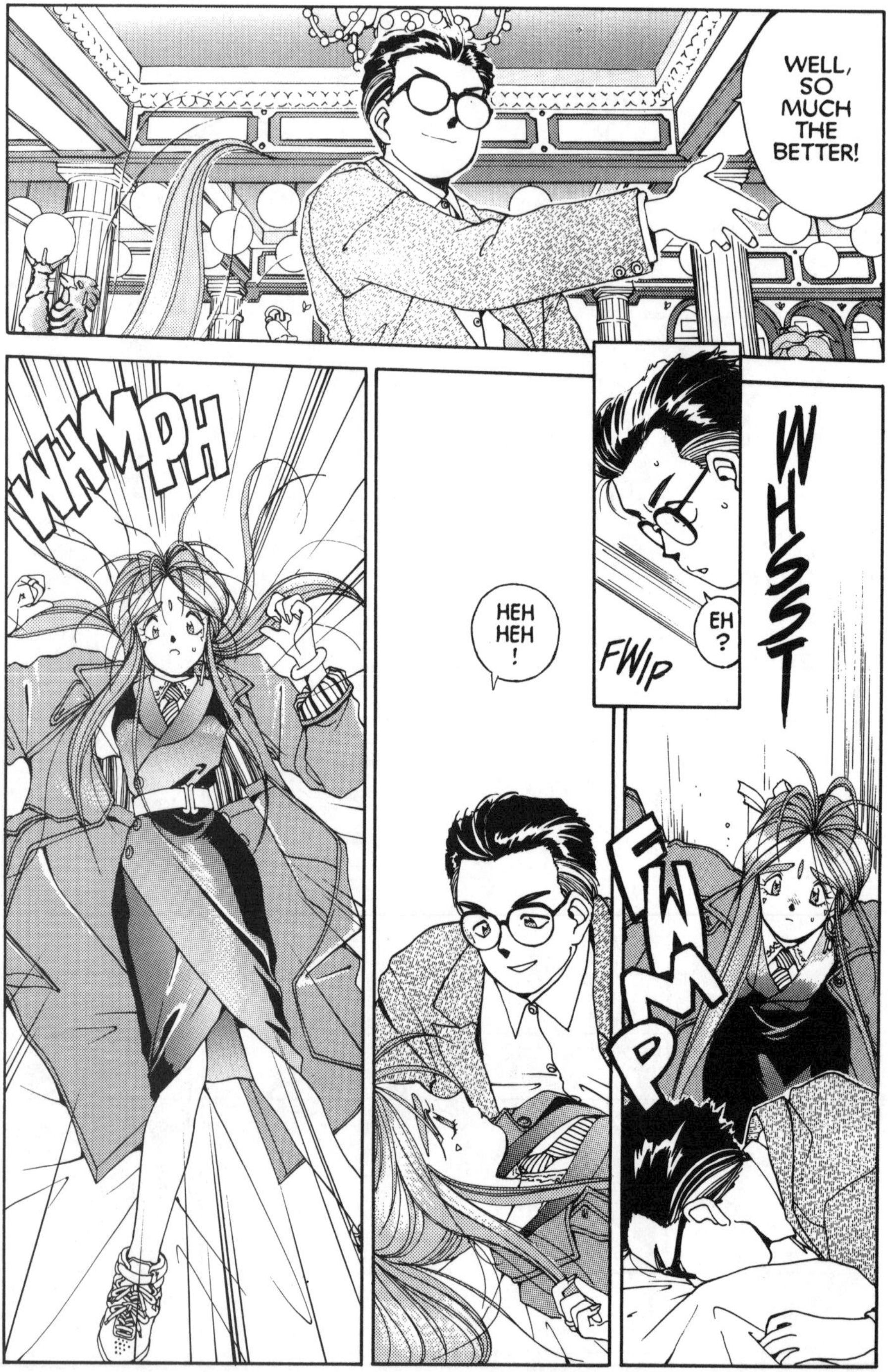
WELL, SO MUCH THE BETTER!
WHMPH
HEH HEH!
EH?
FWIP
WHSST
FWMP

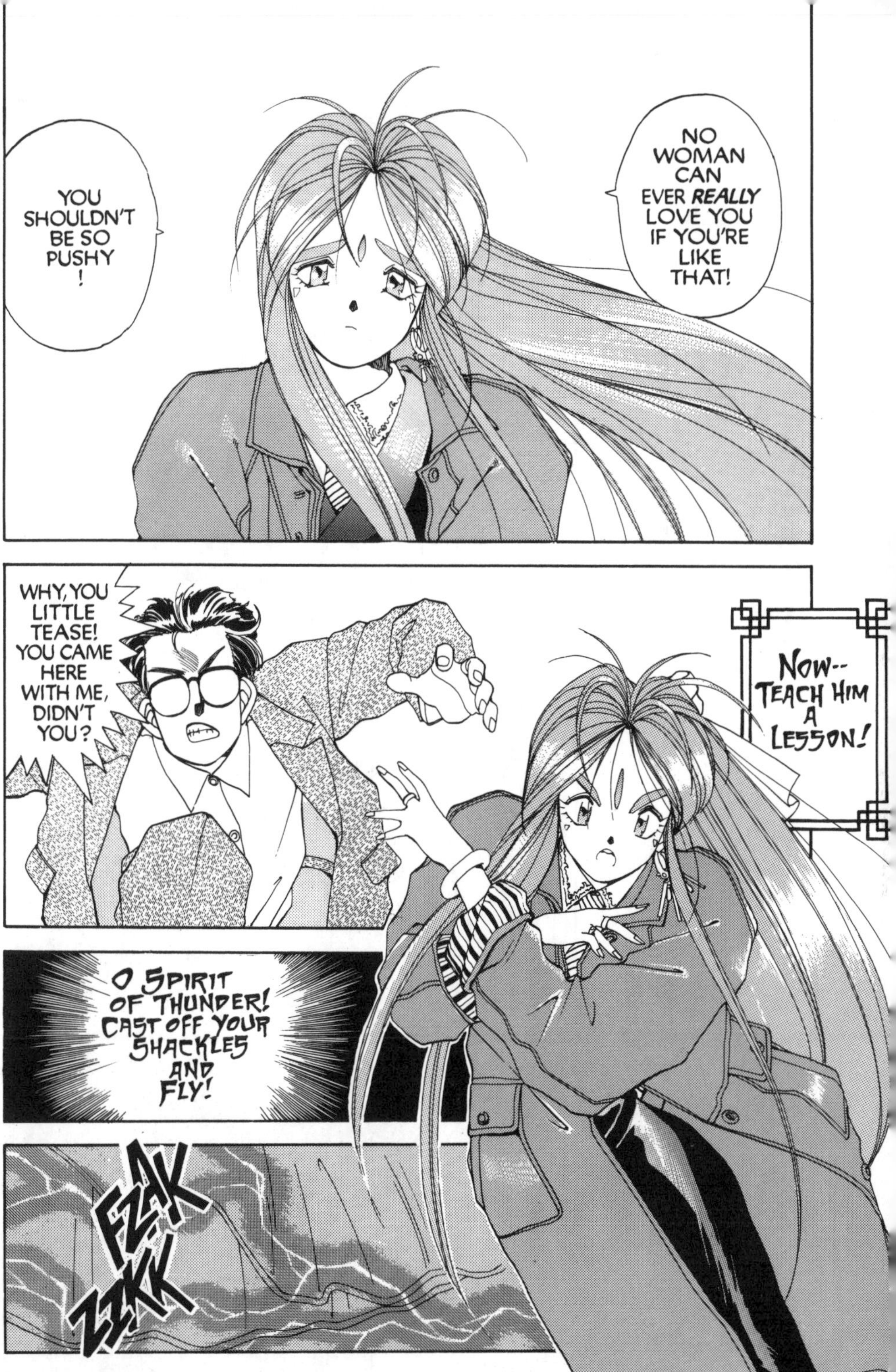
YOU SHOULDN'T BE SO PUSHY !
NO WOMAN CAN EVER *REALLY* LOVE YOU IF YOU'RE LIKE THAT!
WHY, YOU LITTLE TEASE! YOU CAME HERE WITH ME, DIDN'T YOU?
NOW-- TEACH HIM A LESSON!
O SPIRIT OF THUNDER! CAST OFF YOUR SHACKLES AND FLY!
FZAK ZZKK

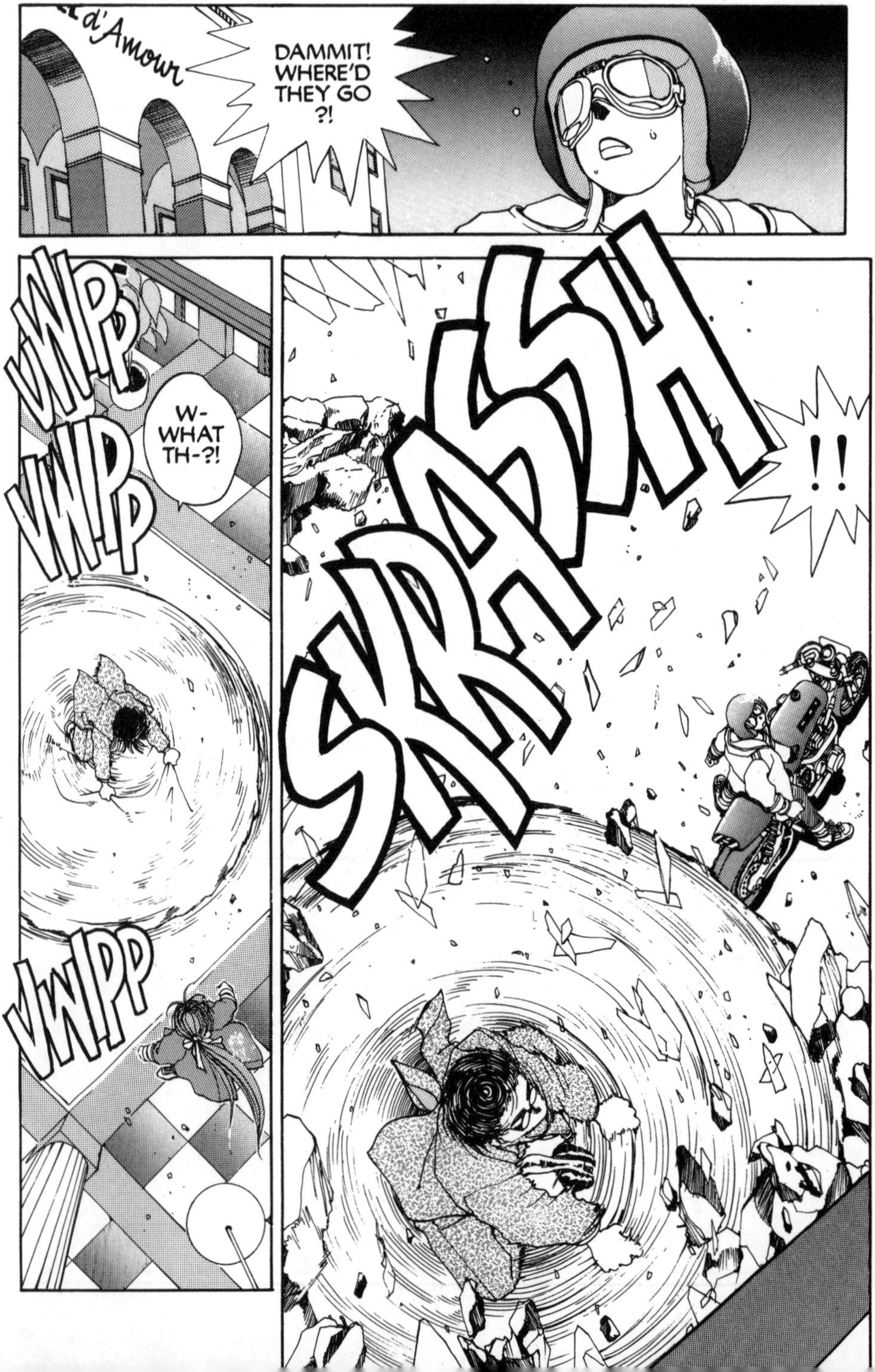
...d'Amour
DAMMIT! WHERE'D THEY GO ?!
VWIPP
VWIPP
W-WHAT TH-?!
VWIPP
SKRASSH
!!

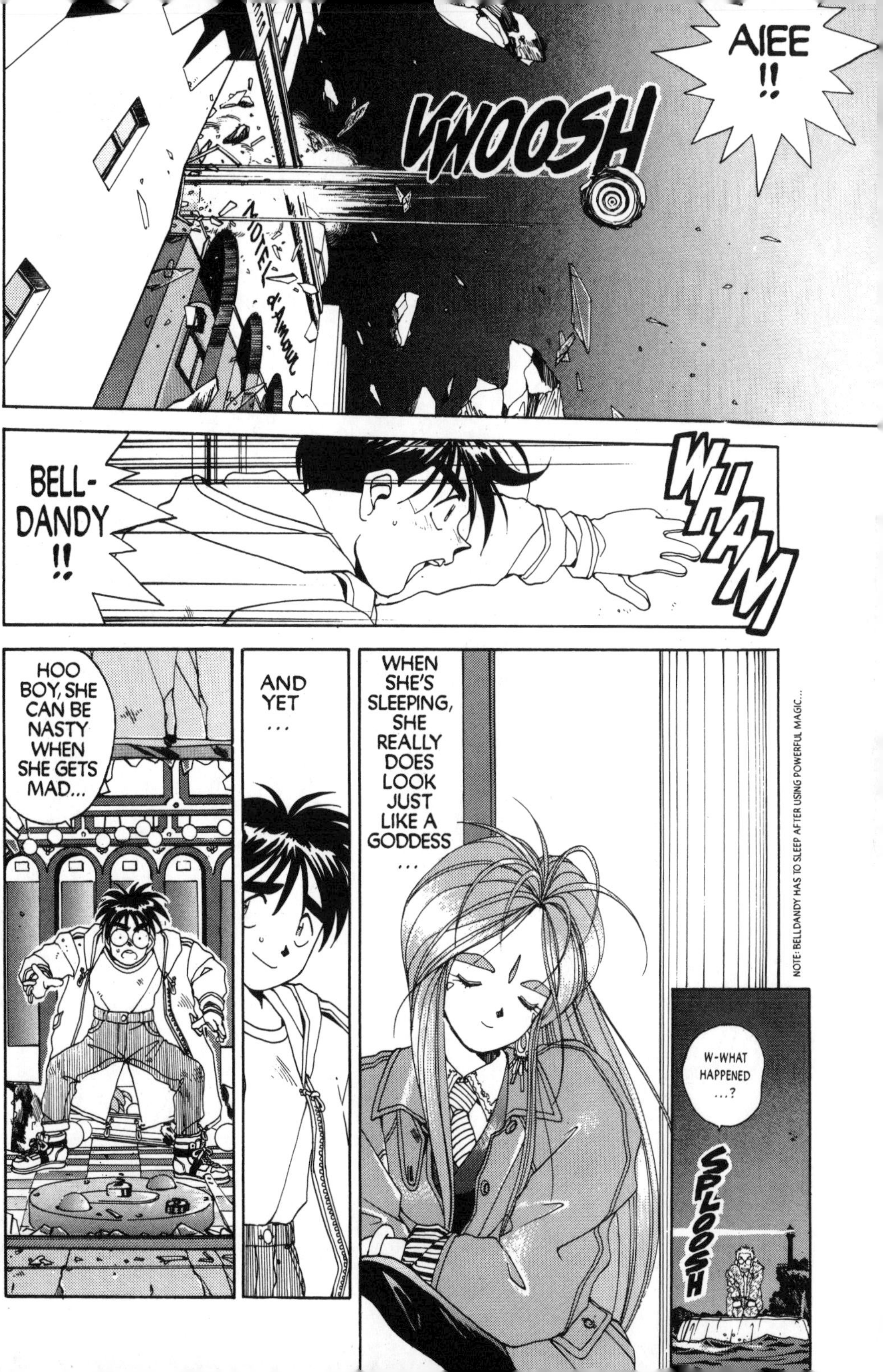
MOTEL d'Amour
VWOOSH
AIEE !!
BELL-DANDY !!
WHAM
HOO BOY, SHE CAN BE NASTY WHEN SHE GETS MAD...
AND YET . . .
WHEN SHE'S SLEEPING, SHE REALLY DOES LOOK JUST LIKE A GODDESS . . .
W-WHAT HAPPENED . . .?
SPLOOSH

NOTE: BELLDANDY HAS TO SLEEP AFTER USING POWERFUL MAGIC...

## Kosuke Fujishima

Born in 1964, Kosuke Fujishima began his comics career just after graduating high school as an editor for comics news magazine, *Puff*. An interview he conducted with *Be Free!* creator Tatsuya Egawa led to becoming Egawa's assistant, which led to Fujishima's first professional panel work, a comics-style report on the making of the live-action *Be Free!* film. Fan mail he received for the piece inspired him to create *You're Under Arrest!* which was serialized in *Morning Party Extra* beginning in 1986.

In 1988, Fujishima created a four-panel gag cartoon that featured the *YUA!* characters praying to a goddess. Fujishima was so pleased with the way the goddess turned out that she became the basis for Belldandy and inspired the creation of the *Oh My Goddess!* series for *Afternoon* magazine, where it still runs today after more than a decade.

Winner, Parent's Choice Award

KOSUKE FUJISHIMA'S

# Oh My Goddess!

*Oh My Goddess!* has proved to be a favorite with manga fans everywhere and is attracting new readers. The stories, following the misadventures of Keiichi Morisato and the trio of lovely goddesses who live with him, quickly explode into a fantastic romantic comedy with a huge cast of wonderful characters.

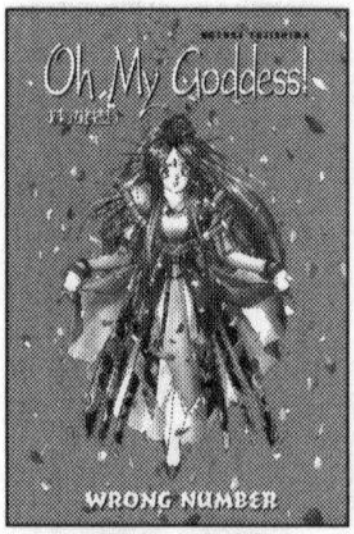
Oh My Goddess!
WRONG NUMBER

**WRONG NUMBER**
ISBN: 1-56971-669-2
softcover Ages 8+ $13.95

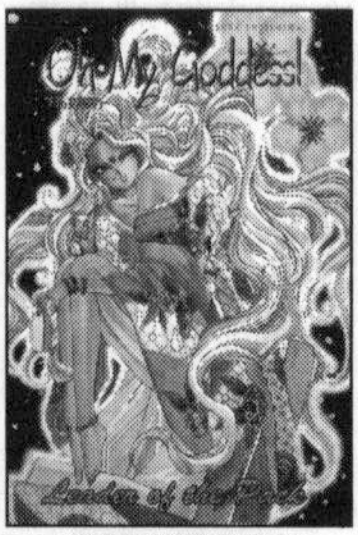
Oh My Goddess!

**LEADER OF THE PACK**
ISBN: 1-56971-764-8
softcover Ages 8+ $13.95

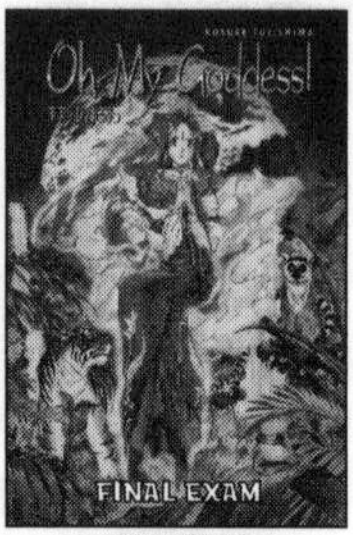
Oh My Goddess!
FINAL EXAM

**FINAL EXAM**
ISBN: 1-56971-765-6
softcover Ages 8+ $13.95

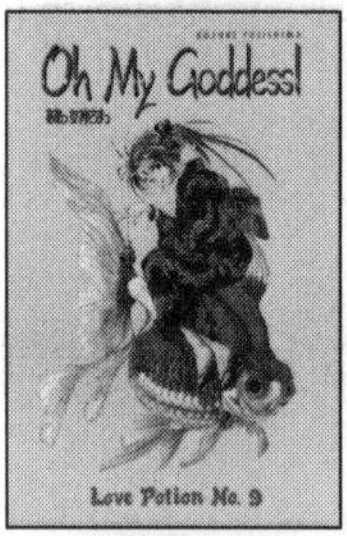
Oh My Goddess!
Love Potion No. 9

**LOVE POTION NO. 9**
ISBN: 1-56971-252-2
softcover Ages 8+ $14.95

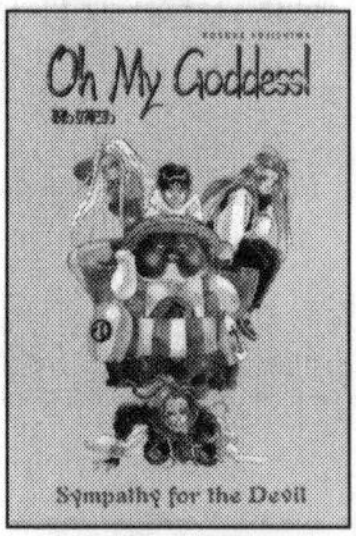
Oh My Goddess!
Sympathy for the Devil

**SYMPATHY FOR THE DEVIL**
ISBN: 1-56971-329-4
softcover Ages 8+ $13.95

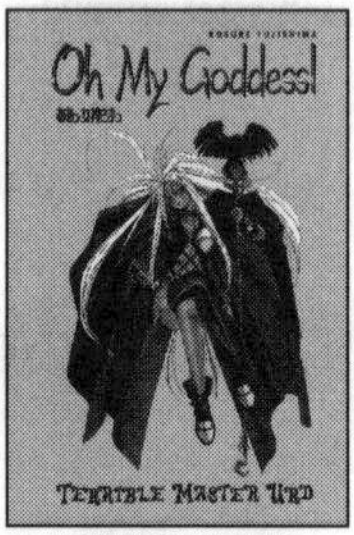
Oh My Goddess!
TERRIBLE MASTER URD

**TERRIBLE MASTER URD**
ISBN: 1-56971-369-3
softcover Ages 8+ $14.95

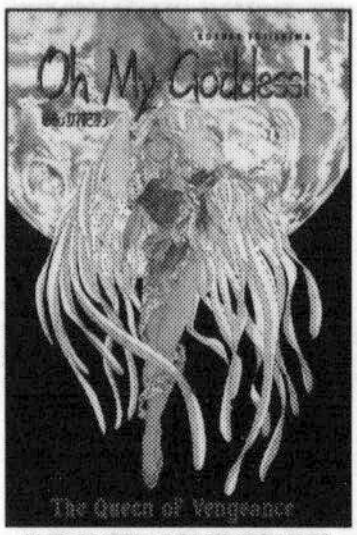
Oh My Goddess!
The Queen of Vengeance

**THE QUEEN OF VENGEANCE**
ISBN: 1-56971-431-2
softcover Ages 8+ $13.95

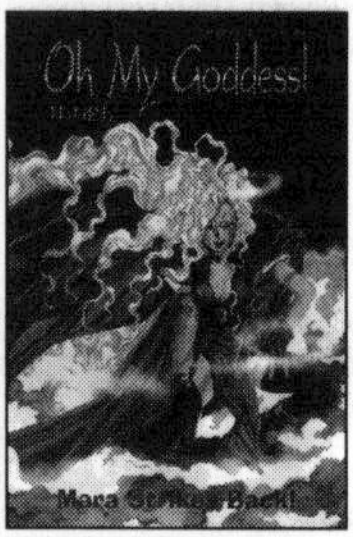
Oh My Goddess!

**MARA STRIKES BACK!**
ISBN: 1-56971-449-5
softcover Ages 8+ $14.95

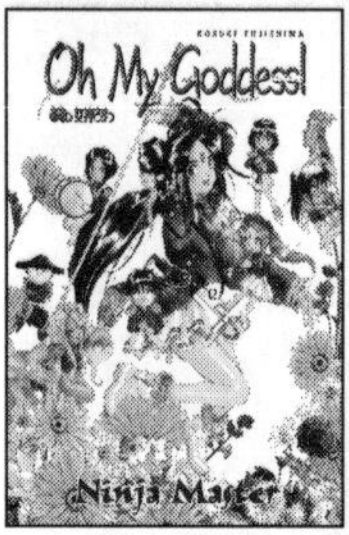
Oh My Goddess!
Ninja Master

**NINJA MASTER**
ISBN: 1-56971-474-6
softcover Ages 8+ $13.95

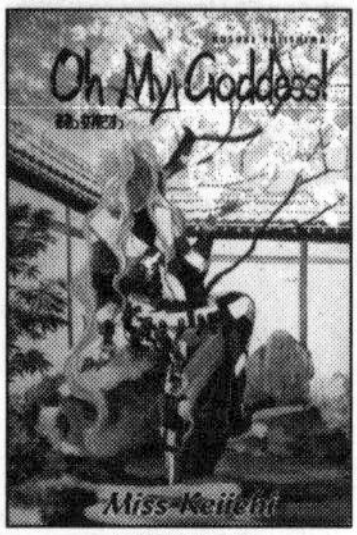
Oh My Goddess!
Miss Keiichi

**MISS KEIICHI**
ISBN: 1-56971-522-X
softcover Ages 8+ $16.95

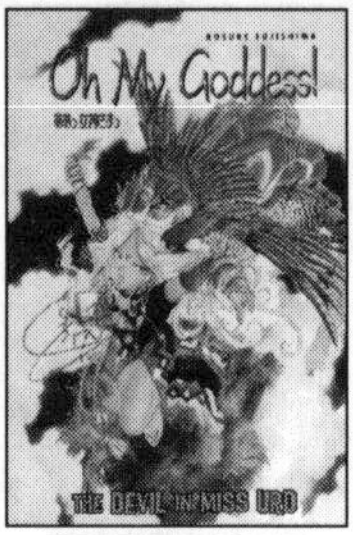
Oh My Goddess!

**THE DEVIL IN MISS URD**
ISBN: 1-56971-540-8
softcover Ages 8+ $14.95

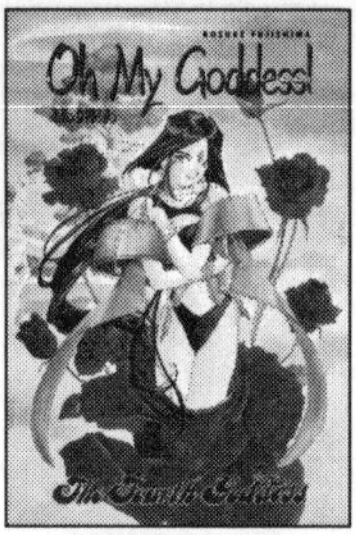
Oh My Goddess!

**THE FOURTH GODDESS**
ISBN: 1-56971-551-3
softcover Ages 8+ $18.95

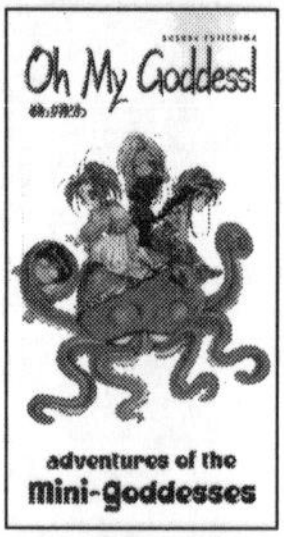
Oh My Goddess!
adventures of the
Mini-Goddesses

**THE ADVENTURES OF THE MINI-GODDESSES**
ISBN: 1-56971-421-5
softcover Ages 8+ $9.95

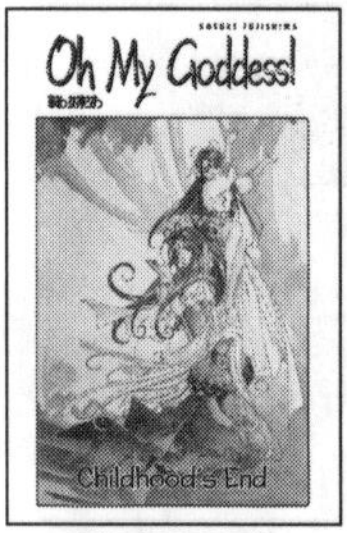
Oh My Goddess!
Childhood's End

**CHILDHOOD'S END**
ISBN: 1-56971-685-4
softcover Ages 8+ $15.95

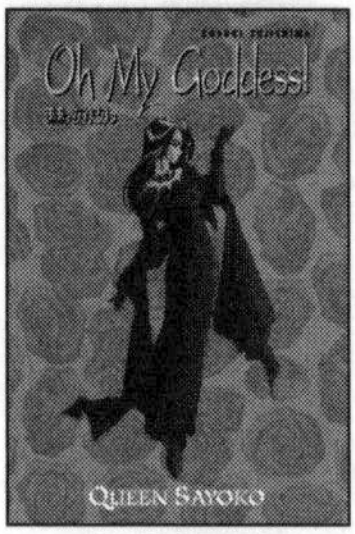
Oh My Goddess!
QUEEN SAYOKO

**QUEEN SAYOKO**
ISBN: 1-56971-766-4
softcover Ages 8+ $16.95

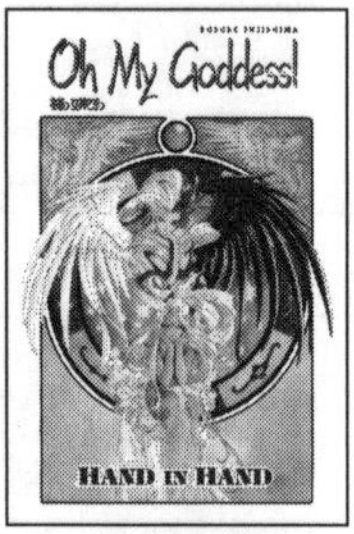
Oh My Goddess!
HAND IN HAND

**HAND IN HAND**
ISBN: 1-56971-921-7
softcover Ages 8+ $17.95

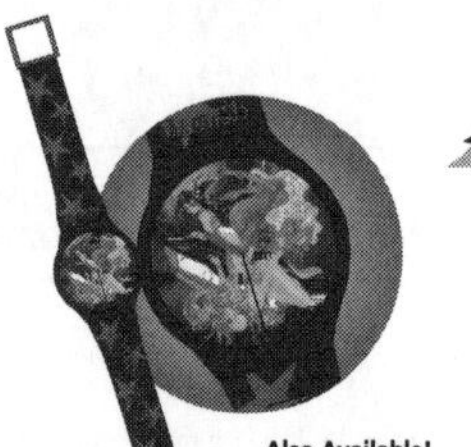

**Also Available!**
**OH MY GODDESS! WATCH**
**ITEM#: 37-517**
**$14.95**

## AVAILABLE AT YOUR LOCAL COMICS SHOP OR BOOKSTORE

To find a comics shop in your area, call 1-888-266-4226

For more information or to order direct: • On the web: www.darkhorse.com • E-mail: mailorder@darkhorse.com
• Phone: 1-800-862-0052 or (503) 652-9701 Mon.-Sat. 9 A.M. to 5 P.M. Pacific Time

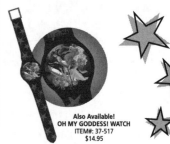

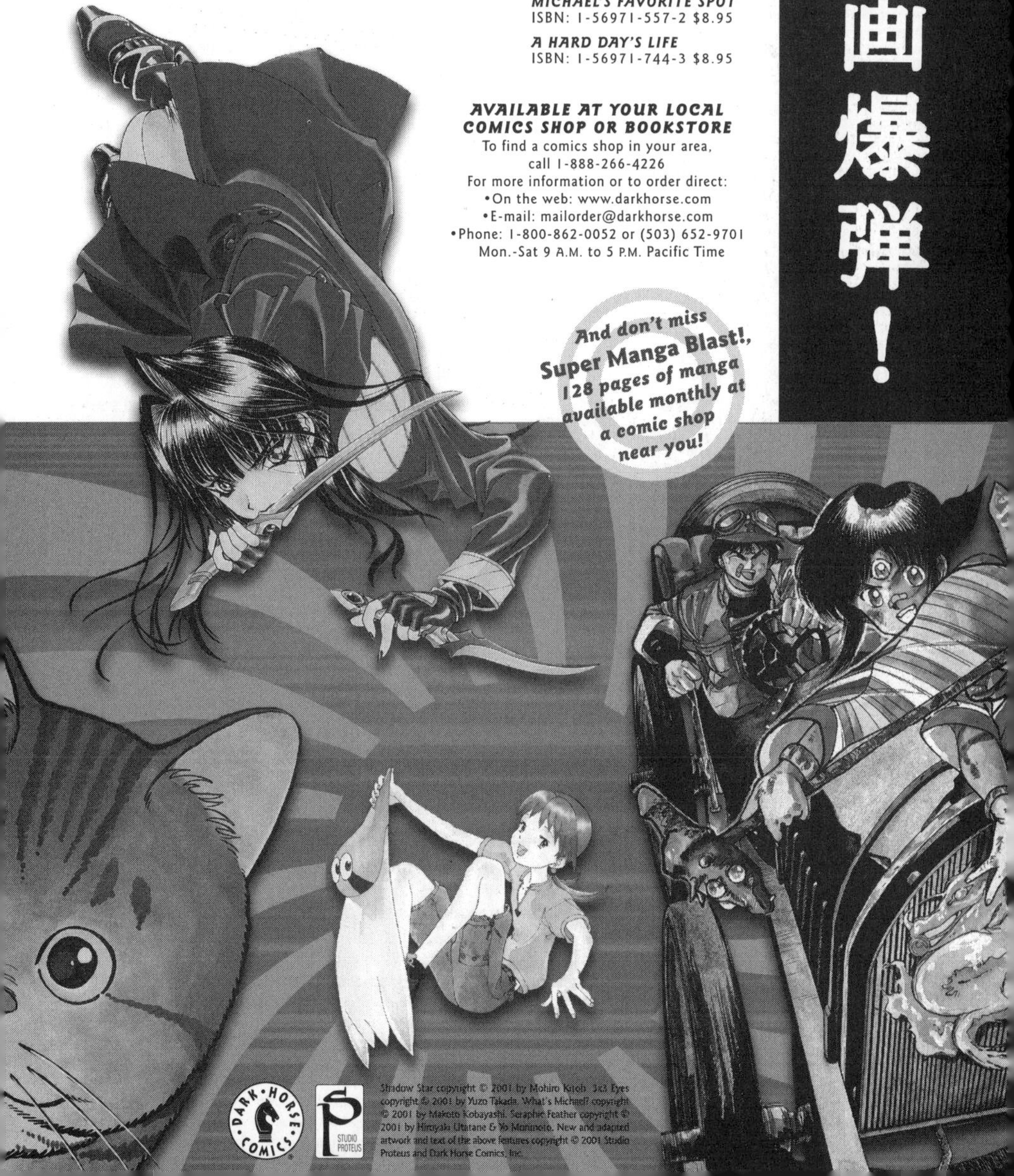

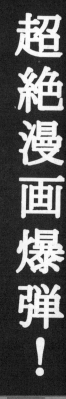